教材项目规划小组
Teaching Material Project Planning Group

严美华   姜明宝   王立峰
田小刚   崔邦焱   俞晓敏
赵国成   宋永波   郭   鹏

加拿大方咨询小组
Canadian Consulting Group

Dr. Robert Shanmu Chen
Mr. Zheng Zhining
University of British Columbia

Dr. Helen Wu
University of Toronto

Mr. Wang Renzhong
McGill University

中国国家对外汉语教学领导小组办公室规划教材
Project of NOTCFL of the People's Republic of China

NEW PRACTICAL CHINESE READER

Textbook

新实用汉语课本

2

主编：刘　珣

编者：张　凯　　刘社会

　　　陈　曦　　左珊丹

　　　施家炜　　刘　珣

英译审定：Jerry Schmidt

北京语言大学出版社
BEIJING LANGUAGE AND CULTURE
UNIVERSITY PRESS

图书在版编目（CIP）数据

新实用汉语课本·第 2 册/刘珣主编；张凯等编.
—北京：北京语言大学出版社，2010 重印
ISBN 978 – 7 – 5619 – 1129 – 7

Ⅰ．新…
Ⅱ．①刘…②张…
Ⅲ．汉语－对外汉语教学－教材
Ⅳ．H195.4

中国版本图书馆 CIP 数据核字（2002）第 083464 号

版权所有　　翻印必究

书　　　名：新实用汉语课本·第 2 册
责任印制：汪学发

出版发行：北京语言大学出版社
社　　址：北京市海淀区学院路 15 号　　邮政编码：100083
网　　址：www. blcup. com
电　　话：发行部　82303648/3591/3651
　　　　　编辑部　82303395
　　　　　读者服务部　82303653/3592
　　　　　网上订购电话　82303668
　　　　　客户服务信箱　service@ blcup. net
印　　刷：北京联兴盛业印刷股份有限公司
经　　销：全国新华书店

版　　次：2002 年 11 月第 1 版　2010 年 3 月第 17 次印刷
开　　本：889 毫米×1194 毫米　1/16　印张：19.25
字　　数：264 千字
书　　号：ISBN 978 – 7 – 5619 – 1129 – 7/H · 02121
　　　　　06700

凡有印装质量问题，本社负责调换。电话：82303590

目　录
CONTENTS

借书　　Borrowing books

还书　　Returning books

认识新朋友　　Making new friends

暂时离开　　Leaving and coming back in a moment

四．阅读和复述　　Reading Comprehension and Paraphrasing 广东的茶楼

五．语法　　Grammar

1．简单趋向补语　　The simple directional complement

2．"把"字句（1）　　The "把" sentence (1)

3．时量补语（1）　　The time-measure complement (1)

六．汉字　　Chinese Characters

汉字的构字法（2）　　Methods of constructing Chinese characters (2)

一．课文　　Text

生词　　New Words

二．注释　　Notes

动词"来、去、到"等带时量补语

　　Verbs "来, 去, 到, etc." with time-measure complement

"极了"、"多了"表示程度　　"极了" or "多了" to express

　　an extent or degree

助词"了"①与"了"②的连用

　　The combined usage of particle "了"① with particle "了"②

三．练习与运用　　Drills and Practice

描述事物　　Describing things

比较　　Comparing things

买衣服　　Buying clothes

四．阅读和复述　　Reading Comprehension and Paraphrasing 高一点儿（相声）

五．语法　　Grammar

1．"的"字短语（1）　　The "的" phrase (1)

2．用介词"比"表示比较（1）　　Comparison using the preposition "比" (1)

3．数量补语　　The complement of quantity

六．汉字　　Chinese Characters

汉字的构字法（3）　　Methods of constructing Chinese characters (3)

一．课文　　Text

生词　　New Words

二．注释　　Notes

量词"些"　　The measure word "些"

五． 语法　　Grammar
　　1. "是…的" 句　　The construction "是…的"
　　2. 方位词　　Location words
　　3. 表示存在的句子　　Sentences indicating existance
六． 汉字　　Chinese Characters
　　汉字的构字法（7）　　Methods of constructing Chinese characters (7)

一． 课文　　Text
　　生词　　New Words
二． 注释　　Notes
　　方位词中"边"的省略　　The omission of "边" in location words
　　指示代词"这么"　　The demonstrative pronoun "这么"
　　指示代词"有的"　　The demonstrative pronoun "有的"
三． 练习与运用　　Drills and Practice
　　谈过去的经历　　Talking about a past experience
　　找工作　　Looking for a job
　　约会　　Making an appointment or a date with someone
　　评价　　Making comments
四． 阅读和复述　　Reading Comprehension and Paraphrasing
　　　　《红楼梦》里的爱情故事
五． 语法　　Grammar
　　1. 过去的经验或经历　　Past experience
　　2. 动量补语　　The action-measure complement
　　3. 虽然…但是/可是…　　The construction "虽然…但是/可是…"
六． 汉字　　Chinese Characters
　　汉字的构字法（8）　　Methods of constructing Chinese characters (8)

一． 课文　　Text
　　生词　　New Words
二． 注释　　Notes
　　"多 + A/ V + 啊!"表示感叹　　The exclamatory construction "多 + A/ V + 啊!"
　　同位短语　　The appositive phrases
　　副词"就"（3）　　The adverb "就"（3）
三． 练习与运用　　Drills and Practice
　　谈计划　　Talking about plans
　　提建议　　Making suggestions

A new semester has begun. As your Chinese level advances, the topics you study in this book will become more interesting.

As you follow Lin Na through this lesson, you will learn how to describe the places you have visited, how to comment on your travel experiences, as well as how to change money at the bank before your departure. You will even learn how to say a sentence in the Shanghai dialect.

第十五课 Lesson 15

她去上海了

一. 课文　Text

gāng cài = just now.

买 mǎi to buy

（一）

林　娜：力波，你来得真早。

v. +de + adv.

丁力波：刚才银行人少，不用排队。林娜，你今天穿得很漂亮啊。

gāng cài　*Pái duì*　*chuān*　*a*

林　娜：是吗？我来银行换钱，下午我还要去王府井买东西。

(really)?　*huàn*　*huàn qian.*　*hái qù wángfújǐng mǐ dōng xī*

【在银行换钱】
Changing money
at the bank

丁力波：今天一英镑换多少人民币？

Yīnbàng

林　娜：一英镑换十一块五毛七分人民币。

Yīnbàng. shí kuài wǔ máo huan.

— 1 —

明天我要去上海旅行，得用人民币。

丁力波：什么？明天你要去上海吗？你刚从西安回北京，① 你真喜

欢旅行！在西安玩儿得好不好？

林　娜：我玩儿得非常好。

丁力波：吃得怎么样？

【评价动作或行为】
Commenting on one's actions

林　娜：吃得还可以。② 这次住得不太好。

丁力波：你参观兵马俑了没有？

林　娜：我参观兵马俑了。我还买了很多明信片，你到我那儿去看看吧。

丁力波：好啊。我也很想去西安旅行，你给我介绍介绍吧。看，该你了。③

林　娜：小姐，我想用英镑换人民币。这是五百英镑。

工作人员：好，给您五千七百八十五块人民币。请数一数。

生词 New Words

| 1. | 得 | StPt | de | (structural particle) 吃得很好，穿得很漂亮，玩儿得很好 |

hai tian
↳ day aft tmo.

gua hào
↳ to register.

compliment
of state structure #

2. 早	A	zǎo	early 来得真早,去得太早,到得很早,睡得不早,你早,都很早
3. 银行	N	yínháng	bank 中国银行
4. 少	A	shǎo	few; little 人少,银行很少,也很少,不少
5. 排队	VO	páiduì	to form a line; to queue up 不用排队,排队买书,排队挂号,排两个队
排	V	pái	to arrange; to put in order
队	N	duì	a row of people; line
6. 换	V	huàn	to exchange; to change 换钱,换书,换光盘
7. 英镑	N	yīngbàng	pound sterling 换英镑,一英镑,五百英镑
8. 人民币	N	rénmínbì	Renminbi (RMB) 换人民币
人民	N	rénmín	people 中国人民银行,加拿大人民
9. 得	OpV	děi *(followed by verb)*	to need; must; to have to 得换钱,得排队,得复习语法
10. 用	V	yòng *(to need)*	to use 用钱,用一下电话,用英镑换人民币,得用人民币,用一用
11. 刚	Adv	gāng	just; only a short while ago 刚回北京,刚去银行
12. 从	Prep	cóng	from 从美国回中国,从上海到北京
13. 非常	Adv	fēicháng	very; extremely; highly 非常早,非常漂亮,非常喜欢中国音乐
14. 次	M	cì	(measure word for actions) 这次,那次,一次
15. 参观	V	cānguān	to visit (a place) 参观学院,参观医院,参观公司
16. 兵马俑	N	bīngmǎyǒng	(ceremonial clay statues of warriors

			and horses which are buried with the dead) 参观兵马俑
兵	N	bīng	soldier; fighter
17. 明信片	N	míngxìnpiàn	postcard 很多明信片,一张明信片,- 美术明信片
信	N	xìn	letter 写信,寄信,给他写信
18. 该	V	gāi	to be sb.'s turn to do sth. 该你了, 该我(换钱)了,该他(念)了
19. 工作人员	N	gōngzuò rényuán	working personnel; staff member 银 行工作人员,邮局工作人员,一位工 作人员
人员	N	rényuán	personnel; staff
20. 千	Nu	qiān	thousand 两千,五千,八千
21. 数	V	shǔ	to count 数一数,数数,数钱,数人民币
22. 王府井	PN	Wángfǔjǐng	(name of a famous commercial district in Beijing)
23. 西安	PN	Xī'ān	(name of the capital of Shaanxi Province)

（二）

【肯定事情已经发生】
Confirming that something has happened

马大为：林娜,早!④ 好久不见,你回英国了吗?
Lín Nà zǎo hǎo jiǔ bú jiàn, nǐ huí yīngguó le ma

林　娜：我没有回英国,我去上海了。昨天刚回北京。
wǒ méi yǒu huí yīngguó, wǒ qù shànghǎi le. Zuótiān gāng huí běijīng

马大为：刚才宋华来了,他也问我,林娜去哪儿了?
gāngcái Sòng huá le, tā yě wèn wǒ, lín Nà qù nǎr le
(a short while ago)

林　娜：我给宋华写信了,他怎么不知道? 他现在在哪儿?
wǒ gěi Sònghuá xiě xìn le, tā zěnme bù zhīdào tā xiànzài zài nǎr
write
(written letter)

hui (return)

马大为：他回宿舍了。上海怎么样？听说这两年上海发展得非常
tā huí sùshè le. Shànghǎi zěnmeyàng? Tīng shuō liǎng nián Fā zhǎn Fēi cháng
zhè   de
快，是不是？
kuài, shì bu shi?
zhè liǎng nián
(these few years)

林　娜：是啊，上海很大，也非常漂亮。那儿银行多，商场也多，我
Shì a, shàng hǎi hěn dà, Fēi cháng nàr yínháng shàng chǎng Yě dōu Wǒ
yě   Piàoliang   dōu
很喜欢上海。
hěn Xǐhuan shànghǎi

gùi = expensive

【描述去过的地方】
Describing a place one has visited

马大为：上海东西贵不贵？
Shàng hǎi dōngxi gùi bu gùi
(Yī Fú)
zòu

林　娜：东西不太贵。上海人做衣服做得真好，我买了很多件。
dōngxi bú tài gùi. zòu Gùuu zhēn hǎo, Jiàn
shuō
zòu yīfú zòu de.
↳ can be dropped

马大为：上海人喜欢说上海话，他们普通话说得怎么样？
shuō huà pǔ tōng huà

林　娜：他们普通话说得很好，年轻人英语说得也很流利。
Pǔ tōng hua Niánqīng Yīnyu shuō liúlì

马大为：你学没学上海话？
huà

林　娜：学了。我会说"阿拉勿懂"。⑤
huì shuō la lai dǒng

马大为：你说什么？我不懂。
shuō dǒng

林　娜：这就是上海话的"我不懂"。⑥
jiù dǒng

生词 New Words

1. 好久不见　IE　hǎojiǔ bú jiàn　haven't seen (sb.) for a very long time
   　好久　IE　hǎojiǔ　a very long time
   　见　V　jiàn　to see
2. 发展　V　fāzhǎn　to develop
3. 快　A　kuài　fast; quick; rapid　发展得非常快,说得很快,念得不快
4. 话　N　huà　dialect; language　上海话,西安话,中国话 / word.
5. 普通话　N　pǔtōnghuà　the common speech (mandarin)　说普通话,学习普通话
6. 年轻　A　niánqīng　young　年轻人,非常年轻
   　轻　A　qīng　light; small
7. 流利　A　liúlì　fluent　说得很流利,念得非常流利,流利的汉语,流利的英语,流利的普通话
8. 懂　V　dǒng　to understand　懂上海话,不懂英语,懂不懂
9. 就　Adv　jiù　exactly; precisely　就是,就是他,就是这个

补充生词 Supplementary Words

1. 美元　N　měiyuán　U. S. dollar
2. 欧元　N　ōuyuán　Euro
★ 3. 加元　N　jiāyuán　Canadian dollar
4. 元　M　yuán　(measure word for Chinese currency *kuai*)
5. 亚洲学系　N　yàzhōuxué xì　Department of Asian Studies
6. 汇率　V　huìlǜ　exchange rate
7. 现金　N　xiànjīn　cash
8. 信用卡　N　xìnyòngkǎ　credit card

9. 城市	N	chéngshì	city
10. 地方	N	dìfang	place
11. 儿子	V	érzi	son
12. 菜	N	cài	food; a dish

zhōng guó cài   (Chinese Food)
Tīng bù dǒng

二. 注释   Notes

Tīng (listen).

① 你刚从西安回北京。

"You just came back to Beijing from Xi'an".

"从+NP" forms a prepositional phrase that precedes the verb, indicating the starting point of an action.

The object of the preposition "从" is usually a word or a phrase denoting location or time (see Lesson 16). For example:

我从学院去邮局。

他从英国来中国。

In order to function as the object of "从", a noun or a pronoun that doesn't denote location must be followed by "这儿" or "那儿", thus completing the prepositional phrase which modifies the verb. For example:

他从力波那儿来。

他从谁那儿来?

陈老师从我这儿去银行。

② (我)吃得还可以。

"The food (I had) was passable."

"可以" is used as an adjective here, meaning "good, not bad". "还可以" means "passable; just so-so". For example:

这个电影还可以。

那位留学生汉语说得还可以。

③ 看,该你了。

"Look, it's your turn now."

"该+NP+(V)+了" means "it's somebody's turn (to do something)". For example:

该你念课文了。

④ 林娜,早!

"Good morning, Lin Na."

"早!" is another expression commonly employed by Chinese people as a greeting. It is usually used to say hello to someone in the morning. The common reply to it is also "早!" For example：

——老师早!

——你们早!

⑤ 我会说"阿拉勿懂"。

"I know how to say 'I don't understand.'"

In the Shanghai dialect, the expression "阿拉勿懂" means "I don't understand." In this dialect, "我" can be pronounced "阿拉"([AʔlA]), whereas "不" is pronounced "勿"([vəʔ]).

⑥ 这就是上海话的"我不懂"。

"This means 'I don't understand' in the Shanghai dialect."

"就"(1) has the function of emphasis. It is used to either confirm a fact, or stress that "this is exactly what the fact is". For example：

这就是北京。

就是这个人。

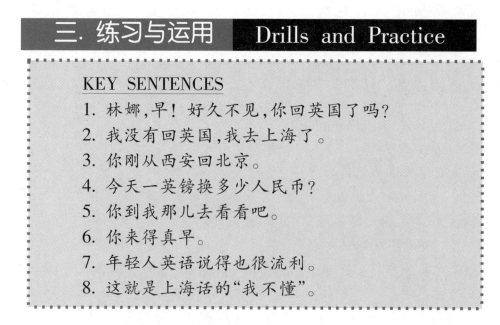

三. 练习与运用 Drills and Practice

KEY SENTENCES

1. 林娜,早! 好久不见,你回英国了吗?
2. 我没有回英国,我去上海了。
3. 你刚从西安回北京。
4. 今天一英镑换多少人民币?
5. 你到我那儿去看看吧。
6. 你来得真早。
7. 年轻人英语说得也很流利。
8. 这就是上海话的"我不懂"。

1. 熟读下列短语 Master the following phrases

(1) 学得怎么样　　玩儿得怎么样　　住得好不好　　写得漂亮不漂亮

　　穿得很好　　　吃得还可以　　　念得太快　　　睡得很晚

　　起得不早　教得不少　说得不流利　数得不对　买得不多

　　发展得非常快　　　休息得不太好

　　(用)钱用得不多　　　(问)问题问得很少　　　(做)练习做得真好

(2) 回家了　买东西了　　去北京了　　学普通话了　　参观兵马俑了

　　喝红葡萄酒了没有　　写信了没有　　练习口语了没有

　　送礼物了没有　　打扫宿舍了没有　　打电话了没有

　　洗没洗衣服　听没听音乐　参加没参加聚会　复习没复习课文

(3) 从学院去医院 从美国到英国 从南方回北京 从他那儿来 从公司租房子

(4) 给妈妈写信　给朋友打电话　给弟弟买礼物　给我介绍西安

　　给他们上语法课

(5) 就是他　　　就是这个人　　　就是那位教授　　　就是陈老师的朋友

(6) 看看　听听　说说　写写　介绍介绍　参观参观　休息休息

　　等一等　问一问　数一数　看一看　听一听　写一写　说一说

2. 句型替换 Pattern drills

(1) 他每天<u>来</u>得<u>早</u>吗？

　　他每天来得很早。

　　你<u>来</u>得<u>早</u>不<u>早</u>？

　　我来得不早。

起	早
睡	晚
吃	多
休息	好

(2) 你<u>说</u> <u>汉语</u> 说得很<u>好</u>。

　　哪里,我说汉语说得不太好。

　　<u>他汉语</u> 说得怎么样？

　　他汉语说得还可以。

写	汉字	漂亮
学	语法	好
念	课文	流利
做	练习	快

（3）谁教你们<u>语法</u>？

　　梁老师教我们<u>语法</u>。

　　他<u>语法</u>教得怎么样？

　　他教得<u>太快</u>。

口语	很好
汉字	非常快
英语	不太好
文学	还可以

（4）昨天你<u>看电影</u>了吗？

　　我没有<u>看电影</u>。

　　你去哪儿了？

　　我去<u>我哥哥</u>那儿了。

上课	医院
参观中学	银行
参加聚会	我朋友那儿
锻炼身体	老师那儿

（5）上午你做什么了？

　　我去银行了。

　　你<u>换</u>没<u>换钱</u>？

　　我没<u>换钱</u>。

买东西	买礼物
去邮局	排队
打扫宿舍	洗衣服
回家	复习中文

（6）明天你要去<u>王府井</u>吗？

　　我要去。

　　你从哪儿去？

　　我从<u>学院</u>去。

　　你跟谁一起去？

　　我跟<u>力波</u>一起去。

租房公司	我家	我弟弟
商场	宋华那儿	宋华
外语学院	美术学院	陈老师

（7）请问，现在一<u>英镑</u>换多少人民币？

　　一<u>英镑</u>换<u>十一块六毛五分</u>人民币。

　　我想用<u>英镑</u>换人民币，这是<u>300</u>英镑。

美元(měiyuán)	八块一毛九分	500 美元
欧元(ōuyuán)	七块一毛二分	200 欧元
加元(jiāyuán)	五块二毛三分	700 加元

3. 课堂活动 Classroom activity

Complete and answer the following questions with your classmates

(1) 1美元(měiyuán)换8.19元(yuán)人民币

A：100美元换多少人民币？　　B：100美元换819元人民币。

A：200美元＿＿＿＿＿＿？　　B：＿＿＿＿＿＿＿＿＿＿。

A：250美元＿＿＿＿＿＿？　　B：＿＿＿＿＿＿＿＿＿＿。

(2) 1欧元(ōuyuán)换7.12元(yuán)人民币

A：500欧元＿＿＿＿＿？　　B：＿＿＿＿＿＿＿＿＿。

A：620欧元＿＿＿＿＿？　　B：＿＿＿＿＿＿＿＿＿。

A：780欧元＿＿＿＿＿？　　B：＿＿＿＿＿＿＿＿＿。

(3) 1加元(jiāyuán)换5.23元(yuán)人民币

A：1300加元＿＿＿＿＿？　　B：＿＿＿＿＿＿＿＿＿。

A：1500加元＿＿＿＿＿？　　B：＿＿＿＿＿＿＿＿＿。

A：1900加元＿＿＿＿＿？　　B：＿＿＿＿＿＿＿＿＿。

4. 会话练习 Conversation exercises

[打招呼 Saying hello]

(1) A：早。

B：你早。今天天气很好。

A：是啊,今天天气真好。

(2) A：张师傅早!

B：您早。

A：昨天您睡得好吗？

B：＿＿＿＿＿,今天起得很晚。您呢？

A：我休息得很好。

[肯定事情已经发生 Confirming that something has happened]

(1) A：昨天你去哪儿了？我下午到你宿舍找你了，你不在。

　　B：我去看朋友了，真对不起。

　　A：没关系。我没有给你打电话，你不知道我要去。

(2) A：好久不见，你去哪儿了？

　　B：我_____了。

　　A：你为什么现在回英国？

　　B：我妈妈住院了，我去看她。

[评价动作或行为 Commenting on one's actions]

(1) A：你知道吗？我去_____了。

　　B：你真喜欢旅行！你_____？

　　A：玩儿得还可以。

　　B：这次你吃得怎么样？

　　A：_____。

(2) A：你是亚洲学系(yàzhōuxué xì)的学生吗？

　　B：是，我学习汉语。

　　A：你汉语说得很流利。

　　B：哪里，_____。

　　A：谁教你们口语？

　　B：_____。

　　A：老师教得怎么样？

　　B：_____。

　　A：这是你写的汉字吗？写得很漂亮。

　　B：我写得不快。请多帮助。

(3) A：你看他汉字写得怎么样？

　　B：_____。

A：他这个字写得对不对？

B：_____。

A：应该怎么写？

B：_____。

[在银行换钱 Changing money at the bank]

(1) A：小姐，我想用美元换人民币。

B：您要换多少美元？

A：今天的汇率(huìlǜ)是多少？

B：现在100美元换_____。

A：我换_____。

B：好。这是_____，请您数一数。

(2) A：您好，我想换800元现金(xiànjīn)。这是我的信用卡(xìnyòngkǎ)。

B：换人民币还是换美元？

A：_____。

[描述去过的地方 Describing a place one has visited]

A：听说你刚去_____了。

B：是啊。_____得很快。

A：你买东西了吗？那儿的东西好不好？

B：_____，东西也很多。

A：吃的东西贵不贵？

B：_____。

A：那儿天气怎么样？

B：_____。

A：那儿的人说普通话吗？

B：那儿的人普通话说得_____。你应该去看看。

5. 看图说话 Describe the following pictures

（起得很晚） （练习做得不对） （吃得很多）

（来得很早） （买得很多） （写得不对）

6. 交际练习 Communication practice

（1）You went to the bank to exchange money, but after talking to the teller, you noticed that the exchange rate was not very good. Therefore, you decided to change the money later.

（2）After visiting different places, you and your friend are asking about each other's travel experiences.

（3）You are discussing language studies with your Chinese friend. You hope that he/she will make some comments on the various aspects of your spoken Chinese, grammar, and character-writing.

四. 阅读和复述 Reading Comprehension and Paraphrasing

张教授去上海

张教授在北京语言学院工作,他很喜欢旅行。他刚从英国回北京,上海的一个学院请他去上课。这个星期五他去上海了。张教授给那儿的学生上英国文学课,他课上得非常好,学生都很喜欢他的课。

上海是一个大城市(chéngshì)，这两年发展得很快。上海的商场很多，商场的东西也非常好，上海人做的衣服很有名。张教授去参观了很多有名的地方(dìfang)，他买了不少衣服，还买了很多明信片。他儿子(érzi)在上海工作，是中国银行的工作人员。星期六儿子请他去吃饭，那个餐厅上海菜(cài)做得很好，也不太贵。张教授在上海玩儿得非常好，吃得也很好，住得还可以，一个星期过得真快。

张教授会说西安话，也会一点儿上海话。可是他上海话说得不太好。他说："现在上海人会说普通话，年轻人普通话和英语都说得很流利，在上海我不用说上海话。"

五. 语法　　　　　Grammar

1. 情态补语(1) The complement of state (1)

In Chinese, a verb or an adjective is frequently followed by an element providing further detail or explanation. This is called the complement. Among the various forms of complements, the one that describes or comments on the achieved state of an action is called the complement of state. It is usually formed by an adjective or an adjectival phrase. The structural particle "得" must be placed between the verb and the complement of state. To create the negative form, "不" should be put before the complement of state.

→ must always hence on adv. before an adj. (doesn't sound complete).

V	+	得	+	Adv	+	A
来		得		很		早
住		得		不		好

zhù to reside/live.

The V/A-not-V/A question form is constructed by juxtaposing the affirmative form of the complement with its negative form.

V	+	得	+	A	+	不A
玩儿		得		好		不好?
发展		得		快		不快?

In this kind of sentence, if there is an object following the verb, the verb needs to be reduplicated and then placed after the object, but before "得". The first verb is often omitted.

$$(V) + O + V + 得 + Adv + A$$

Subject	Predicate						Particle
	(V)	O	V	"得"	Adv	A	
他			来	得	很	早。	
她			住	得		好	吗?
上海			发展	得		快不快?	
他们	(说)	普通话	说	得		怎么样?	
老师	(教)	语法	教	得	不	快。	

(handwritten note above V column: "must have" with arrow)

Notes:

(1) A complement formed by an adjective is usually preceded by "很". This is similar to the case in which the adjective is used as a predicate. For example:"来得很早","说得很快".

(2) The focus of a sentence containing a complement of state is centered on the complement. Therefore, both its question form and related answer form are usually made from variations on the complement. Its negative form is made by negating the complement rather than by placing "不" before the verb. Hence, it is incorrect to say ⊗[1] "他不来得很早。"

(3) In this kind of sentence, the elliptical form can be used to answer a question. For example:

Question	Answer
他汉语说得流利吗?	他汉语说得很流利。
	说得很流利。
	很流利。

(handwritten note: "Can answer w/ either.")

2. 助词"了"②:肯定事情的完成或实现 Particle "了" ②: Confirming the completion or realization of something

In Lesson 13, we learned that the particle "了"① can follow a verb to denote the completion or realization of an action. In this lesson, we see that "了"② always appears at the end of a sentence. It emphatically confirms the completion or realization of some event or situation. Compare the sentences in groups A and B:

---

[1] Incorrect sentences are marked by ⊗ in this book.

	A		B

你去哪儿?

Where are you going?

你去哪儿了?

Where have you been? *Or*
Where did you go?

我去商场。

I am going to the shopping mall.

我去商场了。

I've been to the shopping mall. *Or*

I went to the shopping mall.

你买什么?

What are you going to buy?

你买什么了?

What have you bought? *Or*
What did you buy?

我买衣服。

I am going to buy some clothes.

我买衣服了。

I've bought some clothes. *Or*
I bought some clothes.

In group A, "去商场" and "买衣服" are not completed actions in the past. In group B, however, these two actions are definitely completed or realized.

To negate a sentence with the particle "了"②, place the adverb "没（有）" rather than "不" before the verb, and omit "了" from the end of the sentence. To form a V/A-not-V/A question, juxtapose the affirmative form of the verb with its negative（"…没…"）, or add "…了没有" to the end of an affirmative sentence.

V + O + 了

Subject	Predicate				
	Adv	**V**	**O**	**Pt**
我		换	钱	了。
他	没有	去	上海。	
宋华		回	家	了吗?
林娜		去	西安	了没有?
她		参观没参观	兵马俑?	

Notes：

（1）When present, the particle "了"② always indicates that actions or events have taken place in the past. However, it is not true that "了"② is always required to express past events. To narrate a past event （especially several events taking place consecutively） or to describe a scene at a specific moment, without confirming the realization of the action, we can leave out "了". For example：

星期六他上午去看电影，下午去参加一个聚会。

（2） If "了" simultaneously follows the verb and stands at the end of the sentence，it then performs both functions mentioned above. For example：

他去了。

我懂了。 } "了" expresses the completion and realization of the action and confirms the completion or realization of some event or situation.

刚才宋华来了。

3. 动词的重叠 Reduplication of the verb

In Chinese， verbs can be reduplicated. The form for reduplicated monosyllabic verbs is "AA" or "A—A". However， the form for reduplicated bisyllabic verbs is "ABAB"， and "—" cannot be added between the two syllables of bisyllabic verbs. For example：看看，说说，等一等，用一用，数一数，介绍介绍，复习复习，etc. Reduplicating a verb has the function of implying a short duration for that action or the idea of giving something a try. In this sense， it is similar to adding "一下" to the verb.

4. 100~10000的称数法 Numeration for numbers from 100 to 10,000

101 一百○一	102 一百○二	……	109 一百○九	110 一百一十
111 一百一十一	112 一百一十二	……	119 一百一十九	120 一百二十
⋮	⋮		⋮	⋮
⋮	⋮		⋮	⋮
191 一百九十一	192 一百九十二	……	199 一百九十九	200 二百
201 二百○一	202 二百○二	……	209 二百○九	210 二百一十
⋮	⋮		⋮	⋮
⋮	⋮		⋮	⋮
991 九百九十一	992 九百九十二	……	999 九百九十九	1000 一千

| 1001 一千○一 | 1010 一千○一十 | 1052 一千○五十二 | 1100 一千一百 |
| 1109 一千一百○九 | 3543 三千五百四十三 | 8990 八千九百九十 | 9999 九千九百九十九 |

yī wàn
10 000.

六. 汉字　　Chinese Characters

1. 汉字的构字法(1) Methods of constructing Chinese characters (1)

　　When constructing Chinese characters, certain rules are followed in the combination of sound, structure and meaning. Though the forms of modern characters are frequently very different from these ancient ones, Chinese characters still maintain the characteristics of a logographic writing system. Therefore, understanding the process by which Chinese characters are formed will facilitate learning them.

　　Pictographic method (象形法): This method of construction depicts either the whole image or the partial characteristic of an object. It is the original method of forming characters.

　　a. Depicting the whole image of the object. For example:

　　　人,大,目,见,口,牙,耳,心,手,足,女,木,水,火,土,丁,刀,日,月,井,田,
　　　子,儿,工,弓,衣,车,舟,门,户,虫,马,立.

　　b. Depicting a characteristic of the object. For example:

　　　母,羊,牛,犬,身.

　　c. Depicting both the object and other associated things. For example:

　　　果,天,匕,见.

　　In antiquity, these single-component characters, which we have already learned, were originally pictographic. Nowadays, they are no longer very pictographic but are similar to codes. However, when they are used as the basic components for multi-component characters, the fact that they maintain either their original sounds or meanings certainly helps our understanding of the latter.

2. 认写基本汉字 Learn and write basic Chinese characters

(1) 民　　　　乛 乛 尸 尸 民

　　mín　　the people　　　　　　　　　　　　5 strokes

(2) 币(幣)　　一 丆 币 币

　　bì　　currency　　　　　　　　　　　　4 strokes

(3) 千　　　　千

qiān　　thousand　　　　　　　　　　3 strokes

(4) 久　　　　　久

jiǔ　　long　　　　　　　　　　　3 strokes

(5) 奂(奐)　ノ ク ク 々 名 奂 奂

huàn　　abundant　　　　　　　　7 strokes

(6) 丘　　ノ イ 乍 斤 丘

qiū　　mound, hillock　　　　　　5 strokes

(7) 甬　　フ マ ア 月 月 甬 甬

yǒng　　road; path　　　　　　　7 strokes

(8) 亚(亞)　(一 + 业)

Yà　　Asia　　　　　　　　　　6 strokes

(9) 车(車)　一 左 左 车

chē　　vehicle　　　　　　　　　4 strokes

(10) 重　　ノ 一 一 千 千 盲 盲 重 重

zhòng　　heavy　　　　　　　　9 strokes

(11) 尤　　一 ナ 尤 尤

yóu   especially   4 strokes

3. 认写课文中的汉字 Learn and write the Chinese characters appearing in the texts

(1) 早 zǎo

早 → 日 + 十   6 strokes

(2) 银行 yínháng （銀行）

银 → 钅 + 艮   11 strokes

(3) 排队 páiduì （排隊）

排 → 扌 + 非   11 strokes

队 → 阝 + 人   4 strokes

(4) 换 huàn （換）

换 → 扌 + 奂   10 strokes

立 (pángzìtóu) 丶 亠 亠 六 立 立   6 strokes

(5) 英镑 yīngbàng （英鎊）

镑 → 钅 + 立 + 方   15 strokes

(6) 从 cóng （從）

从 → 人 + 人   4 strokes

(7) 次 cì

次 → 冫 + 欠   6 strokes

(8) 参观 cānguān（參觀）

观 → 又 ＋ 见   6 strokes

(9) 兵马俑 bīngmǎyǒng（兵馬俑）

兵 → 丘 ＋ 八   7 strokes

俑 → 亻 ＋ 甬   9 strokes

(10) 明信片 míngxìnpiàn

信 → 亻 ＋ 言   9 strokes

(11) 工作人员 gōngzuò rényuán（工作人員）

员 → 口 ＋ 贝   7 strokes

(12) 王府井 Wángfǔjǐng

府 → 广 ＋ 付   8 strokes

(13) 西安 Xī'ān

安 → 宀 ＋ 女   6 strokes

(14) 发展 fāzhǎn（發展）

展 → 尸 ＋ 艹 ＋ 民   10 strokes

(15) 普通话 pǔtōnghuà（普通話）

普 → 丷 ＋ 亚 ＋ 日   12 strokes

通 → 甬 ＋ 辶   10 strokes

(16) 年轻 niánqīng （年輕）

轻 → 车 ＋ 圣　　　　　　　9 strokes

(On the left side of a character, the fourth stroke of "车" is written as "㇀".)

㐬(liúzìpáng)　　丶　一　云　云　产　产　㐬　　　7 strokes

(17) 流利 liúlì

流 → 氵 ＋ 㐬　　　　　　10 strokes

利 → 禾 ＋ 刂　　　　　　7 strokes

(18) 懂 dǒng

懂 → 忄 ＋ 艹 ＋ 重　　　15 strokes

(19) 就 jiù

就 → 京 ＋ 尤　　　　　　12 strokes

| 文化知识 | Cultural Notes |

Xi'an and the Ancient Chinese Capitals

Xi'an is a renowned ancient Chinese capital. Back in the 11th century BC, King Wu of the Western Zhou Dynasty established his capital, named Haojing, where Xi'an is currently located. After that, the Qin Dynasty (221 BC—206 BC), the Western Han Dynasty (206 BC—25 AD), the Sui Dynasty(581 AD—618 AD), and the Tang Dynasty (618 AD—907 AD), all had their capital cities at Xi'an. Xi'an was the capital city of Chinese civilization for over one thousand years of its five-thousand-year history. In antiquity, Xi'an was called Chang'an. In the year

1369, its name was changed to Xi'an, and has remained the same to the present day. Now the modern city of Xi'an is the capital of Shaanxi Province.

Nanjing is another ancient Chinese capital. The Kingdom of Wu during the Three Kingdoms' Period (229 AD—277 AD) and the Eastern Jin(晋) Dynasty (317 AD—420 AD) all established their capitals in this city. After the outbreak of the 1911 Revolution, Dr. Sun Yat-sen took office as the acting president in Nanjing. From 1927 to 1949, Nanjing performed the role of capital city of the Nationality government of China. Now it is the capital of Jiangsu Province.

Beijing was the capital city of the Jin(金), Yuan, Ming, and Qing Dynasties for a period of more than eight hundred years. After 1949, it became the capital city of the People's Republic of China.

In addition, Luoyang, Kaifeng, and Hangzhou are among what are called the six major ancient Chinese capitals.

Líhécí

Xiān (1st) 先
Jiā bì 加币 (canadian currency)
  yuán / bì (currency)

kǎo shì (test).

adv. preceeds vb. mostly.

  从 + NP + V + O.
  " 美国 回 中国

dào 到 (to arrive)

jì (post)

gāi must be followed by 了

niàn (read) 念

kèwén (lesson) 课

zuò fàn (to cook)
yóu jú 邮局 (Post office)

cì (m word time)
ie; zhè cì
  liáng cì
    jǐ cì?

zhè → zhèi] both
          ] OK.
nà → nèi   ]

shǔshù (to count the #)
shǔ shu (to count) (how many (muc)
  → ie, how many strawberries?

- 24 -

Filling out forms, getting a library card, going to the library to borrow and return books, paying fines for overdue books: these are some of the things that you are very likely to do in your school life. This lesson will teach you how to express these activities in Chinese. You will also learn two sentence patterns particular to the Chinese language.

第十六课 Lesson 16

我把这事儿忘了

一. 课文　　Text

（一）

宋　华：这是北京图书馆。我们进去吧。
zhè shì Běijīng túshūguǎn. wǒmen jìn qu ba
(zhèi)

丁力波：这个图书馆真大。
zhì ge túshūguǎn zhēn dà

层　楼 floor/building
céng　lóu

宋　华：办公室在三楼，我们上楼去，先把借书证办了。
bàngōngshì zài sān　wǒmen shàng qu, bǎ jiè shū zhèng bàn le.

丁力波：今天就可以借书吗？①
jīntiān jiù kéyǐ jiè shū ma?

宋　华：可以，一会儿下来借书……
kéyǐ, yíhuìr xià lai jièshū…
(a little while).

-25-

三楼到了。我看看，是这个办公室。
Sān lóu le. Wǒ kàn kan, shì zhè ge bàngōngshì.

丁 力 波：先生，我想办借书证。
Xiān sheng, wǒ xiǎng bàn jièshūzhèng

工作人员：您带照片来了吗？
Nín dài Zhàopiàn lai le ma?

丁 力 波：带来了。
dài lai le.

工作人员：请先填一张表。
qǐng xiān tián yì zhāng biǎo

北京图书馆借书证

姓名　　丁力波
性别　　男
职业　　学生
学校　　北京语言学院

宋　　华：力波，你从那儿拿一张表来。我告诉你怎么填。
dà wěi, Nǐ cóng nàr ná yì zhāng biǎo lai. Wǒ　　Nǐ zěnme tián.

丁 力 波：我汉字写得太慢，你来填吧。
wǒ wèn xiě de tài màn, Nǐ lái tián ba.

宋　　华：不行。现在你在中国生活，你应该自己填表。②
bù xíng. Xiànzài Nǐ zài Zhōngguó shēnghuó, Nǐ　　zìjǐ tián biǎo.

丁 力 波：好吧，我自己写。"姓名"？
hǎo ba, Wǒ zìjǐ xiě. "xìngmíng"

宋　　华："丁力波"。
"Ma dà wěi."

【填表】Filling out forms

丁 力 波："性别"写什么？
"Xìngbié" xiě shénme?

宋　　华：自己看。③
zìjǐ kàn.

丁 力 波：自——己——看？啊，性别应该写"男"。"职业"呢？
Zì　　jǐ　　kàn? à, xìngbié yīnggāi "Nán". "Zhéyè" ne?

宋 华：写"学生"。好了。你把这张表和照片交了，一会儿那
Xiě. Xuésheng. hǎo le. Nǐ bǎ zhè zhāng biǎo hé jiāo le, Yíhuìr
zhàopiàn.

位先生就给你借书证了。
Wèi xiān sheng jiù gěi Nǐ jièshūzhèng le.

bàn (sit down work / paper work) 它dà (labour)
wǒ bǎ keban wàng le (ba str.)

生词 New Words

1. 把 (informal)	Prep	bǎ	(denoting the disposal of sth.) 把书看了,把钱换了,把练习做了	

ω Verbal predicate to emphasize the disposal of an object (when moving an object or when the state changes for obj.)

2. 忘	V	wàng	to forget 忘了复习课文,把这事儿忘了

↳ always followed by le

3. 图书馆	N	túshūguǎn (↑)	library 去图书馆,进图书馆,参观图书馆, 一个图书馆
图书	N	túshū	books
馆	N	guǎn	↱ a public place shop; a place for cultural activities 饭馆,咖啡馆;美术馆
4. 办公室	N	bàngōngshì	office 经理的办公室,图书馆的办公室,办 公室工作人员,一个办公室
办		bàn	
办公	VO	bàngōng	to handle official business; to work (usu. in an office) 办公时间
室	N	shì	room 休息室
5. 上	V/N	shàng	to go up; to get on / last; previous 上来, 上去,上楼;上次,上星期,上个月
6. 先	Adv	xiān + vb.	first; before 先看电影,先去办公室,先到 图书馆

xiān + bǎ (after)
↳ before verb.

7. 借书证	N	jièshūzhèng	library card 带借书证,办借书证,把借书 证办了,一个借书证
借	V	jiè	to borrow; to lend 借钱,借书,借语法书,

再 again / then. zài.

Xúe sheng zhèng (student card) 借图书馆的书

证	N	zhèng	certificate；card　学生证,出生证,工作证
8. 一会儿	IE	yíhuìr	a little while　一会儿就去,一会儿上楼,
4 +V = in a minute			一会儿去图书馆借书
9. 下	V/N	xià	to go down；to get off/next　下来,下去,
			下楼,一会儿下来；下次,下星期,下个月
10. 带	V	dài	to bring　带本子,带照片,带名片,带礼物,
			带钱,带人民币
11. 填	V	tián	to fill in；to write　怎么填,填什么,填名
			字,填出生年月日
*12. 表	N	biǎo *(watch)*	form；table；list　填表,带表,做一张表
13. 拿	V	ná	to take；to hold；to get　拿报,拿光盘,
			拿一张表来,拿借书证
14. 慢	A	màn	slow；slowly　写得很慢,学得不慢,说得真
			慢,填得太慢
*15. 不行	V	bùxíng	not be allowed；won't do
16. 生活	V/N	shēnghuó	to live/life　在中国生活,在北京学习和
			生活,生活得很好；快乐的生活
17. 自己	Pr	zìjǐ	oneself　你自己,我自己,学生自己,自己
			看,自己写,自己填
18. 姓名	N	xìngmíng	name　学生的姓名,填姓名
19. 性别	N	xìngbié	sex；gender　填性别
20. 职业	N	zhíyè	occupation；profession　什么职业,有职业,
			找职业
21. 交	V	jiāo	to hand in；to hand over；to pay（the rent, etc.）交表,交钱,交照片

（二）

宋　华：我们借书证办了多长时间？
wǒmen jièshū zhèng bàn le duō cháng shíjiān

丁力波：办了十五分钟，办得真快。
bàn le shí wǔ fēnzhōng　bàn de zhēn kuài

宋　华：今天办证的人不多。力波，听说你们上星期考试了，④你考
jīntiān bàn zhèng de rén bù duō. Dà wēi　shuō nǐmen shàng xīngqī kǎoshì le,
nǐ kǎo

得怎么样？
de zěnmeyàng?

丁力波：我口语考得不错，可是翻译考得不太好，语法也有很多问
wǒ kǒuyǔ kǎo de búcuò, kě shì fānyì kǎo de bù tài hǎo, yǔ fǎ yě yǒu hěn duō wèn
(grammar)

题。我想借新的汉语课本看看。
tí. wǒ xiǎng jiè xīn de hànyǔ kè běn kàn kan.

宋　华：现在我们就去借书，我们从这儿出去。我得先把上次借的书
xiànzài wǒmen jiù qù jièshū, wǒmen cóng zhèr chū qu. wǒ děi xiān bǎ shàng cì
jiè de shū

还了。
hái le.

借书厅
借书

wèntí (problem).

丁 力 波：这儿的书可以借多长时间？⑤
Zhèr de shū kěyǐ jiè dōu cháng

宋　　华：可以借一个月。
Kěyǐ jiè yí ge yuè.

先生，我还书。
Xiānsheng, wǒ hái shū.

工作人员：好。……您的书过期了，您得交罚款。
hǎo. Nín de shū guò qī le, Nín děi jiāo Fánkuǎn.
why are we expected to know this…

宋　　华：真对不起，这个月太忙，我把这事儿忘了。罚多少钱？
Zhēn duì bu qǐ, zhè ge yuè tài máng, wǒ bǎ zhè shì wàng le. Fá dōushao qián?

工作人员：一本书过期一天罚两毛，⑥您借了四本书，过了十天，应
Yì běn shū guò qī yì tiān Fá liǎng máo. Nín jiè le sì běn shū, guò le shí tiān,

该交八块钱。
yīngāi xiān bā kuài qián.

宋　　华：给您八块。请问，汉语课本在哪儿？
gěi nín bā kuài. Qǐng wèn, hànyǔ kèběn zài nǎr?

工作人员：那儿有电脑，您可以先查查。
nàr yǒu diànnǎo, nín kěyǐ xiān chá cha.

丁 力 波：有外国人学汉语的新课本吗？
Yǒu gòurén xué hànyǔ de xīn kèběn ma?

工作人员：有。您找一找《新实用汉语课本》。
Yǒu. Nín wǒ yī wǒ xī shíyòng hànyǔ kèběn

【还书】
Returning books

【借书】
Borrowing books

生词 New Words

| 1. | 长 | A | cháng | long　时间很长，借多长时间，办了很长时间 |
| 2. | 考试 | V/N | kǎoshì | to give or take an examination/examination; |

			test　口语考试,语法考试,汉字考试
考	V	kǎo	to give or take an examination; to test 考口语,考生词,考美术,考文化
3. 不错	A	búcuò	not bad　考得不错,填得不错,生活得不错, 很不错
4. 翻译	V	fānyì	to translate; to interpret　翻译英语书,翻译 课文,做翻译练习,考翻译
5. 新	A	xīn	new　新书,新借书证,新问题,新朋友
6. 课本	N	kèběn	textbook　新的汉语课本,借英语课本,他买 的课本
7. 出	V	chū	to go or come out　出来,出去,从这儿出去
8. 还	V	huán	to give back; to return　还书,还课本,还钱
9. 过期	VO	guòqī	to be overdue　过期了,没有过期,什么时候 过期
过	V	guò	to pass
期	N	qī	a period of time
10. 罚款	VO/N	fákuǎn	to impose a fine or forfeit/fine　过期罚款; 交罚款
罚	V	fá	to punish; to penalize　罚钱,罚多少钱,罚 十块钱
款	N	kuǎn	a sum of money
11. 电脑	N	diànnǎo	computer　图书馆的电脑,买电脑,用电脑
电	N	diàn	electricity
脑	N	nǎo	brain
12. 查	V	chá	to check; to look up　查课本,查生词,查语 法,查电脑,用电脑查

13. 《新实用   Xīn Shíyòng Hànyǔ Kèběn
汉语课本》 PN   New Practical Chinese Reader
实用   A   shíyòng   practical

补充生词   Supplementary   Words

1. 阅览室	N	yuèlǎnshì	reading room
2. 杂志	N	zázhì	magazine
3. 问答	N	wèndá	questions and answers
4. 预订	V	yùdìng	to reserve; to book
5. 房间	N	fángjiān	room
6. 国籍	N	guójí	nationality
7. 钥匙	N	yàoshi	key
8. 目录	N	mùlù	catalogue; list
9. 续借	V	xùjiè	to renew
10. 年龄	N	niánlíng	age
11. 广东	PN	Guǎngdōng	Guangdong Province
12. 茶楼	N	chálóu	tearooms; tea house
13. 老人	N	lǎorén	the elderly; the aged; old man or woman
14. 开始	V	kāishǐ	to start; to begin
15. 孩子	N	háizi	child
16. 热闹	A	rènao	lively; bustling with noise and excitement

bāng zhù
帮助 帮助 to help

二. 注释　Notes

① 今天就可以借书吗？

"Can I start borrowing books today？"

The adverb "就"(2) is often used to suggest the earliness or quickness of an action. It is also used to indicate that an action or event takes place immediately after the previous one. For example：

刚七点，他就来了。

我们现在就去借书。

② 现在你在中国生活，你应该自己填表。

"Now that you are living in China, you should fill in the form by yourself."

The pronoun "自己" is frequently used to refer back to the pronoun or noun preceding it for emphasis. e.g. "他自己"，"我们自己"，"力波自己"，"老师自己"，"医生自己".

③ 自己看。

"You yourself know (what to write)."

④ 听说你们上星期考试了。

"I heard that you had an exam last week."

"上" and "下" are both used with reference to the order of things or to time sequence, with "上" meaning "last" or "previous", and "下" meaning "next" or "the following".

last/previous		*this*		*next/the following*	
上次	(last time)	这次	(this time)	下次	(next time)
上星期五	(last Friday)	（这个）星期五	(this Friday)	下星期五	(next Friday)
上月	(last month)	这个月	(this month)	下月	(next month)

⑤ 这儿的书可以借多长时间？

"How long is the loan period here for a book？"

⑥ 一本书过期一天罚两毛。

"The fine for an overdue book is two *mao* per day."

三. 练习与运用　Drills and Practice

KEY SENTENCES

1. 我们进去吧。
2. 我们上楼去,先把借书证办了。
3. 您带照片来了吗?
4. 现在你在中国生活,你应该自己填表。
5. 一会儿那位先生就给你借书证了。
6. 这儿的书可以借多长时间?
7. 您的书过期了,您得交罚款。
8. 真对不起,这个月太忙,我把这事儿忘了。

1. 熟读下列短语 Master the following phrases

（1）现在就去　今天就来　星期六就去看电影　下午就去图书馆借书
一会儿就来　一会儿就回家　一会儿就复习汉语语法　一会儿就写汉字

（2）自己写　自己念　自己拿　自己带　自己复习　自己锻炼　自己旅行
她们自己去借书　她自己去买东西　他自己洗衣服　他们自己翻译课文
马大为自己租房子　我自己打扫宿舍　我们自己练习口语

（3）上来　　上去　　下来　　下去　　进来　　进去　　出来　　出去
上楼去　　下楼来　　寄钱去　寄明信片来　　回宿舍去　　回家来
到西安去　　到北京来　　带照片来　　带英镑去　　拿一本书来

（4）把这本书看了　　把钱换了　　把礼物拿了　　把饭吃了　把咖啡喝了
把衣服洗了　　把这张表交了　　把借书证办了　　把图书馆的书还了
把那本书借了　　把这事儿忘了

（5）借一个月　　等一会儿　　看一个星期　　住两年　　复习三天
睡二十分钟
来了五分钟　等了两小时　用了一个月　参观了三天　学习了一年

2. 句型替换 Pattern drills

(1) 现在几点？

现在10点。

他从王府井 回来了没有？

没有。他一会儿就回来。

8:45	办公室	出来
7:15	八楼	下来
11:30	一楼	上来

(2) 张小姐在吗？

不在,她上课去了。

她带语法书去了吗？

她没有带语法书去。

下楼	今天的报
回家	练习本(子)
到阅览室(yuèlǎnshì)	借书证

(3) 他给你送什么来了？

他给我送《新实用汉语课本》来了。

寄	明信片
拿	电脑
买	普通话光盘

(4) 那张表呢？

他把那张表交了。

他的药	吃
他的咖啡	喝
他写的信	寄
图书馆的杂志(zázhì)	还

(5) 我们出去散步,好吗？

对不起,现在不行。

你有事儿吗？

我得把今天的 练习 做了。

课文	复习
生词	翻译
汉字	写

(6) 上星期六,你跟力波一起去银行 换钱了吗?

没有,我自己去了。

你等了多长时间?

我等了一会儿。

邮局	寄东西	10分钟
医院	看病	半小时
图书馆	还书	5分钟

(7) 下个月我就回美国去了。

是吗? 这次你在美国要住

多长时间?

要住一年。

下星期	到西安	3天
这星期五	到欧洲	2个星期
明天	回上海	2个月

(8) 你外语 考了多长时间?

我考了两个小时。

你考得怎么样?

我口语考得不错,可是翻译考得不太好。

汉语	复习	一星期	语法	汉字
美术	学习	一年	中国画	汉语
练习	做	一个半小时	问答(wèndá)	翻译

3. 课堂活动 Classroom activity

Ask three of your classmates in Chinese, how much time they spend each day on the following activities, and then report your findings to the whole class:

(1)念课文; (2)练习口语; (3)做语法练习; (4)写汉字

4. 会话练习 Conversation exercises

[填表 Filling out forms]

A:先生,我预订(yùdìng)了一个房间(fángjiān)。我姓_____,

叫_____。

B:我查一下。对,请先填一下这张表。

A:请问,怎么填?

B:这儿填您的姓名、性别和国籍(guójí),这儿填您的护照号。

A:您看看,我填得对吗?

B：对。这是钥匙(yàoshi)。您的房间是668号。

[借书 Borrowing books]

(1) A：请问,有新_____?

B：你可以查一查目录(mùlù)。

A：在哪儿查?

B：那儿有电脑,你自己_____。

(2) A：先生,我想借这五本书。

B：好。您带借书证来了吗?

A：_____。请问您这儿的书可以借多长时间?

B：_____。

[还书 Returning books]

A：先生,我还上次借的书。

B：好的。您上次借了五本书,这儿是四本。

A：是吗? 真对不起,我把那本书的名字忘了,您能帮助我查一查吗?

B：可以。您上次借的书是_____。

A：谢谢,我可以续借(xùjiè)这本书吗?

B：您可以续借一个月。

[认识新朋友 Making new friends]

(1) A：您好,您要出去啊?

B：您好! 您也住这儿?

A：我住九楼。这是我的名片。

B：谢谢。对不起,我没有带名片。我姓王,住三楼。

A：王先生,认识您很高兴。有时间上来坐坐。

B：好的。

(2) B：可以进来吗？

A：啊，是王先生，快进来吧。请坐，请喝茶。

B：谢谢。

B：不早了，我该回去了。

A：有时间常来玩儿。

B：谢谢。您不要出来了。

A：好，慢走。

[暂时离开 Leaving and coming back in a moment]

(1) A：张先生，您的电话。

B：好，我就来。

(to C，D)对不起，我＿＿＿＿＿＿＿＿＿＿＿，一会儿就回来。

(2) A：张先生在吗？

B：在，我就是。有事儿吗？

A：经理请你去一下。

B：好，我一会儿就去。

(to C，D)你们先喝咖啡，我一会儿＿＿＿＿＿＿＿＿＿＿。

5. 看图说话 Describe the following pictures

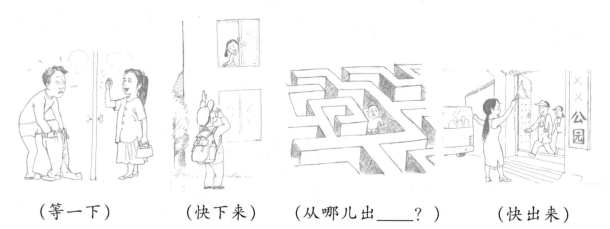

　（等一下）　　　　　（快下来）　　（从哪儿出＿＿？）　　　　（快出来）

－38－

6. 交际练习 Communication practice

（1）You go to the university library to borrow books about the Chinese language. First, you ask the library staff where the grammar books are located, and how to find them. Then you ask whether there are any new or good textbooks for spoken Chinese. The library staff answer all of your questions.

（2）Last time, you borrowed five Chinese books dealing with grammar, spoken Chinese, translation, and Chinese characters. You have kept these books for over a month. Today when you go to the library to return them, you find out that they are overdue and you have to pay fines.

（3）You want to get a library card. You must fill out the following form：

姓名		性别	
年龄(niánlíng)		职业	
国籍(guójí)		学院	
系		专业	

四. 阅读和复述 Reading Comprehension and Paraphrasing

广东(Guǎngdōng)的茶楼(chálóu)

不少广东老人(lǎorén)的每一天都从茶楼开始(kāishǐ)。他们都起得很早，五点半就出来散步，锻炼身体，六点钟就到了茶楼。那儿老人很多，他们跟认识的人问好，跟朋友说说昨天的事儿。王先生每天都带报来，他喜欢自己看看报，喝喝茶，等女儿和小孙女儿来。他等了一会儿，她们都来了。这时候，很多家的爸爸、妈妈、外婆、奶奶，还有孩子(háizi)们，也都来了，一家人在一起吃饭、喝茶、休息。孩子们不想吃，也不想喝，他们喜欢在一起玩儿，真热闹(rènao)啊！很多年轻人也都在这儿看报，他们要知道今天的新事儿和新问题。广东人常说：他们来喝茶，喝的是茶楼里的热闹，喝的是一家人一起吃饭的快乐。把茶喝了,把东西吃了,把报也看了,年轻人就去工作了。老人们新的一天也开始了。

五．语法　　　　　　　Grammar

1. 简单趋向补语 The simple directional complement

"来" and "去" are often placed after certain verbs to act as their complements, showing the direction of their actions. Such complements are called simple directional complements. If the action moves towards the speaker, or proceeds towards the object(s) under discussion, we use "来"; and if the action moves away from the speaker or proceeds away from the object(s) under discussion, we use "去". For example:

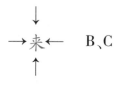

B、C

A:请进来。

(The speaker is standing inside.)

F

G、H

D、E:她上来了。

(The speakers are standing upside.)

B、C:我们进去吧。

(The speakers are standing outside.)

B、C

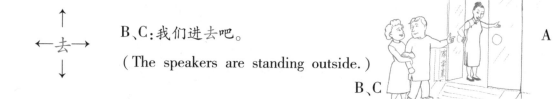

A

G、H：她上去了。

（The speakers are standing downside.）

If a verb with a simple directional complement has an object, it should be placed between the verb and its complement. To negate the completion of an action, the negative adverb "没（有）" is used. To form the V/A-not-V/A question with this construction, use the affirmative and negative forms of the predicative verb.

V ＋ O ＋ 来／去

Subject	Predicate				
	Adverbial	**V**	**O**	**来／去**	**Pt**
我们	先	进		去	吧。
她们		出		来	了。
他们		上	楼	去	了吗？
我	没（有）	回	家	去。	
你	明天	拿不拿	明信片	来？	
他		带没带	照片	来？	

Note: The verb in this type of sentence cannot be modified by the particle "了"①; but the particle "了"② can be used at the end of the sentence to show that something has already happened. Thus, we cannot say ⊗ "你回了家去吗？"

2. "把" 字句 （1） The "把" sentence (1)

The "把" sentence is a kind of sentence with a verbal predicate. It is frequently used in Chinese to show how the action in the sentence disposes of an object and how this disposal affects the object, i.e. whether the object has been transposed, or its state has been changed. For example:

General statement　　　　vs.　　　　Emphasis on disposal

A：你去做什么了？　　　　　　　A：你的书呢？怎么不在这儿了？

B：我去还书了。　　　　　　　　B：我把书还了。（so you can't find it now）

A：她的生日是几号？　　　　　　A：昨天你为什么不参加她的生日聚会？

B：我忘了(她的生日)。　　　　　B：真对不起，我把她的生日忘了。

（so I've made such a mistake）

In the "把" sentence, the preposition "把" and its object — the thing(s) to be disposed of — must function together as an adverbial and be placed after the subject and before the verb.

S + 把 + O + V + other elements

Subject	Predicate					
	OpV	Adverbial	Prep "把"	O (disposed of)	V	Other elements
我			把	这事儿	忘	了。
你			把	那张表和照片	交	了吗？
我	得	先	把	上次借的书	还	了。
你			把	借书证	办	了没有？

We can see the following points from the sentences in the above table：

（1）The main verb in the "把" sentence must be a transitive one, and often it has the meaning "dispose of" or "manipulate". Verbs such as "有，在，是，来，去，回，喜欢，觉得 and 知道"， which do not have the meaning "dispose of" or "manipulate", cannot be used in the "把" sentence.

（2）The object in the "把" sentence is usually definite in the speaker's mind. Therefore，we cannot say：⊗"我先把一本书还了。" We can only say："我先把那本书还了"，or "我先把上次借的书还了。"

（3）The verb in the "把" sentence must take some other element(s) after it. The "把" sentences discussed in this lesson all have the particle "了" at the end (and we will introduce the other "把" sentences with different element(s) later). We cannot say：⊗ "我把这事儿忘"；we must say："我把这事儿忘了" instead.

（4）An optative verb or adverb (functioning as an adverbial) must be put before "把". For example： "我得先把上次借的书还了。"

3. 时量补语 (1) The time-measure complement (1)

The time-measure complement is used after a verb to indicate the duration of an action or state.　When the verb has an object, it is duplicated after the object and then followed by a time-measure complement.　The first verb is usually omitted in this construction, and its interrogative form often uses the phrase "多长时间".

(V) + O + V + time-measure complement

Subject	Predicate				
	(V)	O	V	Pt	Time-measure Complement
你			等		一会儿。
丁力波			学习	了	半年。
我们	(办)	借书证	办	了	多长时间?
我	(考)	外语	考	了	两个小时。

Note：　Only time phrases indicating a period of time can be used as time-measure complements, such as "一分钟, 两小时, 三天, 四个月, 五年 and 一会儿".　Time phrases indicating a point of time on the time scale, such as "三点钟, 一月一号, 2002 年", cannot be used as time-measure complements, since they do not express a duration of time. For example, we　cannot say：⊗ "我等了一点半。"

To create the negative form,　a negative adverb is usually placed before the predicative verb of the sentence with the time-measure complement. For example：

丁力波没有学习半年,他学习了三个月。

你外语考了两个小时吗?

——我外语没有考两个小时。

六. 汉字　Chinese Characters

1. 汉字的构字法(2) Methods of constructing Chinese characters (2)

Ideographic method（指事法）：This is a method in which new characters are created by adding signs to conventional symbols and pictographs.　There is only a small number of characters that fall under this category,　and they are basically of two types:

a. Those created on the basis of the conventional symbols established in primitive times. For example: 一,二,三,四,五,六,七.

b. Those created by adding indicative signs to pictographs. For example: 刃, 本,早,上,中,下.

2. 认写基本汉字 Learn and write basic Chinese characters

(1) 表　　　　一 二 丰 主 丰 寿 表 表

biǎo　　form　　　　　　　　　　　　　　8 strokes

(2) 卅　　　　丿 川 川 卅

sà　　thirty　　　　　　　　　　　　　　4 strokes

(3) 官　　　　丶 丷 宀 宀 宀 宀 官 官

guān　　official　　　　　　　　　　　　8 strokes

(4) 正　　　　一 丁 下 正 正

zhèng　　right　　　　　　　　　　　　5 strokes

(5) 式　　　　一 二 干 王 式 式

shì　　style　　　　　　　　　　　　　　6 strokes

3. 认写课文中的汉字 Learn and write the Chinese characters appearing in the texts

(1) 把 bǎ

把 → 扌 + 巴　　　　　　　　　　　7 strokes

(2) 忘 wàng

忘 → 亡 + 心　　　　　　　　　　7 strokes

(3) 图书馆 túshūguǎn（圖書館）

图 → 囗 + 冬　　　　　　　　　　8 strokes

馆 → 饣 + 官　　　　　　　　　　11 strokes

(4) 办公室 bàngōngshì（辦公室）

室 → 宀 + 至　　　　　　　　　　9 strokes

(5) 借书证 jièshūzhèng（借書證）

借 → 亻 + 龷 + 日　　　　　　　　10 strokes

证 → 讠 + 正　　　　　　　　　　7 strokes

(6) 填 tián

填 → 土 + 真　　　　　　　　　　13 strokes

(7) 带 dài（帶）

带 → 丗 + 冖 + 巾　　　　　　　　9 strokes

(8) 慢 màn

慢 → 忄 + 日 + 四 + 又　　　　　14 strokes

(9) 生活 shēnghuó

活 → 氵 + 舌　　　　　　　　　　9 strokes

(10) 性别 xìngbié

性 → 忄 + 生　　　　　　　　　　8 strokes

别 → 口 + 力 + 刂　　　　　　　7 strokes

(11) 职业 zhíyè（職業）

职 → 耳 + 只　　　　　　　　　11 strokes

(12) 交 jiāo

交 → 亠 + 父　　　　　　　　　6 strokes

(13) 考试 kǎoshì（考試）

考 → 耂 + 丂　　　　　　　　　6 strokes

试 → 讠 + 式　　　　　　　　　8 strokes

(14) 不错 búcuò（不錯）

错 → 钅 + 昔　　　　　　　　　13 strokes

釆 (fānzìtóu)　丿 ㇒ ㇜ 二 平 釆 釆　　　　7 strokes

(15) 翻译 fānyì（翻譯）

翻 → 釆 + 田 + 丬 + 羽　　　18 strokes

译 → 讠 + 又 + 十　　　　　　7 strokes

(16) 新 xīn

新 → 立 + 木 + 斤　　　　　　13 strokes

(17) 罚款 fákuǎn（罰款）

$$罚 \rightarrow 四 + 讠 + 刂 \qquad \text{9 strokes}$$

$$款 \rightarrow 士 + 示 + 欠 \qquad \text{12 strokes}$$

(18) 电脑 diànnǎo（電腦）

$$脑 \rightarrow 月 + 亠 + 凶 \qquad \text{10 strokes}$$

(19) 查 chá

$$查 \rightarrow 木 + 日 + 一 \qquad \text{9 strokes}$$

(20) 实用 shíyòng（實用）

$$实 \rightarrow 宀 + 头 \qquad \text{8 strokes}$$

文化知识　　　Cultural Notes

The Educational System of China

The educational system of China consists of basic education, vocational and technical education, higher education, and adult education. Basic education refers to pre-school, primary, and general secondary education.

Chinese children usually start their schooling at the age of six or seven. They spend six years in an elementary school. After that, they enter junior middle school to study for three more years. These nine years of schooling are generally referred to as "nine-year compulsory education", and are made universal in most parts of China.

After graduating from junior middle school, many students enter senior middle school, whereas some choose to go to specialized secondary school or vocational secondary school (generally called "vocational senior middle school"). The period of study for both types of school is three years. After graduating, students may seek employment, or they may choose to continue their studies at the higher education level.

The length of schooling for a university education is usually four years, but some programs (medicine, for instance) require five years of study. At the time of graduation, if a student meets all the academic requirements, and is given the authorization of the state, a bachelor's degree is then conferred upon him or her by the university. After graduating from university, one may opt for further studies toward master's and doctoral degrees. Each degree usually takes three years to obtain. Like most universities in the world, Chinese universities offer three academic degrees, i.e., the bachelor's, the master's, and the doctorate.

Have you ever worn Chinese-style clothes before? Do you know what a Chinese cheongsam is? When shopping for clothes, do you usually compare colour, price, size and style? In this lesson you will learn how to choose clothes and make comparisons in Chinese.

第十七课 Lesson 17

这件旗袍比那件漂亮

一. 课文　Text

（一）

丁力波：小云，哪儿卖中式衣服？
shǎo yún Nǎr mài zōngshì yīfu?

王小云：你不知道吗？你来北京
Nǐ bù nē dao ma? NY lái běijīng.
→ path (Never learned this...)
　　　　多长时间了？①
dōu chǎng shí wen le?

丁力波：我来北京半年了。可是你在
Wǒ lái běijīng bànnián le. Kě shì ni zài

　　　　北京已经二十年了，你是北京人，
běijīng yǐjīng èr shí nian le, NY shì běijīngrén

　　　　你当然比我知道得多。
NY dāngrán bǐ wǒ nē dào de duō.

王小云：你说得对。现在北京的商店和商场
NY shōu de duì. Xiànzài běijīng de shàng dian né shān chǎng

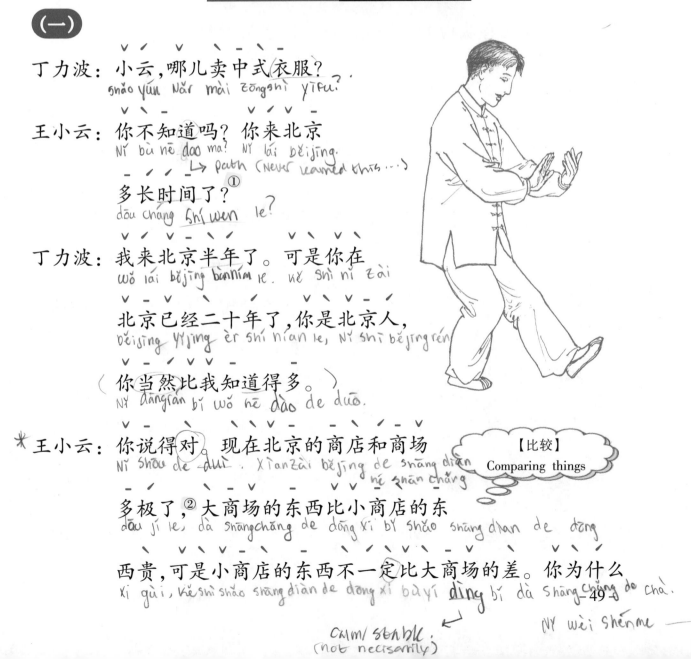

【比较】
Comparing things

　　　　多极了，②大商场的东西比小商店的东
dōu jí le, dà shāngchǎng de dǒng xi bǐ shǎo shàng dian de dòng

　　　　西贵，可是小商店的东西不一定比大商场的差。你为什么
Xi gùi, kě shì shǎo shàng dian de dòng xi bàyí dìng bǐ dà shàng chàng de chā.
NY wèi shénme

chm/ stable (not necessarily)

49

现在想买中式衣服？

丁力波：从下星期开始，我要学太极拳，我得穿一套中式衣服。

王小云：好极了！③ 你穿中式衣服一定很帅。你喜欢什么颜色的，

黑的还是红的？

【描述事物】
Describing things

丁力波：我喜欢白的。

王小云：我也喜欢白的，白的漂亮。你想买好的还是买便宜的？

丁力波：我不要太贵的，也不要太便宜的。你说该去哪儿买？

王小云：去王府井吧。那儿东西多，可能贵一点儿。

丁力波：贵一点儿没关系。我们下午就去吧，我还想去公园走走。

生词 New Words

1. 旗袍	N	qípáo	cheongsam; a long formal dress with a slit skirt 一件旗袍,这件旗袍,中国的旗袍
2. 比	Prep	bǐ	than (indicating comparison) 比那件漂亮,比他好,比今天冷,比这件贵一点儿
3. 卖	V	mài	to sell 卖衣服,卖光盘,卖苹果,卖中药,卖东西
4. 中式	A	zhōngshì	Chinese style 中式衣服,中式房子
式	N	shì	type; style
5. 已经	Adv	yǐjing	already 已经二十年了,已经来了,已经买旗袍了

前宽

氵- language radical.

Zenme mái 二
dou sh qian

讠去 fǎ french.
Fang zi = house.

intended
dǎ suan
打算

6.	商店	N	shāngdiàn (个)	shop; store 小商店,北京的商店,去商店买东西,一个商店
	商	N	shāng	commerce; business
	店	N	diàn	shop; store
7.	极(了)	Adv	jí(le)	extremely 多极了,慢极了,漂亮极了,流利极了
8.	一定	Adv	yídìng	must; surely 一定很新,一定很脏,一定知道,不一定早,不一定懂
9.	差	A	chà	not up to standard; poor; bad 很差,差极了,不一定差,不一定比大商场的东西差
10.	开始	V	kāishǐ	to start; to begin 从下星期开始,从现在开始,从八点开始考试,开始学中文,开始工作
11.	太极拳	N	tàijíquán	Taiji Boxing 学太极拳,打太极拳
12.	套	M	tào	set; suit; suite 一套中式衣服,一套大房子,一套新课本
13.	帅	A	shuài	handsome; smart 很帅,帅极了,比他帅,一定很帅
14.	颜色	N	yánsè	colour 什么颜色,漂亮的颜色,旗袍的颜色,衣服的颜色
15.	黑	A	hēi	black 黑的,黑颜色,黑衣服
*16.	红	A	hóng	red 红的,红颜色,红苹果
17.	白	A	bái	white 白的,白颜色,白旗袍
18.	便宜	A	piányi	cheap 便宜的,一套便宜的衣服,一定很便宜
*19.	没关系	IE	méi guānxi	never mind; it doesn't matter 贵一点儿没关系,慢一点儿没关系,少一点儿没关系
20.	公园	N	gōngyuán	park 去公园玩儿,去公园打太极拳,到公园去,一个公园
21.	走	V	zǒu	to walk; to go 去公园走走,走了一个小时,走得很快

(handwritten annotations: "always." under 7; "necessarily" next to 8; "(bad)" next to 9; "对 duì" next to 店; "mw 1 a set of smt" next to 12)

打 - dǎ practice.

（二）

宋　华：两个小时过去了，你要的
衣服还没买。

林　娜：谁说我没有买？我已经
买了衬衫了。④

宋　华：你要的旗袍呢？

林　娜：刚才看的旗袍都不错，我真想都买了。

宋　华：我们还有时间，可以再多看看。这件绿的怎么样？

林　娜：啊，这件漂亮极了，颜色、样子都比刚才看的旗袍好。

售货员：您可以试一试。

【买衣服】
Buying clothes

林　娜：好。我觉得这件大点儿，是不是？

售货员：我给您换一件小的。这件是三十八号，比那件小两号。您
再拿去试试吧。

林　娜：这件比那件合适，宋华，你看怎么样？

time measure.

(V+O)+V+ time compliment.

women kao le ban ↑ xiaoshi
↳Object must be seperated by V.

shui jiao
V   N   +V (了)+ time measure.
↳ if already happened.

宋　华：我觉得这件太短了。
wǒ júe de zhè jiàn tài duǎn le.

售货员：对,您比我高,得穿长点儿的,我再给您找找。有了,这件
—, nín bǐ wǒ gāo, děi chuān cháng diǎnr de, wǒ zài gěi nín wǒ wǒ, yǒu le, zhè jiàn.

红的比那件绿的长两公分。您再试一试这件。
hóng de bǐ nà jiàn lǜ de cháng liǎng gōngfēn. Nín zài shì yí shì zhè jiàn.

林　娜：小姐,太麻烦您了,真不好意思。⑤ 这件很合适。
xiǎojiě, bài ___ nín le, zhēn bù hǎo yìsi. zhè jiàn hěn néshì.
↳ idea.

宋　华：这件红旗袍比那件绿的漂亮。
zhè jiàn hóng qípáo bǐ nà jiàn lǜ de piàoliang.

林　娜：可是也贵多了。
kě shì yě guì duō le.

宋　华：比那件贵多少?
bǐ nà — guì duō shao?

林　娜：贵九十块钱。
guì jiǔ shí kuài qían.

宋　华：丝绸的当然贵一点儿。
sīchóu de dángrán guì yì diǎnr.

林　娜：好吧,我就买这件。⑥ 宋华,现在该去买你的了。你穿多大
hǎo ba, wǒ ___ mǎi zhè jiàn. Sònghuá xiànzài gāi qù mǎi nǐ de le. nǐ chuān duō dà

号的?想不想试试那套西服?
hào de? Xiǎng bu xiǎng shì shì nà tào xīfú?
↳ cover / case

生词 New Words

↳measure word / Noun
(xīngqī ie; — ↑ xīngxī oﬀ — xīngqī)

1.	小时	N	xiǎoshí	(个)	hour 两个小时,几个小时,多少小时
2.	过去	V	guòqù		to pass 两个小时过去了,三天过去了
3.	衬衫	N	chènshān	(件	shirt 一件衬衫,白衬衫,中式衬衫,买了衬衫了
4.	绿	A	lǜ		green 绿的,绿颜色,绿衬衫,绿香蕉

仁 wéi (handwritten at top)

5.	样子	N	yàngzi	*style of something* (handwritten)	shape; sample; model; pattern 样子好，衬衫的样子，旗袍的样子
6.	售货员	N	shòuhuòyuán		shop assistant; salesclerk
	售	V	shòu		to sell 售书
	货	N	huò		goods
7.	试	V	shì		to try on；to have a try 试试，试一试，试试这件，试一试那件衣服
8.	觉得	V	juéde		to feel；to think 觉得太长，觉得很合适，觉得这件大点儿，觉得非常帅，觉得便宜极了
9.	合适	A	héshì		suitable；appropriate；right 很合适，合适极了，这件绿衬衫比那件红的合适
10.	短	A	duǎn	*+一点儿 (comparitive)* (handwritten)	short 短旗袍，短衬衫，短极了，短一点儿，觉得这件太短了
11.	高	A	gāo		high；tall 比我高，高一点儿，房租高
12.	公分	N	gōngfēn		centimeter 两公分，短一公分，比那套长两公分
13.	麻烦	V	máfan		to bother sb.；to trouble sb. 麻烦您，太麻烦您了，很麻烦，不麻烦
14.	丝绸	N	sīchóu		silk 丝绸的，丝绸衬衫，中国丝绸
15.	西服	N	xīfú	*套件* (handwritten)	Western-style clothes；suit 一套西服，穿西服，西服的样子，合适的西服

补充生词 Supplementary Words

1.	双	M	shuāng	pair
2.	鞋（子）	N	xié(zi)	shoes
3.	头发	N	tóufa	hair
4.	打折	VO	dǎzhé	to sell at a discount；to give a discount 打九折(to sell at ten percent discount)
5.	条	M	tiáo	(a measure word for long, narrow objects, such as trousers, skirt, snake, etc.)

6. 裤子	N	kùzi	trousers；pants
7. 相声	N	xiàngsheng	comic dialogue；repartee
8. 了不起	IE	liǎobuqǐ	amazing；terrific；extraordinary
9. 薄	A	báo	thin
10. 页	M	yè	page
11. 料子	N	liàozi	material for making clothes
12. 布	N	bù	cloth；fabric
13. 总是	Adv	zǒngshì	always
14. 表	N	biǎo	watch

二. 注释 Notes

① 你来北京多长时间了？

"How long have you been in Beijing?"

Some actions, such as "来，去，到", do not endure over time, so a time-measure complement must be used to indicate a period of time from the occurance of this kind of actions until the time of speaking. When the verb is followed by an object, the time-measure complement must be placed after the object. For example：

我来中国已经一年了。

他去图书馆已经两个小时了。

② 现在北京的商店和商场多极了。

"Now there are plenty of stores and shopping malls in Beijing."

In spoken language, "极了" and "多了" are often placed after an adjective or a verb as a complement to indicate an extent or degree. "极了" denotes the highest degree, while "多了" indicates a great extent of difference. For example：

NaIí = bu keqi

A/V + 极了/ 多了

这件旗袍	漂亮	极了。
他	高兴	极了。
那本书比这本书	贵	多了。
他哥哥比他	年轻	多了。

③ 好极了!

"That's wonderful!"

In spoken language, this is an expression indicating absolute agreement or satisfaction. It is more emphatic than "太好了".

Note the range of expressions used to describe the qualities of things:

好极了,太好了 (marvelous; excellent)

↓

非常好,很好 (very good), 好 (good)

↓

不错 (not bad),还可以,马马虎虎 (passable; just so-so), 不太好 (not very good)

↓

不好,差,坏 (bad)

④ 我已经买了衬衫了。

"I have already bought the shirts."

A verb plus the particle "了"① is a perfective construction. If the object does not have an attributive or a numeral classifier compound, it requires the particle "了"② to complete the sentence. These two particles together indicate the completion and realization of the action expressed by the verb. They also emphasize that the event or situation has already occurred. For example:

我买了衬衫了。

我吃了饭了。

⑤ 小姐,太麻烦您了,真不好意思。

"Miss, I'm really sorry to have troubled you so much."

This expression conveys apology as well as heartfelt thanks.

⑥ 好吧,我就买这件。

"All right, I'll buy this one."

This is a common shopping expression. The word "就" shows emphasis.

三. 练习与运用　Drills and Practice

> **KEY SENTENCES**
> 1. 你来北京多长时间了?
> 2. 你喜欢什么颜色的,黑的还是红的?
> 3. 我已经买了衬衫了。
> 4. 这件红旗袍比那件绿的漂亮。
> 5. 这件红的比那件绿的长两公分。
> 6. 这件比那件贵多了。
> 7. 你当然比我知道得多。
> 8. 现在北京的商店和商场多极了。

1. 熟读下列短语　Master the following phrases

(1) 黑的　红的　白的　绿的　早的　晚的　快的　慢的　合适的　有名的
　　这间大的　　那间小的　　这个长的　　那个短的　　这瓶多的　　那瓶少的
　　这套中式的　　那套漂亮的　　这件贵的　　那件便宜的
　　中国的　　外国的　　中文的　　外语的　　语法的　　口语的
　　老师的　　医生的　　外婆的　　女儿的　　司机的　　工作人员的
　　学院的　　办公室的　　图书馆的　　商店的

(2) 比他好　比我忙　比西安大　比这件贵　比今天冷　比我的宿舍脏
　　比我来得早　　比他说得流利　　比他朋友写得好　　比你休息得晚
　　比我们生活得快乐　　比这儿发展得快

(3) 贵三十块钱　便宜六百块　长两公分　短五公分　多一个　少四十张
　　比她大一岁　比他早七个小时　比我晚一个星期　比小云快十分钟
　　比大为慢一点儿　比林娜高两公分

(4) 多极了　疼极了　对极了　好极了　可爱极了　容易极了　便宜极了
　　贵多了　新多了　早多了　长多了　多多了　　差多了　　短多了
　　流利多了　舒服多了　年轻多了　漂亮多了　合适多了

(5) 来北京半年了　去欧洲一年了　去西安十天了　到银行已经半个小时了
　　去公园已经一个半小时了

(6) 写了 50 个汉字了　　问了两个问题了　　看了一本汉语书了

　　复习了十个生词了　　试了三件旗袍了

2. 句型替换 Pattern drills

(1) 他来 中国已经多长时间了?
　　他来中国半年了。

去	上海	两个月
来	语言学院	一年
去	商店	20 分钟
来	公园	一个小时

(2) 这件旗袍怎么样?
　　这件旗袍比那件旗袍漂亮,
　　这件漂亮极了。

(个)电影	有意思
(个)医院	大
(瓶)红葡萄酒	贵
(位)售货员	好

(3) 今天比昨天 冷吗?
　　我觉得今天不比昨天 冷。

上午	下午	忙
小商店的东西	大商场的东西	便宜
这个课本	那个课本	合适
他	他哥哥	帅

(4) 这件衬衫 大还是那件衬衫 大?
　　这件衬衫 大。
　　这件衬衫比那件衬衫大多少?
　　这件衬衫比那件衬衫大两公分。

(套)西服	贵	200 块钱
(双 shuāng)		
鞋(xié)	小	1 号
(件)旗袍	长	一点儿
(个)楼	高	多了

(5) 他比他朋友来得早吗?
　　不,他朋友比他来得早。

走	快
睡	晚
吃	多
介绍	好

(6) 你课文 翻译得真好!
　　哪里,我翻译得不好。
　　她翻译 课文比我翻译得好。

太极拳	学	快
汉语	说	流利
汉字	写	漂亮
口语	考	好

3. 课堂活动 Classroom activity

Complete the following comparisons

(1) 汉语书：23 块；英语书：37 块

　　——▶　汉语书比英语书便宜,汉语书比英语书便宜多少?

　　　　　汉语书比英语书便宜 ＿＿＿14＿＿＿ 块。

(2) 汉字课本：18.50 元；口语课本：26.90 元

　　——▶　口语课本比汉字课本 ＿＿＿＿＿,口语课本比汉字课本 ＿＿＿＿

　　　　　多少?

　　　　　口语课本比汉字课本 ＿＿＿＿＿＿＿ 块。

(3) 我们系：350 人；你们系：240 人

　　——▶　我们系的人比你们系的人 ＿＿＿＿,我们系的人比你们系的人

　　　　　＿＿＿＿ 多少?

　　　　　我们系的人比 ＿＿＿＿＿＿＿＿＿ 人。

(4) 王老师：43 岁；陈老师：30 岁

　　——▶　王老师比陈老师 ＿＿＿＿＿,王老师比陈老师 ＿＿＿＿＿ 多少?

　　　　　王老师比 ＿＿＿＿＿＿＿＿＿ 岁。

(5) 这件旗袍：120 公分；那件旗袍：117 公分

　　——▶　这件旗袍比那件旗袍 ＿＿＿＿＿,这件旗袍比那件旗袍 ＿＿＿＿

　　　　　多少?

　　　　　这件旗袍比 ＿＿＿＿＿＿＿ 公分。

4. 会话练习 Conversation exercises

[描述事物 Describing things]

(1) A：请问,张老师在吗?

　　B：哪位张老师?

　　A：对不起,我不知道他的名字,他在 ＿＿＿＿＿＿＿＿＿ 工作。

B：男的还是女的？

A：男的。他比您高，岁数也比您大一点儿，头发(tóufa)有点儿白。

B：我知道了，他叫张大生，在二楼209办公室。

A：谢谢。

(2) A：好久不见，你今天穿得真漂亮。

B：谢谢。这是我刚在 ＿＿＿＿＿＿＿＿＿ 买的新衣服。

A：颜色好极了，样子也很新，我喜欢中式的。

B：是啊，中式的比西服 ＿＿＿＿＿＿＿＿＿。

[比较 Comparing things]

(1) A：小云，你是北京人，给我们介绍介绍北京吧。你应该
　　　比 ＿＿＿＿＿＿＿＿＿＿＿＿＿。

B：好。北京这两年发展得很快，现在大商场和银行多 ＿＿＿＿＿＿＿＿。

A：听说上海的商场也非常多。

B：你说得对，上海的商场可能比 ＿＿＿＿＿＿＿＿＿。

(2) A：力波，你来北京多长时间了？

B：＿＿＿＿＿＿＿＿＿＿＿＿。

A：我觉得你汉语比我说得 ＿＿＿＿＿＿＿＿＿。

B：哪里，你的语法和汉字 ＿＿＿＿＿＿＿＿＿＿＿ 多了。

[买衣服 Buying clothes]

(1) A：小姐，我想买双鞋。

B：您穿多大号的？

A：我穿42号的。

B：您看看这双。

A：可以试一下吗？

B：可以。合适吗？

A：我觉得小点儿。

B：您再试试这双。这双比那双大半号。

A：这双真合适。多少钱？

B：280 块。

A：能便宜点儿吗？

B：好吧，打九折(zhé)。

(2) A：你觉得这条(tiáo)裤子(kùzi)怎么样？

B：比刚才那条好。小姐，多少钱一条？

C：350 块。

A：有便宜点儿的吗？

C：有。您穿多少公分的？

A：我穿 75 公分的。

C：这条合适。

A：多少钱？

C：199 块。

A：太贵了。

C：您给多少？

A：100 块。

C：100 块不行。

B：我们走吧。

C：等一等。150 块，给您。

A：不要。

C：好吧，做个朋友，120 块怎么样？

5. 看图会话 Describe the following pictures

这儿的苹果比那儿的苹果 _____。
那儿的苹果比 _____。
这儿的苹果比那儿的苹果 _____ 多了。
那儿的苹果比 _____ 多了。

你看,哥哥比 _____。
弟弟比 _____。
哥哥 _____ 多了。
弟弟 _____ 多了。

这件衣服比那件衣服 _____,
那件衣服 _____。
这件衣服 _____,
那件衣服 _____。
你说,哪件衣服好?
_____。

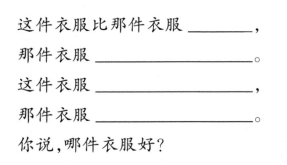

这间房子比 _____。 这间房子 _____。
那间房子比 _____。 那间房子 _____。
你喜欢哪间房子?

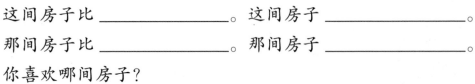

6. 交际练习 Communication practice

（1） You have just returned from Beijing. Describe to your relatives the difference between China and your own country, or compare Beijing to a city in your country.

（2） What does your friend like? What does he/she like to do on the weekends? Call and talk to your friend now.

（3） You went shopping in a mall. At first you wanted to buy a suit, but it was too expensive, so you didn't buy it. Then you wanted to buy some shirts, but they were either too big or too small, or too long or too short. You didn't find the colours or styles suitable, so you didn't buy any shirts. Finally, you bought a Chinese-style dress that appealed to you.

四. 阅读和复述 Reading Comprehension and Paraphrasing

"高一点儿"（相声，xiàngsheng）

A：王先生,听说你也开始写相声了?

B：我写得很少,今年写了五个很短的相声,您呢?

A：我工作很忙,也写得不多。今年写了十五个不太短的相声。

B：比我多十个！您真了不起（liǎobuqǐ）。

A：不客气。你写相声有问题,可以来问我。你还翻译了一本书,对不对?

B：对,书很薄（báo）,两百页（yè）。

A：我也翻译了一本很薄的书。

B：多少页?

A：五百页。

B：比我的多三百页！您真了不起。

A：不客气。你翻译有问题,可以来问我。你的衬衫是什么料子（liàozi）的?

B：是布（bù）的。

A：我穿的衬衫是丝绸的。

B：您的比我的好多了。

A：不客气。你今年多大？

B：我今年三十，您呢？

A：我今年三十一。

B：您比我大一岁。

A：不客气。你多高？

B：172 公分，您呢？

A：我现在 173 公分，比你高一点儿。

B：是啊，您总是(zǒngshì)比我高一点儿。

A：不客气。你的表(biǎo)现在几点？

B：九点。

A：我的现在十点。

B：您的表也比我们的快一个小时。

A：不客气。——啊？

五．语法　　Grammar

1. "的"字短语(1)　The "的" phrase (1)

The "的" phrase is constructed by placing "的" after a noun, a pronoun, an adjective, a verb, or a noun or verbal phrase. It is equivalent to a noun and expresses some distinction.

Pr / N / A + 的

我　　　　　的 (mine)

老师　　　　的 (the teacher's)

丝绸　　　　的 (the silk one)

大　　　的 (the big one)

yánsè
colour. hǎ

本 ms.
600k

件 → refers
to upper ware.
↳ measure word for clothes.

lù (green).

The "的" phrase can be used as a subject or an object in a sentence. For example：

丝绸的很贵，我没有丝绸的。

套 tào
↳ measure word
for clothes (suit)

我喜欢绿的，他喜欢红的。

✳ 2. 用介词"比"表示比较(1) Comparison using the preposition "比" (1)

The preposition "比" may be used to compare the qualities and characteristics of two things. "比" and its object form a prepositional phrase and are often placed before the adjective, in sentences with an adjectival predicate.

bǐ
no adverb! ↳ compared to

$$S + Prep"比" + N/Pr + A$$

x + 比 + y + Adj.

Subject	Predicate		
	Prep "比"	N/Pr	A
这件旗袍	比	那件旗袍	漂亮。
大商场的东西	比 (compared to) →	小商店的	多。(large)
这件衬衫	比	那件衬衫	合适。
小云	比	他	忙。

diàn (shop)

→ large shopping mall has more things than the small shopping mall.

The preposition "比" with its object may be placed before a verb to express comparison in sentences with a verbal predicate.

$$S + Prep"比" + N/Pr + VP$$

(compared to)

Subject	Predicate			
	N	Prep "比"	N/Pr	VP
你		比	我	知道 得 多。
田小姐		比	我	翻译 得 好。
他们	汉语	比	我们	说 得 流利。

✳ Negative

The adverb "不" is placed before "比" to form a negative comparative sentence. "x 不比 y + A" means "x < y" or "x = y". For example：

他不比我高。(meaning "I am taller than him" or "he is as tall as me")

cha
小商店的东西不比大商场的东西差。 (meaning "things in small stores are better than those in big shopping malls" or "things in small stores are as good as those in big shopping malls")

没有 notas.

（1）The auxiliary verbs and adverbs must be placed before "比".

For example：

你应该比我知道得多。

他可能比我忙。

这件衣服当然比那件衣服好。

（2）The adverbs "很，真，非常" cannot be used before the adjective in a "比" sentence with an adjectival predicate. For example, we can not say ⊗ "他比我很忙。"

3. 数量补语 The complement of quantity

In a "比" sentence with an adjectival predicate, the complement of quantity（a numeral-measure word phrase）can be used after the main element of the predicate to express specific differences between two things or persons.

A + Numeral-measure word phrase

Subject	Predicate			
	"比"	N/Pr （the object of comparison）	A （the aspect of comparison）	Numeral-measure word phrase （the result of comparison）
这件衣服	比	那件衣服	大	一号。
这本书	比	那本书	贵	20块钱。
这件	比	那件	长	两公分。
我们系	比	他们系	多	90个学生。

The word "一点儿" is used to indicate a slight difference between two things or persons, while "多了" is used to indicate that the difference is great. For example：

这件衣服比那件贵一点儿。

这个电脑比那个新多了。

The question form for this type of sentence is "A + 多少?". For example：

你们系比他们系多多少人?

这件衣服比那件贵多少（钱）?

1. 汉字的构字法(3) Methods of constructing Chinese characters(3)

Associative method（会意法）: This method of construction combines two or more words to create a new word with a new meaning, which is derived from the association of the original meanings of all the individual components. For example, "从" is constructed by placing one "person" after another, to signify the meaning "to follow". We have learned the following characters in this category:

林, 比, 北, 明, 信, 友, 孙, 多, 步, 出, 看, 拿, 坐, 休, 分, 品.

2. 认写基本汉字 Learn and write basic Chinese characters

(1) 比　　　　ㄥ ㄐ 比 比

bǐ　　to compare　　　　　　4 strokes

(2) 已　　　　㇕ ㇕ 已

yǐ　　already　　　　　　　3 strokes

(3) 及　　　　㇛ 乃 及

jí　　and　　　　　　　　3 strokes

(4) 产　　　　丶 亠 六 㡀 立 产

chǎn　　to produce; to give birth to　　6 strokes

(5) 黑　　　　丶 冂 冂 冂 回 罒 甲 里 里 黑 黑 黑

hēi　　black　　　　　　　12 strokes

(6) 丝　　　　ㄥ ㄠ 纟 纠 丝

sī　　silk　　　　　　　　5 strokes

3. 认写课文中的汉字 Learn and write the Chinese characters appearing in the texts

衤 (yīzìpáng)　`　㇇　礻　礻　礻　　　　5 strokes

("衣" is written as "衤" on the left side of a character.)

(1) 旗袍 qípáo

旗 → 方 + ㇉ + 其　　　　14 strokes

袍 → 衤 + 包　　　　10 strokes

(2) 卖 mài（賣）

卖 → 十 + 买　　　　8 strokes

(3) 商店 shāngdiàn

店 → 广 + 占　　　　8 strokes

(4) 极 jí（極）

极 → 木 + 及　　　　7 strokes

(5) 一定 yídìng

定 → 宀 + 疋　　　　8 strokes

(6) 开始 kāishǐ（開始）

始 → 女 + 厶 + 口　　　　8 strokes

关 (quánzìtóu)　`　丷　丷　⺀　丷　关　　　　6 strokes

(7) 太极拳 tàijíquán（太極拳）

拳 → 关 + 手　　　　10 strokes

-68-

(8) 套 tào

套 → 大 + 镸   10 strokes

(9) 帅 shuài（帥）

帅 → ⺗ + 巾   5 strokes

⺈（dāozìtóu）ノ ⺈   2 strokes

（"刀" is written as "⺈" on the top side of a character.）

(10) 颜色 yánsè（顏色）

颜 → 产 + 彡 + 页   15 strokes

色 → ⺈ + 巴   6 strokes

(11) 便宜 piányi

便 → 亻 + 更   9 strokes

宜 → 宀 + 且   8 strokes

yí

(12) 没关系 méi guānxi（沒關係）

关 → ⾊ + 天   6 strokes

(13) 公园 gōngyuán（公園）

园 → 囗 + 元   7 strokes

(14) 衬衫 chènshān（襯衫）

衬 → 衤 + 寸   8 strokes

衫 → 衤 + 彡   8 strokes

(15) 绿 lǜ（綠）

绿 → 纟 + 录   11 strokes

(16) 售货员 shòuhuòyuán （售貨員）

售 → 隹 + 口　　　　　11 strokes

货 → 化 + 贝　　　　　8 strokes

(17) 合适 héshì （合適）

适 → 舌 + 辶　　　　　9 strokes

(18) 短 duǎn

短 → 矢 + 豆　　　　　12 strokes

(19) 麻烦 máfan （麻煩）

麻 → 广 + 林　　　　　11 strokes

烦 → 火 + 页　　　　　10 strokes
fán

(20) 丝绸 sīchóu （絲綢）

绸 → 纟 + 冂 + 土 + 口　　11 strokes

Urban transportation in China currently depends mainly on buses and the subway. Beijing has a very advanced public transit system. The bus routes are so numerous that it is possible to take the wrong bus. Our friend, Ma Dawei, took the wrong bus this time because he didn't remember the place name of his destination correctly.

第十八课 Lesson 18

我听懂了,可是记错了

ji (mail/post)
(to mail something)

一. 课文　　Text

（一）

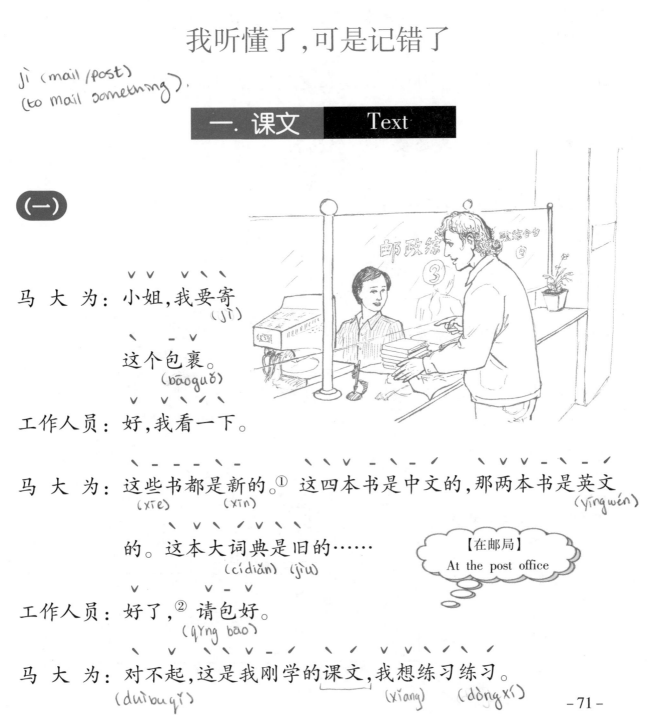

马 大 为：小姐,我要寄
　　　　　　　　(jì)
　　　　这个包裹。
　　　　　(bāoguǒ)

工作人员：好,我看一下。

马 大 为：这些书都是新的。① 这四本书是中文的,那两本书是英文
　　　　　　(xiē)　　　(xīn)　　　　　　　　　　　　　　　　　(yīngwén)
　　　　的。这本大词典是旧的……
　　　　　　　(cídiǎn)　(jiù)

【在邮局】
At the post office

工作人员：好了,② 请包好。
　　　　　　　　(qǐng bāo)

马 大 为：对不起,这是我刚学的课文,我想练习练习。
　　　　　(duìbuqǐ)　　　　　　　　　　　(xiǎng)　　(dōngxi)

-71-

工作人员：您汉语说得很流利。您要往哪儿寄？③
(wǎng) (jì)

马 大 为：美国。

工作人员：您寄航空还是海运？
(hángkōng) (hǎiyùn)

马 大 为：寄航空比海运贵，可是比海运快多了。寄航空吧。
(jì hángkōng bǐ hǎiyùn)

工作人员：邮费是 106 块。请在这儿写上您的名字。 "at here"
(Yóufèi) (xiě) (zì)

马 大 为：小姐，我还要取一个包裹。
(qǔ) (bāoguǒ)

工作人员：请把包裹通知单给我。对不起，您的包裹不在我们邮局
(bǎ) (tōngzhīdān gěi) (duìbuqǐ)

取，您得去海关取。④
(qǔ) (hǎiguān)

【提醒】
Reminding

马 大 为：请问，海关在哪儿？

工作人员：在建国门。别忘了把您的护照带去。⑤
(jiànguó mén) (bié wàng) (hùzhào dài)

马 大 为：谢谢。
(Xièxie)

工作人员：不客气。
(bú kèqi)

国内普通包裹详情单 （通知单联）

收件人	1 0 0 0 8 0	寄件人声明 如包裹无法投递,请 1. 退还寄件人 2. 抛弃处理 3. 改寄	包裹号码: 接收局号码:
	详细地址: 北京语言学院留学生宿舍 15楼204号		
	姓 名: 马大为 电话:010-82301234		
寄件人	详细地址: 上海外国语学院第二宿舍楼 307号	内装何物	收寄人员签章: 检查人员签章:
	姓 名: 王文清		
	邮政编码: 200030 电话:021-64131234	保价金额: 元	重 量: 克
领取人证件内容		领取人签章	单 价: 元
证件名称:			保价费: 元
证件号码:			其 他: 元
发证机关:		收件单位公章	共 计: 元

填写本单前，请真阅读背面的"使用须知"，若认可并遵守，请在此签字

-72-

做字
zòu
to do.

生词
new words.
(sheng ci).

礼 牛勿
lǐ wù   gift.

生词　New Words

1.	记	V	jì	to remember; to bear in mind 记生词,记汉字,记得快,记得慢
2.	错	A	cuò	wrong; erroneous　记错,听错,写错,说错,做错,坐错
3.	包裹	N	bāoguǒ	parcel; package 寄包裹,一个包裹,寄这个包裹
4.	些 _(these)_	M _zhe_ xiē _(these)_		some 一些,这些,那些,这些书,那些学生
5.	英文	N	Yīngwén	English　英文书,这些英文书,那些英文课本,英文的
6.	词典	N	cídiǎn	dictionary　英文词典,中文词典,一本大词典,查词典
7.	旧	A	jiù	old; past; used　旧词典,旧书,旧衣服,旧衬衫
8.	包 → thapaen	V	bāo	to wrap　包书,包包裹,包好
9.	往	Prep	wǎng	to; toward　往美国,往西安,往欧洲寄,往哪儿走
10.	航空	N	hángkōng	aviation 寄航空,航空公司,航空小姐
	空	N	kōng	sky; air
11.	海运	N	hǎiyùn	sea transportation; ocean shipping; ocean freight　寄海运,海运公司
	海	N	hǎi	sea; big lake
12.	邮费	N	yóufèi	postage 交邮费,多少邮费
	费	N	fèi	fee; expenses; charge　车费,书费,学费,水电费
13.	取	V	qǔ	to take; to get; to fetch　到银行取钱,到邮局取包裹,取照片,取东西
14.	通知单	N	tōngzhīdān	advice note;letter of notice 包裹通知单,取通知单
	通知	V/N	tōngzhī	to notify; to inform/notification
	单	N	dān	sheet, paper

15.	海关	N	hǎiguān	customhouse; customs 去海关, 海关工作人员
16.	别	Adv	bié	don't 别忘了, 别过期了, 别写错了
17.	护照	N	hùzhào	passport 带护照, 办护照, 取护照, 看护照
18.	客气	A	kèqi	polite; courteous 不客气, 不要客气, 别客气, 太客气
19.	建国门	PN	Jiànguó Mén	Jianguo Men (a place in Beijing)
	门	N	mén	door; gate; entrance

（二）

丁力波：大为,现在该去海关办你的事儿了。从这儿怎么去海关?
(gāi) (hǎiguān bàn) shìr. (hǎiguān)

马大为：海关在……我想想,叫什么门。
(Jiào shénme mén)。

【不能确定】
Uncertainty

丁力波：看,这儿有803路公共汽车,经过前门。
(lù gōng gòng qì chē), Jīngguò Qiánmén。

马大为：对,好像是前门吧。车来了,咱们先上去。⑥
(Xiàng) (Qiánmén) (Chē lái le), (zán men) xiān shàng qù。

售票员：请大家往里走。⑦ 下一站,前门。下车的乘客请拿好自己
(chūan wǎng lǐ zǒu)。 (Zhàn, Qiánmén)。 (chē de chéng kè) (zì jǐ)

的东西;刚上车的请买票。⑧
(Chē) (piào)。

马大为：小姐，请问海关是不是在前门？
(hǎiguān) (Qiánmén)

售票员：海关是在建国门，不是在前门。
(jiànguó mén) (Qiánmén)

【坐公车汽车】
Taking the bus

丁力波：我们坐错车了。
(zuò cuò)

售票员：没关系，您可以在前门下车，在那儿换地铁到建国门。
(méi guān xi) (chē) (huàn dì tiě, dào jiànguó mén)

马大为：没有坐错？好极了！买两张到前门的。
(jí le) (zhāng)

售票员：一块一张。您这是五块，找您三块。请拿好票。⑨
we did NOT learn this.

丁力波：大为，你说昨天邮局的工作人员告诉你了，你听懂了没有？
(zuó tiān, yóu jú) (gōngzuò rényuán) (tīng dǒng)

马大为：我听懂了，可是记错了。
(jì cuò le).

丁力波：我得查一查：你把护照带来了吗？
(chá yi chá) (hùzhào dài lai le ma)?

马大为：当然带来了，你放心吧！
(dāngrán) (fàngxīn ba)!

丁力波：包裹通知单呢？
(bāoguǒ tōngzhīdān ne)?

马大为：糟糕，我把包裹通知单忘了。
(zāogāo), (bāoguǒ tōngzhīdān wàng le).

北京巴士股份有限公司(五)专线票
A17 票价: 2元 066790
1	2	3	4	5	6	7	8	9	10	11	12	13
14	15	16	17	18	19	20	21	22	23	24	25	26
27	28	29	30	31	32	33	36	37	38	39
40	41	42	43	44	45	46	47	48	49	50	51	52
53	54	55	56	57	58	59	60	61	62	63	64	65
报销凭证
支持公交事业
投放巴士广告

生词 New Words

1. 路	N	lù	route 803路,323路,331路
2. 公共汽车	N	gōnggòng qìchē	bus 810路公共汽车,726路公共汽车
公共	A	gōnggòng	public; common; communal 公共厕所

汽车	N	qìchē	automobile; motor vehicle; car
车	N	chē	vehicle
3. 经过	V	jīngguò	to pass; to go through; to go by 经过王府井,经过建国门,经过家美租房公司,经过美国
4. 好像	V	hǎoxiàng	to seem; to be like 好像是前门,好像是陈老师,好像是《新实用汉语课本》
像	V	xiàng	to seem; to look as if; to appear
5. 咱们	Pr	zánmen	we, us 咱们认识一下,咱们一起去
6. 售票员	N	shòupiàoyuán	ticket seller; conductor
票	N	piào	ticket 车票,汽车票,公共汽车票,电影票
7. 大家	Pr	dàjiā	all; everybody 大家好,请大家进来,请大家多帮助
8. 里(边)	N	lǐ(bian)	in; inside; within 往里走
9. 站	N	zhàn	station; stop 两站,下一站,汽车站,公共汽车站
10. 乘客	N	chéngkè	passenger 下车的乘客,刚上车的乘客,到王府井的乘客
乘	V	chéng	to ride 乘车,乘汽车,乘公共汽车
客	N	kè	visitor; guest
11. 地铁	N	dìtiě	underground railway; subway 乘地铁,换地铁,坐地铁
12. 放心	VO	fàngxīn	to set one's mind at rest; to be at ease; to feel relieved 请放心,放心吧,不放心
13. 糟糕	A	zāogāo	in a wretched state; in a mess; too bad 太糟糕,真糟糕
14. 前门	PN	Qiánmén	Qianmen (a place in Beijing)

1.	公斤	M	gōngjīn	kilogram（kg.）
2.	邮票	N	yóupiào	stamp
3.	纪念	N	jìniàn	commemorate
4.	然后	Adv	ránhòu	then
5.	准备	N/V	zhǔnbèi	preparation/to prepare；to get ready
6.	聪明	A	cōngming	clever；bright
7.	儿子	N	érzi	son
8.	封	M	fēng	(measure word for letter)
9.	信封	N	xìnfēng	envelope
10.	贴	V	tiē	to stick；to paste
11.	孙子	N	sūnzi	grandson

二. 注释　　Notes

① 这些书都是新的。

"These books are all new."

"些" represents uncertain quantities, commonly used with "这"，"那" and "哪"，to modify nouns.　For example：

"这些书"(these books)，"那些老师"(those teachers)，"哪些电影"(which movies).

It is also commonly used with "一".　For example：

"一些书"(some books)，"一些人"(some people).

② 好了。

"All right."

"好了" here is used to express the wish to discontinue an action. For example：

好了,不要再说了。

③ 您要往哪儿寄？

"Where do you want to mail it to?"

The preposition "往" and nouns that indicate place or direction together make up the preposition-object phrase. "Prep 往 + PW" represents the direction of the action. For example：

往学院去, 往里走, 往欧洲寄.

Compare："Prep 在 + PW" represents the place of the action. For example：

在这儿写, 在北京学习.

④ 对不起,您的包裹不在我们邮局取,您得去海关取。

"Sorry, your package is to be picked up at customs, not at our post office."

Foreign packages sent to China are usually picked up at the local post office. Sometimes it is necessary to go to the customs office for pick-up.

⑤ 别忘了把您的护照带去。

"Don't forget to take your passport with you."

"别忘了" here indicates reminding.

⑥ 车来了,咱们先上去。

"The bus is here; let's get on first."

The meaning of "咱们" is almost the same as "我们", and is commonly used in spoken Chinese. However, "咱们" includes the listener; "我们" usually does not include the listener. For example：

A and B go to the library to borrow books; A says to the librarian：先生,我们来借书。(Sir, we want to borrow books.)

Then, A says to B：咱们借几本书? (How many books are we going to borrow?)

⑦ 请大家往里走。

"Please move inside."

The pronoun "大家" indicates everyone in a certain area or group. For example：

大家好。

请大家进来。

大家都来了。

我告诉大家一件事儿。

"大家" is often used after "你们,我们,咱们" for emphatic purposes. For example：

明天我们大家都去上海。

你们大家都想学汉语吗?

In China, most buses have a person selling tickets on board. Buses without ticket agents are becoming more numerous in some large cities.

⑧ 刚上车的请买票。

"Passengers who just boarded should purchase tickets, please."

"刚上车的" is a form of the "的" phrase, which means "刚上车的乘客"。"V+的" or "VP+的" can also form the "的" phrases. For example：

这本书是借的，不是买的。

（是借的书，不是买的书：borrowed book, not purchased）

买两张到前门的。（到前门的票：tickets to Qianmen）

⑨ 您这是五块，找您三块。请拿好票。

"You gave five dollars; three dollars is your change. Please hold onto your ticket."

These are common phrases used by bus ticket sellers. In some Chinese cities, a ticket check is conducted at the time of getting off the bus; thus the ticket sellers say, "Please hold onto your ticket."

三. 练习与运用　Drills and Practice

KEY SENTENCES
1. 这些书都是新的。
2. 这四本书是中文的，那两本书是英文的。
3. 请把包裹通知单给我。
4. 别忘了把您的护照带去。
5. 买两张到前门的。
6. 请大家往里走。
7. 下车的乘客请拿好自己的东西。
8. 我听懂了，可是记错了。

1. 熟读下列短语 Master the following phrases

(1) 一些书　一些咖啡　这些词典　那些包裹　这些专业　那些医院

　　看一些课本　买一些衣服　吃这些中药　记那些生词

(2) 往里走　往这儿看　往哪儿去　往美国寄　往33楼来　往宿舍走

往宋华家去　　往加拿大打电话

(3) 咱们先上车　　咱们去锻炼身体　　咱们一起去商场　　咱们来念课文
　　咱们去海关取包裹

(4) 大家好　　　　大家都很高兴　　祝大家快乐
　　请大家参观　　请大家喝咖啡　　请大家吃烤鸭　　请大家看电影
　　请大家放心　　请大家进来　　　请大家帮助我　　请大家参加生日聚会
　　你们大家都来玩儿吧　　我们大家都说汉语　　咱们大家一起去公园

(5) 是新的　是旧的　是贵的　是便宜的　是对的　是错的　　是容易的
　　是我的　是咱们的　是你们大家的　是文学的　是美术的　是丝绸的
　　是买的　是租的　是借的　是寄的　是送的　是喝的　是吃的
　　是看病的　是来参观的

(6) 写上名字　带上护照　包好包裹　拿好车票　　看懂英文　听懂上海话
　　记错名字　做错练习　写错汉字　拿错包裹　　坐错公共汽车
　　穿错衣服

(7) 把通知单给我　把礼物送他　把课本还你　把中文词典给他
　　把名片拿来　　把护照带去　把教授请来
　　把借书证带去　把新课本借来

2. 句型替换 Pattern drills

(1) 你<u>听懂</u><u>他</u>的话了吗？
　　我听懂了一些，一些没有听懂。

听	老师讲的语法
听	这个电影
看	今天的课文
看	这张通知单

(2) <u>她写对</u>你的<u>名字</u>了没有？
　　没有，她<u>写错</u>了。

做对	练习	错
听错	他的话	对
记错	你的电话号	对
坐错	公共汽车	对
念对	这些生词	错
打错	电话	对

(3) 她说什么了？
她说请大家拿好自己的东西。

排	队
写	汉字
练习	口语
复习	这一课课文
带	护照和通知单

(4) 你把钱 给 司机了没有？
我把钱给他了。

票	给	售票员
那些照片	给	大家
那些书	还	图书馆
英文报	还	老师
蛋糕	送	你朋友

(5) 他想把什么寄 去？
他想把那本新书寄去。

寄	来	兵马俑的明信片
带	来	他家的小狗
带	去	那张光盘
拿	来	刚买的苹果
拿	去	这个包裹

(6) 那本词典是你的吗？
哪本词典？
那本英文的。
那不是我的,是图书馆的。

（间）	房子	大	我姐姐
（件）	衬衫	丝绸	我朋友
（套）	西服	新	我哥哥
（个）	电脑	白	办公室
（张）	明信片	兵马俑	林娜

(7) 这张票是不是你买的？
这张票不是我买的。
我买的是下星期二的。

（本）	书	你借	中文
（些）	练习	他做	翻译
（些）	苹果	你要	红
（个）	包裹	他取	海运

(8) 他往哪儿寄包裹?

他往西安寄包裹。

他给谁寄包裹?

他给他弟弟寄包裹。

寄信	公司	经理
寄钱	家	外婆
送礼物	学生宿舍	女朋友
打电话	加拿大	他妈妈

3. 课堂活动 Classroom activity

Complete the following question-and-answer exercises (A asks the first question, B answers it; B asks the second question, C answers it; ...)

(1) 马大为要寄什么东西?

(2) 他要往哪儿寄包裹?

(3) 寄航空贵还是寄海运贵? 航空比海运快吗?

(4) 邮局的工作人员让马大为去哪儿取包裹?

(5) 邮局的工作人员让马大为把什么带去?

(6) 海关是不是在前门?

(7) 马大为买了几张票?

(8) 马大为买的票是到哪儿的?

(9) 他们为什么要在那儿下车?

(10) 马大为听懂邮局工作人员的话了吗?

(11) 马大为把什么忘了?

4. 会话练习 Conversation exercises

[在邮局 At the post office]

(1) A：先生,我要寄这个包裹。

B：我看一下。

A：这些都是 _____。

B：好了,请包好。您要往哪儿寄?

A：_____。

B：您想寄航空还是海运?

A：我要寄 _____。邮费多少钱?

B：你的包裹一共五公斤(gōngjīn),邮费是 _____。

A：请问这个包裹几天能到？

B：要一星期。

(2) A：小姐,您好。我来取一个包裹。

B：请把包裹通知单 _____。

A：给您。

B：我要看一看您的护照。好,请写上您的姓名。

A：在这儿吗？

B：对。这是您的包裹,请拿好。

(3) A：我要买邮票(yóupiào)：十张八毛的,十张六毛的。

B：一共 14 块。

A：我还要买纪念(jìniàn)邮票。

B：你要什么样儿的？

A：我要买兵马俑的。

B：要几套？

A：五套。

[描述事物 Describing things]

(1) A：我的本子在哪儿？

B：_____ 吗？

A：那不是我的,我的本子是新的。

B：你的本子是什么颜色的？

A：_____。

B：这儿有红的、白的、黑的……,这是不是你的？

A：对,这是我的。

[不能确定 Uncertainty]

(1) A：你知道那位先生是谁？

B：他是……,我想想,好像是王什么中。

A：对，是王华中。

(2) A："休息"的"休"字怎么写？

B：先写"人"，然后(ránhòu)……，写什么？好像是"本"。

A：不对，是"木"。

[提醒 Reminding]

(1) A：力波，下午没有课，咱们一起去图书馆吧。

B：＿＿＿＿＿＿＿＿＿＿＿＿。

A：我下午等你，别忘了把要还的书带去。

B：＿＿＿＿＿＿＿＿＿＿＿＿。

(2) A：我明天去邮局。

B：＿＿＿＿＿＿＿＿＿＿＿＿＿？

A：我要取一个包裹，是朋友从美国寄来的。

B：别忘了＿＿＿＿＿＿＿＿＿＿＿＿＿＿。

[坐公共汽车 Taking the bus]

(1)　　　 A：＿＿＿＿＿＿路公共汽车来了，咱们上去吧。

B：好。往里走，我来买票。买两张票，到＿＿＿＿＿＿。

售票员：一张＿＿＿＿＿＿。您这是＿＿＿＿＿＿，找您＿＿＿＿＿＿。请拿好票。

B：谢谢。

售票员：下一站，王府井。下车的乘客请准备(zhǔnbèi)好。王府井到了，下车的乘客请拿好自己的东西。

(2) 乘　客：小姐，请问去王府井是不是坐这路车？

售票员：这路车不到王府井。

乘　客：糟糕，我坐错车了。

售票员：您＿＿＿＿＿＿＿。您可以在前门下车，换810路公共汽车到王府井。

乘　客：谢谢，到站请告诉我们一下儿，好吗？

售票员：没问题，还有三站。

5. 看图说话 Describe the following pictures

A：这件西服是 _____ 的,
　　那件衬衫是 _____ 的。
B：那件衬衫是 _____ 的,
　　这件西服是 _____ 的。

这本书是 _____ 的,
它是 _____ 的。
那本书是 _____ 的,
它是 _____ 的。

学　　　生：小姐,我来办借书证。
工作人员：请把你的 _____ 给我。
学　　　生：好。
工作人员：请把你的 _____ 给我。
学　　　生：好的。
工作人员：请把你的 _____ 给我。
学　　　生：给您。
工作人员：请把 _____ 给我。
学　　　生：给。
工作人员：好了,您的借书证办好了。

6. 交际练习 Communication practice

(1) You go to the post office to mail a parcel to a friend back home. There are many things in the parcel and you show them to the clerk one by one. Initially you want to send it by air, since that is faster, but you change your mind after you find out that the postage is very costly because you have so many things to mail.

(2) Describe one incident where you had to go to the post office to pick up a package or to withdraw money.

(3) You get on a bus and while buying a ticket, find out that you are on the wrong bus. The ticket seller tells you how to change buses to reach your destination.

四. 阅读和复述 Reading Comprehension and Paraphrasing

聪明(cōngming)的爸爸和儿子(érzi)

1. 寄信

爸爸写了两封(fēng)信,一封信的信封(xìnfēng)是大的,一封信的信封是小的。他让儿子去邮局寄。过了一会儿,儿子回家了。爸爸问:"你把信寄了吗?"儿子说:"寄了。爸爸,您把邮票贴(tiē)错了。往西安寄的信是小的,您贴了五块钱邮票;往加拿大寄的信是大的,您贴了八毛钱邮票。"爸爸问儿子:"你把邮票换了吗?"儿子说:"您已经贴好了邮票了,我不能换邮票,我把里边的信换了。"

2. 把我寄去

爸爸买来一套音乐光盘,说:"把这套光盘给奶奶,她喜欢听音乐。"他包好光盘,贴上邮票,和儿子一起到邮局把光盘寄了。过了两个星期,奶奶来信了,她说:"下个月让我的小孙子(sūnzi)到上海来玩儿吧,我很想他。"爸爸想了一会儿,说:"下个月我和你妈妈都很忙,谁送你去啊?"儿子说:"没关系,爸爸,您在我身上贴上邮票,把我寄去!"

3. 爸爸没有帮我

儿子每天的练习都做得不对,可是昨天的练习都做对了。老师很高兴,问他:"每天你练习都做得不好,为什么昨天做得很好?你爸爸昨天一定帮助你了。"儿子说:"没有。老师,我爸爸昨天晚上没有回家,我想我应该自己做了。"

1. 结果补语 The resultative complement

The resultative complement explains the result of the action. It usually consists of a verb or an adjective.

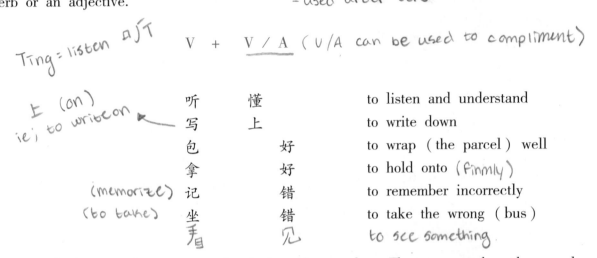

听	懂		to listen and understand
写	上		to write down
包		好	to wrap (the parcel) well
拿		好	to hold onto
记		错	to remember incorrectly
坐		错	to take the wrong (bus)
看	见		

Resultative complements are closely bound to verbs. There cannot be other words in between. The particle "了" or any objects must be placed behind the resultative complement.

	Predicate				
Subject	**V**	**V/A (complement)**	**Pt "了"**	**O**	**Pt "了"**
我	听	懂			了。
马大为	包	好	了	那个包裹。	
下车的乘客	拿	好		自己的东西。	
我们	坐	错		车	了。

If expressed by verbs with resultative complements, the action is usually complete. Thus, "没(有)" is commonly used in the negation, while "…了没有" is used for the V/A-not-V/A question. For example：

你听懂了没有?

——我没听懂。

马大为包好包裹了没有?

——他没有包好包裹。

The adjective "好" in this lesson is used as a resultative complement, indicating that an action is completed to satisfaction. For example：

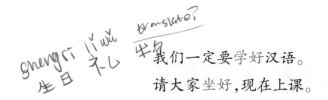

我们一定要学好汉语。

请大家坐好，现在上课。

2. "把"字句（2） The "把" sentence（2）

There are two types of "把" sentence in this lesson：

A. "把" sentence with the predicative verb "to give", such as "给"，"送"，"找（钱）"，"还"，etc.

This type of "把" sentence commonly indicates giving a certain object to a certain person.

$$S + "把" + O_{把}（sth.）+ V（"to give"）+ O（sb.）$$

Subject	Predicate					
	Adv	"把"	O_把 (**something**)	V (**to give**)	O (**somebody**)	Pt
你		把	你的护照	给	我。	
你		把	护照	给	我。	
我	没(有)	把	包裹	给	你。	
他		把	礼物	送	我	了。
他		把	钱	找	我	了。

B. "把" sentence with simple directional complement

The basic form of the "把" sentence with a simple directional complement is：

$$S + Adv + "把" + O + V + 来/去 + （了）$$

Subject	Predicate					
	Adv	"把"	O_把	V	来/去	Pt
你		把	你的护照	带	去。	
我	今天	把	护照	带	来。	了。
马大为	没有	把	那本书	拿	去。	
我		把	借图书馆的书	拿	来	了。
我	也	把	林娜	请	来	了。

3. "是"字句（2） The "是" sentence （2）

We have already learned the "是" sentence; for example "我是马大为". Its subject and object are nouns or pronouns. The function of the "的" phrase is equivalent to that of a noun; thus it can also serve as the subject and the object of a "是" sentence.

上 - last
下 - next

S + 是 + N/A/Pr/Vp + 的

Adj + de
→ Noun.

you can add an adverb.

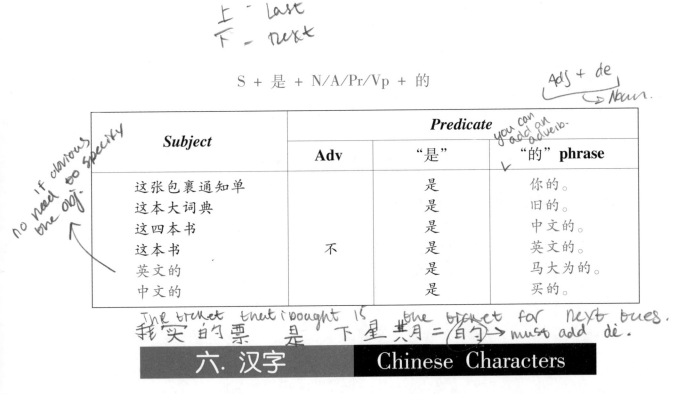

Subject	Predicate		
	Adv	"是"	"的" phrase
这张包裹通知单		是	你的。
这本大词典		是	旧的。
这四本书		是	中文的。
这本书	不	是	英文的。
英文的		是	马大为的。
中文的		是	买的。

no need to specify the obj. if obvious

我买的票 是 下星期二的 → must add de.
The ticket that i bought is the ticket for next tues.

六. 汉字　Chinese Characters

1. 汉字的构字法(4) Methods of constructing Chinese characters(4)

Phonetic loan method（假借法）: This method uses the shape and sound of a readily available character to represent another word that has the same sound. For example, the original meaning of "斤" was "axe"; it is now borrowed as a measure word to represent "a unit of weight", which has the same sound. "我" was originally used to represent a type of weapon; now it is used to write the first person pronoun. "来" originally meant "wheat"; it is now borrowed to mean "come", because the sounds were the same in ancient times. All foreign words borrowed through transliteration are applications of the phonetic loan method. For example, "沙发"（sofa）, "可乐"（coke）, etc.

2. 认写基本汉字 Learn and write basic Chinese characters

(1) 巳　 フ コ 巳

sì　　　the sixth of the twelve Earthly Branches　　3 strokes

(2) 弗　 �ㄱ ㄱ 弓 弗 弗

fú　　not　　　　　　　　　　　　　　　　5 strokes

(3) 象　 ⺈ ⺈ ⺈ ⺈ 户 户 免 免 象 象 象　　　　

xiàng　　elephant　　　　　　　　　　11 strokes

(4) 聿   ⊐ ⊐ ⊐ 圭 圭 聿

    yù   a pencil   6 strokes

(5) 乘   ⼂ ⼀ 千 千 千 乖 乖 乖 乘 乘

    chéng   to ride   10 strokes

(6) 失   ⼂ ⼂ ⼆ 失 失

    shī   to lose   5 strokes

3. 认写课文中的汉字 Learn and write the Chinese characters appearing in the texts

(1) 记 jì（記）

$$记 \longrightarrow 讠 + 己$$ 5 strokes

(2) 包裹 bāoguǒ

$$包 \longrightarrow 勹 + 巳$$ 5 strokes

$$裹 \longrightarrow 亠 + 果 + 亻$$ 14 strokes

(3) 些 xiē

$$些 \longrightarrow 止 + 匕 + 二$$ 8 strokes

(4) 词典 cídiǎn（詞典）

$$典 \longrightarrow 曲 + 八$$ 8 strokes

(5) 旧 jiù（舊）

$$旧 \longrightarrow 丨 + 日$$ 5 strokes

(6) 往 wǎng

往 → 彳 + 主　　　　　　　　8 strokes

(7) 航空 hángkōng

航 → 舟 + 亠 + 几　　　　10 strokes

空 → 穴 + 工　　　　　　　8 strokes

(8) 海运 hǎiyùn（海運）

运 → 云 + 辶　　　　　　　7 strokes

(9) 邮费 yóufèi（郵費）

费 → 弗 + 贝　　　　　　　9 strokes

(10) 取 qǔ

取 → 耳 + 又　　　　　　　8 strokes

(11) 通知单 tōngzhīdān（通知單）

单 → 丷 + 甲 + 一　　　　8 strokes

(12) 护照 hùzhào（護照）

护 → 扌 + 户　　　　　　　7 strokes

(13) 客气 kèqi（客氣）

客 → 宀 + 夂 + 口　　　　9 strokes

(14) 建国门 Jiànguó Mén（建國門）

建 → 聿 + 廴　　　　　　　8 strokes

(15) 路 lù

路 → 𧾷 + 夂 + 口　　　　13 strokes

(16) 汽车 qìchē（汽車）

汽 → 氵 + 气　　　　　　7 strokes

(17) 好像 hǎoxiàng

像 → 亻 + 象　　　　　13 strokes

(18) 咱们 zánmen（咱們）

咱 → 口 + 自　　　　　9 strokes

(19) 售票员 shòupiàoyuán（售票員）

票 → 覀 + 示　　　　　11 strokes

(20) 里（边）lǐ(bian)

边 → 力 + 辶　　　　　5 strokes

(21) 站 zhàn

站 → 立 + 占　　　　　10 strokes

(22) 地铁 dìtiě（地鐵）

地 → 土 + 也　　　　　6 strokes

铁 → 钅 + 失　　　　　10 strokes

(23) 放心 fàngxīn

放 → 方 + 攵　　　　　8 strokes

(24) 糟糕 zāogāo

糟 → 米 + 一 + 曲 + 日　17 strokes

(25) 前门 Qiánmén（前門）

前 → 丷 + 一 + 月 + 刂　9 strokes

-92-

Transportation in China

The Chinese transportation industry has developed rapidly since the economic reforms.　By late 1997,　the total national railroad network comprised 57566 km. The network has expanded to reach every province, every region, and cities, except in Tibet. (The Qinghai–Tibet railway is now under construction.) 80% of all the cities in the country have access to railways.

In 1997 the total length of roads was 1.2 million kilometers.　Roads have expanded to all cities and counties throughout the country, with a coverage of 98% of townships （xiāng, 乡） and 80% of villages.　Modern highway construction first started in the mid 1980's.　Now the total length of the modern highway is 19 thousand kilometres, ranking the second in the world.

There were a total of 967 commercial passenger airline routes in 1997,　which was approximately a seven-fold increase from 1978.

Have you ever seen traditional Chinese painting? Our friend Ding Libo not only appreciates it, he also knows how to paint traditional Chinese paintings. He is going to tell us the differences between traditional Chinese painting and oil painting. In this lesson, you will learn a new way to make comparisons between things.

第十九课 Lesson 19

中国画跟油画不一样

一. 课文　　Text

（一）

丁力波：咱们来早了，美术馆还没有开门呢。①
　　　　　　　　　　　（měishùguǎn）　　（kāimén）.

林　娜：来早了比来晚了好。今天我一定要参观一个上午。
　　　　　　　　　　　　　　　　　　　　　　（yídìng）　（cānguān）

丁力波：你真喜欢中国画！
　　　　　　　　　（zhōngguóhuà）

【表达持续时间】
Expressing a duration of time

林　娜：是啊，我非常喜欢徐悲鸿画的马。
　　　　　　（fēicháng）（Xú Bēihóng）

丁力波：我跟你一样，也很喜欢中国画。从我十岁开始，妈妈就教我
(yíyàng)   (kāishǐ) (māmahù)

画中国画。你说说，我中国画画了多少年了？
(shōu shou)

林　娜：啊，已经画了十一年了！我真不知道您还是一位"老画家"。
(yǐ jing)   (zài)(lǎo huà jiā)

丁力波：不敢当。② 我爸爸跟我妈妈一样喜欢中国画，可是他自己
(bù gǎng dāng)   (yí yàng)   (zì jǐ)

不会画。我爸爸也有很多爱好，他喜欢唱中国京剧。现在
(bú huà huà)   (aìhào)   (chàng) (jīngjù)

他在家还常常唱京剧。
(hái chángcháng chàng jīngjù)

【谈爱好】
Talking about hobbies

林　娜：他唱得怎么样？
(chàng)

丁力波：他唱京剧跟我画中国画一样，马马虎虎。
(yí yàng)   (mǎmǎhūhū)

林　娜：我想买一幅中国画。大画家画的一定很贵，是不是？
(fú)

丁力波：徐悲鸿画的马当然贵极了。我认识一位"老画家"，他画的
(xú bēi hóng)   (mǎ) (dāngrán)

马不贵。

林　娜：这位老画家是谁？
(shéi)

丁力波：是丁力波啊！我可以把我画好的马送你③。

生词　New Words

1. 中国画	N	zhōngguóhuà	traditional Chinese painting 看中国画，喜欢中国画，买中国画，介绍中国画
画儿	N	huàr	painting
2. 油画	N	yóuhuà	oil painting　送油画，买油画，卖油画，看油画
油	N	yóu	oil
3. 一样	A	yíyàng	the same; alike 一样快，一样美，一样帅，一样高，一样糟糕
4. 美术馆	N	měishùguǎn	art gallery　参观美术馆，到美术馆去
5. 开门	VO	kāimén	to open the door; to begin a day's business 商店开门，邮局九点开门，银行不开门，还没有开门呢
6. 画	V	huà	to paint 画画儿，画马，画中国画，画油画
7. 老	A	lǎo	old; experienced　老人，老师傅，老先生，老教授
8. 画家	N	huàjiā	painter; artist 老画家，年轻的画家，有名的画家
家	N	jiā	specialist 旅行家，文学家，美术家
9. 不敢当	IE	bù gǎndāng	I really don't deserve this
10. 爱好	N/V	àihào	hobby/to like　有很多爱好，有什么爱好，爱好画画儿
11. 唱	V	chàng	to sing

*12. 京剧	N	jīngjù	Beijing opera	唱京剧
13. 马马虎虎	A	mǎmǎhūhū	so-so；careless	唱得马马虎虎,写得马马虎虎,翻译得马马虎虎,考得马马虎虎
马虎	A	mǎhu	careless	
14. 幅	M	fú	(measure word for painting, cloth, etc.)	一幅画儿,一幅油画,两幅中国画
15. 徐悲鸿	PN	Xú Bēihóng	(name of a well-known Chinese painter)	

（二）

丁力波：咱们已经看了一个半小时的画儿了,二楼的还没有看呢。

现在是不是坐电梯上楼去?④

林　娜：好吧。力波,你觉得中国画跟油画一样不一样?

丁力波：当然一样,都是画儿啊。

【比较】
Comparing things

林　娜：别开玩笑。

丁力波：我没有开玩笑,我是说中国画跟油画一样美。

林　娜：你说说哪儿不一样?

丁力波：你找对人了，我来告诉你吧。⑤ 中国画和油画用的材料不

一样。

林　娜：怎么不一样？

丁力波：中国画用纸，油画常常用布；中国画主要用墨和水画，油画

一定要用油彩画。

林　娜：对，还有别的吗？

丁力波：油画没有空白，中国画常常有空白。你看这幅徐悲鸿的画

儿：画家只画了一匹马，没有画别的。

林　娜：可是我们觉得还有别的东西。让我们来想像一下：那匹

马往咱们这儿跑来了，我觉得它跑得非常快，好像还有风。

丁力波：对了。这就跟齐白石画的虾一样,它们游来游去,⑥真可爱!

你看,画家画水了吗?

林　娜：没画,可是我觉得有水。

丁力波：中国画是不是跟油画很不一样?

林　娜：谢谢你的介绍。可是我还想看看"老画家"画的马怎么样。

生词 New Words

1. 电梯	N	diàntī	elevator 坐电梯上楼,等电梯,电梯司机
2. 开玩笑	V O	kāi wánxiào	to crack a joke; to make fun of 别开玩笑,开我的玩笑
3. 美	A	měi	beautiful 很美的中国画,很美的姑娘,北京很美
4. 材料	N	cáiliào	material 用的材料,画画儿的材料,做衣服的材料
5. 纸	N	zhǐ	paper 用纸,买纸,一张纸
6. 布	N	bù	cloth 布衬衫,布衣服,用布做衣服
7. 主要	A	zhǔyào	main 主要用,主要是,主要有,主要的语法,主要的问题
8. 墨	N	mò	Chinese ink 用墨画,用墨写
9. 油彩	N	yóucǎi	greasepaint 用油彩画
10. 别的	Pr	biéde	other 别的画儿,别的画家,别的乘客,别的时间,别的颜色,别的样子
11. 空白	N	kòngbái	blank space 有空白,空白的表
12. 只	Adv	zhǐ	only 只有,只说,只觉得,只画马,只唱京剧,只考课文,只记汉字
13. 匹	M	pǐ	(measure word for horses) 一匹马

14.	想像	V	xiǎngxiàng	to imagine 想像一下，喜欢想像
15.	跑	V	pǎo	to run　跑来，跑去，跑得很快，往宿舍跑
16.	它	Pr	tā	it
17.	风	N	fēng	wind 有风，没有风，大风
18.	虾	N	xiā	shrimp 画虾，吃虾
19.	它们	Pr	tāmen	they (refering to things, animals)
20.	游	V	yóu	to swim 游得很快，游了一个小时，游来游去
21.	齐白石	PN	Qí Báishí	(name of a well-known Chinese painter)

补充生词　Supplementary Words

1.	骑	V	qí	to ride；to sit on the back of
2.	自行车	N	zìxíngchē	bike; bicycle
3.	远	A	yuǎn	far
4.	跑步	VO	pǎobù	to run, jog
5.	书法	N	shūfǎ	handwriting; calligraphy
6.	业余	A	yèyú	spare time; amateur
7.	节目	N	jiémù	program
8.	以前	N	yǐqián	before; formerly; previously
9.	瘦	A	shòu	thin
10.	减肥	VO	jiǎnféi	to reduce; to be on diet
11.	管	V	guǎn	to discipline
12.	生气	VO	shēngqì	to get angry; to take offense
13.	钢琴	N	gāngqín	piano
14.	孩子	N	háizi	child; children
15.	书店	N	shūdiàn	bookstore; bookshop
16.	教育	V	jiàoyù	to teach; to educate
17.	观点	N	guāndiǎn	opinion

二. 注释　　Notes

① 咱们来早了,美术馆还没有开门呢。

"We came too early. The art gallery is not open yet."

The structure "还没(有)+ V + 呢" indicates that a certain event or situation has not happened yet, but it will happen. Compare the following：

> 他回家了没有？
>
> 他没有回家。(He didn't go home.)
>
> 他还没有回家呢。(He hasn't gone home yet.)

② 不敢当。

"I don't deserve this."

This phrase is used commonly as a reply to someone's compliment. For example：

> 您给了我很多帮助,您真是我的老师。
>
> 不敢当。您也常常帮助我,我非常感谢。

Lin Na's statement, calling Libo an "experienced painter," has the hint of a joke to it. Libo's answer is also meant to be a joke.

③ 我可以把我画好的马送你。

"I can give you the horse that I drew."

When used as a resultative complement, the word "好" can also convey the meaning of completion. For example：画好画儿,做好练习,写好信,填好表,办好借书证,换好人民币.

④ 现在是不是坐电梯上楼去？

"Should we take the elevator upstairs now?"

We have already learned the interrogative sentence "…,是不是？" in Lesson 10. The structure "是不是" can be placed not only at the end of a sentence, but also at the beginning or in the middle of a sentence. The meanings these different arrangements convey are basically the same. For example：

> 他是不是已经来了？　　（＝他已经来了,是不是？）
>
> 是不是林娜真去上海了？（＝林娜真去上海了,是不是？）

The affirmative answer to this kind of sentence can be "是啊". The negative answer, however, needs to negate the part about which the question asks. For example, the negative answers of the above example sentences can respectively be：

> ——他没有来。
>
> ——(不是,)林娜没有去上海。

⑤ 我来告诉你吧。

"Let me tell you."

The structure "来+V/VP" is commonly used in spoken Chinese. Here, the word "来" does not express concrete action, but rather the meaning of, "will do something". The structure with "来" has the same meaning as that without "来". For example：

> 我来介绍一下。 （ = 我介绍一下。）
> 你来试试。 （ = 你试试。）

⑥ 它们游来游去。

"They swim back and forth."

三. 练习与运用　Drills and Practice

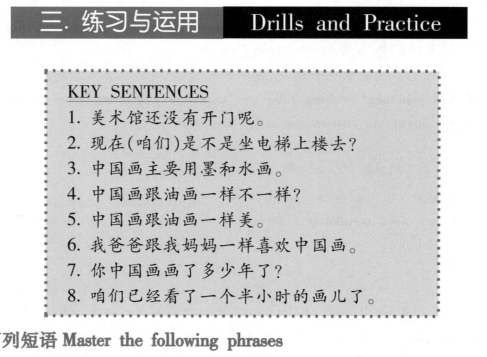

KEY SENTENCES
1. 美术馆还没有开门呢。
2. 现在(咱们)是不是坐电梯上楼去?
3. 中国画主要用墨和水画。
4. 中国画跟油画一样不一样?
5. 中国画跟油画一样美。
6. 我爸爸跟我妈妈一样喜欢中国画。
7. 你中国画画了多少年了?
8. 咱们已经看了一个半小时的画儿了。

1. 熟读下列短语 Master the following phrases

(1) 跟那个问题一样　　跟油画不一样　　跟那个公司一样不一样
　　跟他哥哥一样帅　　跟中国人一样流利　　跟那个学院一样有名
　　跟她一样想去旅行　　跟他一样喜欢音乐　　跟我一样会唱京剧

(2) 参观了一个上午了　　锻炼了四十分钟了　　在北京生活了一年了
　　汉语学习了半年了　　英语教了十年了　　课文念了二十分钟了
　　做了一个小时的练习　　打了十分钟的电话　　睡了八个小时的觉
　　排了一刻钟的队　　散了一会儿步

(3) 我来查一查　我来说说　我来画　我来告诉你　我来打扫房间
　　我来帮助你

(4) 坐电梯上楼　　　　坐公共汽车去美术馆　　　　坐地铁去王府井

　　　用墨画　　用油彩画　　用纸做练习　　用丝绸做旗袍

(5) 还没有呢　　还没有开门呢　　还没有写好呢　　还没有办好呢

　　　还没有走呢　　还没有吃饭呢　　还没有复习呢　　还没有取呢

　　　还没有懂呢　　还没有开始呢

2. 句型替换 Pattern drills

(1) 这本词典跟那本(词典)一样吗？
　　 这本词典跟那本不一样。
　　 这本比那本新。

你的电脑	他的	新
这儿的房租	那儿的	便宜
北京的天气	你们那儿(的)	冷

(2) 这件旗袍跟那件一样长吗？
　　 这件旗袍跟那件不一样长。
　　 这件比那件短一点儿。

这个公园	那个	大	小一点儿
这位画家	那位	年轻	老一点儿
那个电梯	这个	快	慢多了
北京美术馆	上海美术馆	新	旧多了

(3) 你有什么爱好？
　　 我喜欢学 中国画。
　　 我跟你一样喜欢学中国画。

打	太极拳
唱	京剧
开	玩笑
看	电影

(4) 昨天你锻炼了多长时间？
　　 昨天我只锻炼了半个小时。
　　 今天你锻炼了多长时间了？
　　 今天我锻炼了一个小时了。

跑	1个小时
游	45分钟
走	1.5小时
参观	2个小时

（5）你做好练习了没有？

还没有做好呢。

你已经做了多长时间的练习了？

我已经做了50分钟的练习了。

画	画儿
翻译	课文
写	生词
填	表
查	词典

（6）你（排）队排了多长时间了？

我排了一刻钟了。

是不是工作人员太慢了？

换	钱	十分钟	人	多
寄	包裹	二十分钟	工作人员	少
办	证	十天	工作人员	忙
坐	车	一个半小时	车	慢
买	衣服	两小时	好衣服	多

（7）他用什么写 课文？

他用电脑写课文。

画	中国画	墨
包	书	纸
做	衬衫	丝绸
介绍	上海	汉语
换	人民币	英镑

（8）你每天怎么回家？

我每天坐公共汽车回家。

来学院	坐375路车
到公司	坐地铁
回家	走
去办公室	骑(qí)自行车(zìxíngchē)

3. 课堂活动 Classroom activity

（1）Divide the class into two groups (A and B). Group A chooses two items or things to ask group B about, "x 跟 y 一样不一样？" Group B replies quickly and then chooses two other items or things to ask Group A about.

(2) Ask your partner to identify the similarities and differences between the two characters in each of the following groups of words (key words：左边 left side, 右边 right side, 意思 meaning, 读音 dúyīn pronunciation).

   A 妈、吗 B 爸、吧 C 音乐、快乐 D 他、她 E 法、汉

(3) Take turns making up questions and answers with the following patterns：

   Q：你锻炼了多长时间？   A：我锻炼了半个小时。

   Q：你写了多长时间(的)汉字？ A：我写了一个小时(的)汉字。

4. 会话练习 Conversation exercises

[表达持续时间 Expressing the duration of time]

(1) A：你汉语说得很流利,跟中国人一样。

  B：不敢当,还差得远(yuǎn)呢。

  A：你学了几年的中文了？

  B：_____。

  A：你要在中国学习几年？

  B：_____,还有一年的时间。

(2) A：你(教)书教了多少年了？

  B：我教了十年了。

  A：啊,您是老教师了。

  B：_____。

(3) A：咱们跑步(pǎobù)跑了多长时间了？

  B：_____。

  A：还跑不跑了？

  B：再跑一会儿吧。

[谈爱好 Talking about hobbies]

(1) A：你有什么爱好？

  B：我喜欢中国的书法(shūfǎ)。

  A：_____?

  B：我学了两年了。

A：你学得怎么样？

B：马马虎虎。

(2) A：业余(yèyú)时间你常常做什么？

B：我常常看电视。

A：你喜欢什么节目(jiémù)？

B：＿＿＿＿＿＿＿＿＿＿＿＿＿＿。

A：我喜欢看京剧。

[寒暄 Exchanging greetings]

(1) A：好久不见了，你还跟以前(yǐqián)一样。

B：哪里，我老多了。你比以前瘦(shòu)一点儿。

A：是啊，我减肥(jiǎnféi)了。

(2) A：您来中国多长时间了？

B：我来了一年了。

A：生活过得怎么样？

B：我过得很好，跟在英国一样。

A：你觉得这儿的天气怎么样？

B：这儿的天气跟我们那儿不一样，比我们那儿冷。

[告别 Saying good-bye]

A：您忙吧，我该回去了。

B：还早呢，再坐一会儿吧。

A：我还有点事儿，我得回学院去。

B：在这儿吃饭吧。

A：不用了，谢谢。

B：别客气，在这儿就跟在自己家一样。

5. 看图说话 Describe the following pictures

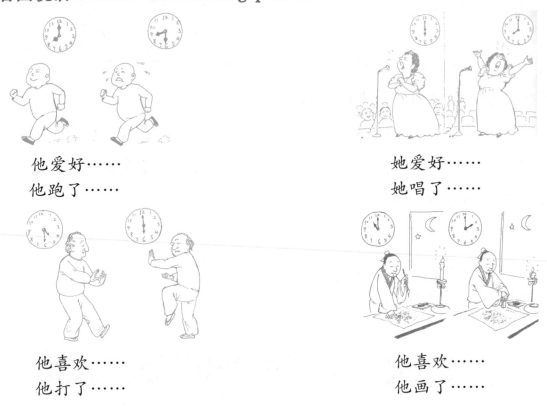

他爱好……
他跑了……

她爱好……
她唱了……

他喜欢……
他打了……

他喜欢……
他画了……

6. 交际练习 Communication practice

（1）Talk about your hobbies with your friends to find out if you have any common interests.

（2）Talk about your study or work experiences with your friends.

（3）Discuss a picture or a movie with your friends and talk about your different opinions.

四. 阅读和复述 Reading Comprehension and Paraphrasing

管(guǎn)孩子还是不管孩子

我女儿今年14岁,她已经开始不听我们的话了,常常让我和她妈妈生气(shēngqì)。我们让她学画画儿,每个星期天我都不休息,跟她一起坐公共汽车到老师家去。可是刚学了两个月,她说画画儿不容易,她不想学了。我们让她学钢琴(gāngqín),把钢琴也买来了。现在刚学了一个月,她说学钢琴跟学画儿一样没意思。我们不知道该怎么办?是不是别的孩子(háizi)都跟我的女儿一样?

huà huàr
draw painting.

昨天我到书店（shūdiàn）去，想找一本怎么教育（jiàoyù）孩子的书。售货员给我找出了三本书：一本是《别管孩子》，一本是《孩子不能不管》，还有一本是《管还是不管孩子》。我把三本书都买来了，也都看了，可是三本书的观点（guāndiǎn）一本跟一本不一样。

我常常想，应该怎样教育孩子，大人的观点跟孩子不一样，外国人的观点跟中国人不一样，孩子跟孩子也不一样。大人让孩子学钢琴，可是这个孩子可能听到钢琴就头疼；大人想让孩子学画儿，可是孩子喜欢唱京剧。听说外国的孩子下课就可以做自己喜欢的事情，中国的孩子晚上 11 点还要做练习。我朋友的孩子不用她爸爸妈妈管，可是我女儿……

管孩子还是不管孩子，真是一个大问题啊！

五·语法　　　　Grammar

1. "跟……（不）一样" 表示比较 Using "跟…（不）一样" to make comparisons

The comparative structure "跟…一样" indicates that two things are the same, or similar. If they are different, the structure "跟…不一样" is used. In a V/A-not-V/A question, the structure "一样不一样" is used.

跟 / ne + NP + （不） + 一样 + A / V O
gen

Subject	Predicate			
	跟	NP	（不）一样 yàng	A / V O
这张表	跟	那张（表）	一样。	
上海话	跟	普通话	不一样。	
中国画	跟	油画	一样不一样？	
这个中学	跟	那个（中学）	一样	有名。
这件西服	跟	那件（西服）	不一样	长。
我爸爸	跟	我妈妈	一样	喜欢 中国画。

can be dropped

If the central words of the two sides being compared are the same, the second central word may be omitted.

When de is put btw Vb. and Noun becomes a noun

2. 时量补语（2）The time-measure complement (2)

In a sentence with a time-measure complement, if the particle "了" is both after the verb and at the end of the sentence, it means that the action is still continuing. Compare the following:

（我）已经画了 11 年了。(I have been drawing for 11 years.)

（The practice of drawing is still continuing.）

（我）已经画了 11 年。(I have drawn for 11 years.)

（This does not indicate whether or not the practice of drawing is

continuing at present.）

If the verb in a sentence with a time-measure complement takes an object, the time-measure complement can also be placed between the verb and the object. The particle "的" can be inserted between the time-measure complement and the object.

→ Same as s + (V) + O + V + Time-measure compliment.

V	+	Time-measure complement	+ （的）+	O (N)	
你要	听		多长时间	（的）	音乐？
我要	听		半小时	（的）	音乐。
你	学 了		多长时间	（的）	汉语？
我	学 了		两年	（的）	汉语。
你	看 了		多长时间	（的）	画儿 了？
我	看 了		一个半小时	（的）	画儿 了。
好	睡 了		八个小时	（的）	觉。

↳ shuì | jiào ∴ don't include in the V (no noun) ✱

Note：If the object is a personal pronoun, it cannot be placed after the time-measure complement. We cannot say：⊗ "我等了一个小时的他。"

我等了他一个小时.

3. 连动句（2）：表示工具方式 Sentences with serial verb phrases (2)： means or manner

In the sentences with serial verb phrases in this lesson, the first verb usually expresses the means or manner that the action of the second verb performs. For example：

我们坐电梯上楼去。　　　　　*Fēi jī (aeroplane)*

他每天坐公共汽车回家。

画家用墨和水画中国画。

林娜用汉语介绍西安。　　　　*开车 driving*

1hr ½　　　　　　　　　*gōng kè (school work)*
一个半时

1. 汉字的构字法(5) Methods of constructing Chinese characters (5)

The pictophonetic method（形声法）：The majority of Chinese characters are "pictophonetic". Most consist of one component indicating the sound of the character, the phonetic, combined with one semantic component, the radical, which shows the category of meaning to which the character belongs. The pictophonetic characters fall into several categories:

(1) In its basic form, a pictophonetic character is constructed by placing the component indicating the sound on the right side and the component indicating the meaning on the left side. For example: 饭,姑,妈,吗,吧,锻,机,快,块,理,们,哪,娜,请,情,物,泳,钟,洲,住,俑,懂,把,馆,证,慢,职,极,样,幅,像,虾,衬,护,试.

2. 认写基本汉字 Learn and write basic Chinese characters

(1) 夭　　　ノ 二 チ 夭

yāo　　　　young　　　　　　　　　　　4 strokes

(2) 斗　　　丶 冫 二 斗

dǒu　　　(an object shaped like a cup or dipper)　4 strokes

(3) 石　　　一 丆 丆 石 石

shí　　　stone　　　　　　　　　　　5 strokes

(4) 氏　　　ノ 匚 乇 氏

shì　　　a clan　　　　　　　　　　　4 strokes

3. 认写课文中的汉字 Learn and write the Chinese characters appearing in the texts

(1) 油画 yóuhuà （油畫）

油 → 氵 + 由　　　　　　　　　　8 strokes

画 → 一 + 田 + 凵　　　　　　　　8 strokes

耳 (gǎnzìpáng) 一 二 尸 兵 兵 耳 耳   7 strokes

(2) 不敢当 bù gǎndāng（不敢當）

敢 → 耳 + 夂   11 strokes

(3) 唱 chàng

唱 → 口 + 日 + 日   11 strokes

虍 (hǔzìtóu) 丨 卜 卢 卢 卢 虍   6 strokes

(4) 马马虎虎 mǎmǎhūhū （馬馬虎虎）

虎 → 虍 + 几   8 strokes
hǔ

(5) 幅 fú

幅 → 巾 + 畐   12 strokes

(6) 徐悲鸿 Xú Bēihóng（徐悲鴻）

徐 → 彳 + 人 + 一 + 木   10 strokes
悲 → 非 + 心   12 strokes
鸿 → 氵 + 工 + 鸟   11 strokes

(7) 电梯 diàntī（電梯）

梯 → 木 + 弟   11 strokes

(8) 开玩笑 kāi wánxiào

笑 → 竹 + 天   10 strokes

(9) 材料 cáiliào

材 → 木 + 才   7 strokes
料 → 米 + 斗   10 strokes

(10) 纸 zhǐ（紙）

纸 → 纟 + 氏　　　　　7 strokes

(11) 布 bù

布 → ナ + 巾　　　　　5 strokes

(12) 墨 mò

墨 → 黑 + 土　　　　　15 strokes

(13) 油彩 yóucǎi

彩 → ⺀ + 木 + 彡　　　11 strokes

(14) 匹 pǐ

匹 → 匚 + 儿　　　　　4 strokes

(15) 跑 pǎo

跑 → 𧾷 + 包　　　　　12 strokes

(16) 它 tā（牠）

它 → 宀 + 匕　　　　　5 strokes

(17) 风 fēng（風）

风 → 几 + 乂　　　　　4 strokes

(18) 虾 xiā（蝦）

虾 → 虫 + 下　　　　　9 strokes·

(19) 游 yóu

游 → 氵 + 方 + 𠂉 + 子   12 strokes

(20) 齐白石 Qí Báishí（齊白石）

齐 → 文 + 刂   6 strokes

文化知识　　　Cultural Notes

Traditional Chinese Painting

A traditional Chinese painting is created using a special Chinese writing brush and ink, according to traditional Chinese painting techniques. It is very different from Western oil painting. Because of the tools and materials employed, traditional Chinese painting could be called "water-and-ink painting" (shuǐmòhuà, 水墨画) or "color-and-ink painting" (cǎimòhuà, 彩墨画), to distinguish it from oil painting, watercolor painting, and gouache. Depending on subject matter, much traditional Chinese painting can be classified into three categories: figure painting, landscape painting, and flower-and-bird painting. In addition, many traditional Chinese painting methods can be classified as either "fine, detailed brush work paintings" (gōngbǐ, 工笔), or "free hand paintings" (xiěyì, 写意).

Traditional Chinese painting often finds spiritual sustenance from mountains, rivers, flowers, and birds, and it is through such images that painters express their feelings. Another essential aspect of much traditional Chinese painting is that it emphasizes "likeness in spirit" (shénsì, 神似) and does not insist on "strict likeness in appearance" (xíngsì, 形似). The composition of a picture should rather be "between likeness and unlikeness." Because the images and the composition of the traditional Chinese painting have to be subordinated to the requirement that the content should be expressed through the expression of the painter's spirit and lyricism, painters usually stress things that they want to represent and omit things that they do not want to represent. In this way, the artistic style of traditional Chinese painting developed the quality of being realistic, yet not depicting every aspect of reality.

Lin Na and Ding Libo are going to Song Hua's place for a treat—a hotpot dinner. In the evening, they will go to a concert of traditional Chinese music. This is the way in which they will celebrate the New Year in China. In this review lesson, we will summarize the grammar points covered in the five previous lessons.

第二十课 Lesson 20(复习 Review)

过 新 年

一·课文　　　　Text

王小云：中午咱们都去宋华家吃

　　　　火锅,他爸爸、妈妈要

　　　　我们跟他们一起过新年。

林　娜：在北京过新年一定很有

　　　　意思。小云,为什么北京很多饭馆都有火锅? 是不是因为现

　　　　在天气冷,所以北京人常吃火锅?①

【问原因】
Asking for reasons

王小云：不是。北京人就爱吃火锅,主要是涮羊肉,天气热的时候也

　　　　吃。② 北京的涮羊肉跟北京烤鸭一样有名。

林　　娜：过新年的时候北京人都吃涮羊肉吗？

王小云：不一定。

林　　娜：你说说北京人怎么过新年。

王小云：跟西方人一样，很多人去旅行。也可能开车去郊区玩儿，或者去锻炼身体。③

【催促】
Hurrying somebody up

林　　娜：晚上常常做些什么？

王小云：晚上看京剧、听音乐会或者跟朋友聚会。我说林娜，快点儿吧！④ 你化妆化了半个小时了。咱们得早点儿走。

林　　娜：一会儿就好。今天晚上咱们还要去听音乐会，所以得正式一点儿。

王小云：你知道吗？今天晚上听中国民乐，它跟西方音乐很不一样。

林　　娜：我知道，中国民乐主要是用民族乐器演奏的中国音乐。刚来的时候我不太习惯听民乐，可是现在我很爱听。

王小云：你喜欢《春江花月夜》吗？

林　　娜：啊，《春江花月夜》美极了。⑤

我已经买了这个乐曲的光盘，今天还要再买一些，给我朋

友寄去。咱们怎么去宋华家？坐出租车还是坐公共汽车？

王小云：今天路上的车一定很多。出租车比公共汽车快多了，坐

出租车吧。

林　　娜：咱们还没有买礼物呢。送花儿是西方人的习惯，我们参加聚会

的时候也可以带吃的、喝的。中国人去朋友家的时候送什么？

王小云：过去常送一些吃的、喝的或者用的，现在的年轻人跟西方人

一样，也常送花儿。

林　　娜：咱们买些花儿，再带些吃的吧。

王小云：好。别忘了把照相机带去。

林　娜：我的照相机呢？⑥

王小云：在电话旁边。

林　娜：大为和力波怎么不给咱们打个电话？

王小云：我不知道大为能不能去，因为他要跟女朋友一起去旅行。

力波一定去，他说要从这儿出发。

林　娜：再等一等他吧。

王小云：好。咱们把陆雨平也叫去，让他写一篇文章，介绍留学生在

中国怎么过新年。

＊　　　　＊　　　　＊

丁力波：小云，林娜，新年好！恭喜恭喜！⑦

【新年祝愿】
New Year's greetings

林　娜：恭喜你！大为呢？

丁力波：大为昨天晚上就坐火车去南方了。

王小云：你又来晚了。⑧

丁力波：真不好意思。二位小姐别着急，出租车已经来了。

王小云：你把出租车叫来了，太好了。⑨咱们快走。

林　娜：你给宋华带什么礼物去？

丁力波：今年是马年，我又画了一匹马。你们看，画得怎么样？

生词　New Words

1. 新年	N	xīnnián	new year 新年好,过新年,祝贺新年	
2. 火锅	N	huǒguō	hotpot　吃火锅,在饭馆吃火锅	
火	N	huǒ	fire；heat	
锅	N	guō	pot；pan	
3. 饭馆	N	fànguǎn	restaurant　有名的饭馆,去饭馆吃饭	
4. 因为	Conj	yīnwèi	because	
5. 所以	Conj	suǒyǐ	so	
6. 爱	V	ài	to love　爱妈妈,爱音乐,爱唱,爱画,爱开玩笑,爱吃火锅	
7. 涮羊肉	N	shuànyángròu	thin slices of mutton boiled in water 吃涮羊肉,爱吃涮羊肉,主要是涮羊肉	
涮	V	shuàn	to cook thin slices of meat in boiling water	
羊	N	yáng	sheep	
肉	N	ròu	meat	
8. 热	A	rè	hot　天气很热,天热,热天	

9. 开车	VO	kāichē	to drive a car	开车去饭馆,开车到王府井,开车回学院
开	V	kāi	to drive; to operate	开汽车,开公共汽车,开电梯
10. 郊区	N	jiāoqū	suburb; outskirts	上海郊区,在郊区,去郊区玩儿,开车去郊区
11. 或者	Conj	huòzhě	or	你或者他,今天或者明天,寄航空或者海运,去郊区玩儿或者锻炼身体
12. 音乐会	N	yīnyuèhuì	concert	听音乐会,参加音乐会,买音乐会的票
13. 化妆	VO	huàzhuāng	to put on makeup	爱化妆,得化妆,不用化妆,化妆化了半个小时
化	V	huà	to change	
妆	N	zhuāng	makeup	
14. 正式	A	zhèngshì	formal	正式学习,正式上课,正式参加,穿得正式一点儿
15. 民乐	N	mínyuè	folk music played with traditional instruments	中国民乐,民乐光盘,听民乐,爱民乐
16. 西方	N	xīfāng	western; the West	西方人,西方音乐,西方美术,西方文学,西方电影
西	N	xī	west	
17. 民族	N	mínzú	nation; nationality	中国的民族,每个民族,民族音乐,民族音乐会
18. 乐器	N	yuèqì	musical instrument	民族乐器,西方乐器,主要乐器
器	N	qì	utensil	
19. 演奏	V	yǎnzòu	to give an instrumental performance	演奏了一个半小时,正式演奏,用民族乐器演奏
演	V	yǎn	to perform; to play	
奏	V	zòu	to play a musical instrument	
20. 习惯	V/N	xíguàn	to be accustomed to/habit	很习惯,不太习惯,习惯这儿的生活,习惯听民乐,西方人的习惯

21.	乐曲	N	yuèqǔ	musical composition	民族乐曲,西方乐曲,有名的乐曲
	曲	N	qǔ	tune; melody	
22.	出租车	N	chūzūchē	taxi; cab	叫出租车,坐出租车,开出租车,出租车站,出租车司机
	出租	V	chūzū	to hire; to rent	
23.	路上	N	lùshang	on the road; on the way	路上的车,路上的人,路上要多长时间
24.	花儿	N	huār	flower	买花儿,卖花儿,送花儿,画花儿
25.	过去	N	guòqù	in or of the past	过去的事情,过去的习惯,过去的生活
26.	照相机	N	zhàoxiàngjī	camera	用一下照相机,带照相机
	照相	VO	zhàoxiàng	to take a picture; to photograph	
	机	N	jī	machine	
27.	旁边	N	pángbiān	side	旁边的画儿,旁边的厕所,商店旁边,邮局旁边,在电话旁边
28.	出发	V	chūfā	to set out; to start off	从学院出发,从这儿出发,九点出发
29.	篇	M	piān	(a measure word for essays and articles)	一篇课文,两篇翻译
30.	文章	N	wénzhāng	essay; article	写一篇文章,看文章,长文章
31.	恭喜	IE	gōngxǐ	congratulations	恭喜你,恭喜恭喜
32.	火车	N	huǒchē	train	坐火车去南方,开火车,火车票,火车站
33.	又	Adv	yòu	again	又来晚了,又去上海,又买光盘,又画了一匹马
34.	着急	VO/A	zháojí	to feel anxious/anxious	不用着急,别着急,很着急,非常着急
35.	《春江花月夜》	PN	《Chūn Jiāng Huā Yuè Yè》	(a famous, traditional Chinese music composition)	
	春	N	chūn	spring	
	江	N	jiāng	river	
	月	N	yuè	moon	
	夜	N	yè	night	

1. 小学	N	xiǎoxué	primary school
2. 辆	M	liàng	(a measure word for vehicle)
3. 音乐厅	N	yīnyuètīng	concert hall
4. 幸福	A	xìngfú	happy
5. 万事如意	IE	wàn shì rú yì	May all your wishes come true.
6. 条	M	tiáo	(a measure word for long, narrow objects, such as trousers, skirt, snake, etc.)
7. 蛇	N	shé	snake
8. 最	Adv	zuì	the most
9. 添	V	tiān	to add
10. 脚	N	jiǎo	foot
11. 完	V	wán	to finish
12. 多余	A	duōyú	superfluous; uncalled for; surplus
13. 足	N	zú	foot

二. 注释　Notes

① 是不是因为现在天气冷,所以北京人常吃火锅?

"Is it because the weather has now become colder that people in Beijing are having hotpot more frequently?"

The paired conjunctions "因为…所以…" are used to connect two clauses in a complex cause-effect sentence. The "因为" clause, which states the cause, usually comes first, and is followed by the "所以" clause, which states the effect. One may also use only one of the two conjunctions in a sentence. For example:

因为大为感冒了,所以他没有来上课。

(因为)他们要去听音乐会,所以得穿得正式一点儿。

因为银行排队的人多,(所以)他想明天再去换钱。

② 北京人就爱吃火锅,主要是涮羊肉,天气热的时候也吃。

"The people in Beijing just love hotpot, mostly boiled mutton slices, and they eat it even when the weather is hot."

The construction "…的时候" is often used in the sentence as an adverbial of time (similar to "when" and "while" in English), indicating the period of time when an action or event takes place. "的时候" can be preceded by a verb, a verbal phrase, or a subject-predicate phrase. For example：

上课的时候,老师让我们多说汉语。

去图书馆的时候,别忘了带你的借书证。

天气热的时候,要多喝水。

中国人去朋友家的时候,常送吃的、喝的或者用的。

③ 也可能开车去郊区玩儿,或者去锻炼身体。

"(They) might also drive to the suburbs for fun, or they might go out to exercise."

The conjunctions "或者" and "还是" can both be used to connect two alternatives; "还是" is used in the interrogative sentence, and "或者" is normally used in the declarative sentence. For example：

明天你去找我还是我来找你?

明天我去找你,或者你到我那儿去。

④ 我说林娜,快点儿吧!

"Hey, Lin Na. You'd better hurry."

The expression "我说" is used to attract attention, to break in on a conversation, or to introduce a new topic for discussion.

⑤ 啊,《春江花月夜》美极了。

"Oh, *Moonlit Night on the Flowery Spring Riverside* is extremely beautiful."

"*Moonlit Night on the Flowery Spring Riverside*" is a famous, ancient Chinese musical composition which depicts the beautiful scenery by the riverside on a moonlit night in spring, when all the flowers are in full bloom.

⑥ 我的照相机呢?

"Where is my camera?"

In Lesson Seven, we learned how to form an elliptical interrogative sentence with "呢", and we know that what is asked in this type of question is made clear by the context. However, "呢" can also be used to ask the location of a person or an object, without any dependence on the context, as shown in the question above. In this case, "NP+呢?" is equivalent to "NP 在哪儿?" For example:

你的文章呢？（＝你的文章在哪儿？）

大为呢？　　　（＝大为在哪儿？）

⑦ 恭喜恭喜！

"Best wishes (for a happy New Year)!" This literally means, "Congratulations!"

This is an idiomatic expression used frequently for congratulating people on happy occasions; for example, "恭喜你！" or "恭喜你买了新房子！" Here, the "恭喜" is the same as "祝贺" in usage, except that "祝贺" is more formal. In the Spring Festival or on New Year's Day, we often say, "恭喜恭喜！" to extend our New Year's greetings (the word "祝贺" is not used this way).

⑧ 你又来晚了。

"You are late again."

The adverbs "又"(1) and "再"(1) both express the recurrence of an action or a state. "再"(1) is used in a situation where the action or state has yet to recur, whereas "又"(1) is normally used in a situation where the action or state has already occurred again. For example:

他上午来了,他说下午<u>再</u>来。

(The action has yet to happen, so we cannot say ⊗ "他说下午又来。")

他上午来了,下午<u>又</u>来了。

(The action has already happened, so we cannot say ⊗ "下午再来了。")

⑨ 你把出租车叫来了,太好了。

"You have hired a taxi. That's great."

"叫出租车" means "to hail or to hire a taxi".

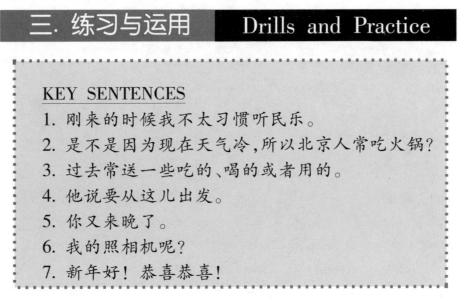

三. 练习与运用　Drills and Practice

KEY SENTENCES

1. 刚来的时候我不太习惯听民乐。
2. 是不是因为现在天气冷,所以北京人常吃火锅?
3. 过去常送一些吃的、喝的或者用的。
4. 他说要从这儿出发。
5. 你又来晚了。
6. 我的照相机呢?
7. 新年好! 恭喜恭喜!

1. 熟读下列短语 Master the following phrases

(1) 开学的时候　锻炼的时候　休息的时候　感冒的时候　旅行的时候

　　演奏的时候　打扫的时候　上课的时候　排队的时候　打工的时候

　　考试的时候　挂号的时候　发烧的时候　睡觉的时候

　　过新年的时候　在北京的时候　取包裹的时候　画画儿的时候

　　坐公共汽车的时候　买衣服的时候

　　邮局开门的时候　银行休息的时候　天气热的时候　他住院的时候

　　我们去朋友家的时候

(2) 演奏中国乐曲　演奏民乐　演奏了《梁祝》　演奏了《春江花月夜》

　　用民族乐器演奏　演奏了两个小时　演奏得好极了　演奏得马马虎虎

(3) 开车去郊区玩儿　　　(开)车开得不快　　　(开)车开了一个上午

　　开了四个小时的车　　把车开来

(4) 又来晚了　又去早了　又感冒了　又过期了

　　又学了一百个汉字　　又买了一件旗袍

2. 句型替换 Pattern drills

(1) 这个星期天你想去哪儿？

　　我想去美术馆或者去图书馆。

　　上午去还是下午去？

　　上午去。

商场	商店
银行	邮局
公司	朋友家
王府井	前门
美术学院	音乐学院

(2) 过新年的时候, 你做什么了？

　　过新年的时候, 我跟朋友去

　　饭馆吃饭了。

过圣诞节	给爸爸妈妈打电话
过生日	跟朋友一起吃蛋糕
参观美术馆	买画儿
上语法课	问老师问题
办借书证	填表

(3) 天气热的时候,他也吃火锅吗?
天气热的时候,他也吃火锅。

天气非常冷	散步
学习忙	去公园玩儿
路上的车多	自己开车
嗓子发炎	上课

(4) 昨天你是不是去 办公室了?
是啊,今天上午我又去了。
你什么时候再去?
明天下午再去。

听	中国民乐
用	这个电脑
送	她花儿
练习	那个乐曲

(5) 你习惯吃 涮羊肉吗?
我已经习惯了。
他还有点儿不习惯。

吃	中国饭
喝	咖啡
听	中国民乐
用	这儿的电脑
坐	公共汽车

(6) 他为什么没有来参加聚会?
因为他不爱吃火锅。
(所以没有来参加聚会。)

上课	病了
回家	公司有事儿
去公园玩儿	要写一篇文章
听音乐会	没有票
开车来	身体不太舒服

3. 课堂活动 Classroom activity

This game is to be played by two groups of students. The students in "Group A" ask ten questions regarding the five previous lessons, using "为什么", and the students in "Group B" answer these questions, using "因为…所以…". The scoring method is as follows: each time that Group B gives a correct answer, they will get one point; if they give an incorrect answer and Group A can then give the correct answer, Group A will get the point, instead. When all ten questions have been asked, the two groups reverse roles, so that Group B asks a new set of ten questions. The group with the higher score wins.

4. 会话练习 Conversation exercises

[问原因 Asking for reasons]

(1) A：老师，咱们为什么八点上课？

   B：这是我们这儿的习惯，中学、小学(xiǎoxué)也都是八点上课。

   A：这儿的商店或商场每天几点开门？

   B：＿＿＿＿＿＿＿＿。银行、邮局、海关或者公司也是九点开始办公。

(2) A：今天你怎么没有把照相机带来？

   B：因为我起(床)晚了，出来的时候我把照相机忘了。

   C：没关系，我带照相机来了，你们＿＿＿＿＿＿＿＿。

[催促 Hurrying somebody up]

(1) A：大为，你的电话。

   B：等一下。

   A：快，是你女朋友！

   B：是吗？我就来。

(2) A：快点儿，该出发了。

   B：咱们说好几点出发？

   A：＿＿＿＿＿＿＿＿＿。

   B：现在五点二十五，还有五分钟呢，别着急。

   A：别忘了，咱们得先到图书馆，从那儿出发！

(3) A：咱们坐几路车？

   B：应该坐＿＿＿＿＿＿＿。

   A：看，"307"来了，快跑！

   B：(To the bus driver)师傅，请等一下。

(4) A：喂,是出租汽车公司吗?

B：是啊。您哪里?

A：我是语言学院留学生宿舍楼,我要一辆(liàng)出租车。

B：_____?

A：我去北京音乐厅(yīnyuètīng)。能不能快点儿?

B：没问题,车一会儿就到。

[新年祝愿 New Year's greetings]

(1) A：新年好!

B：_____!

(2) A：祝你新年快乐!

B：祝你全家幸福(xìngfú)!

(3) A：恭喜恭喜!

B：恭喜你新的一年万事如意(wàn shì rú yì)!

5. 看图说话 Describe the following pictures

(不一样)

(习惯)

(送礼物,或者)

(坐出租车)

6. 交际练习 Communication practice

(1) Tell your friend about what people eat and do to celebrate the New Year in your hometown.

(2) You are waiting for your friend to get ready to go to the park. What would you say to hurry him/her up?

(3) You are in a hurry to get to the concert hall; how do you tell this to the taxi driver?

四. 阅读和复述 Reading Comprehension and Paraphrasing

画 蛇 添 足

一天，几个朋友在一起喝酒。他们人很多，可是酒太少，只有一瓶。应该把这瓶酒给谁呢？一个年轻人说："我们每人都画一条(tiáo)蛇(shé)，画得最(zuì)快的人喝这瓶酒，好吗？"大家都说："好。"

他们开始画蛇。那个年轻人比别的人画得快，他非常高兴，说："你们画得太慢了！我比你们画得快多了！看，现在我还有时间，我再给蛇添(tiān)上脚(jiǎo)吧。"他就开始画蛇的脚了。

一会儿，他旁边的一个人说："我画完(wán)了，这瓶酒应该给我。"年轻人听了很着急，说："不对！你画得比我慢，我早就画完了。你看，我还给蛇添了脚呢。这瓶酒是我的。"旁边的那个人说："大家都知道蛇没有脚，你画了脚，所以你画的不是蛇。最早画完蛇的是我，不是你。"

大家说："他说得对。我们应该把这瓶酒给他。"

一个人做了多余(duōyú)的事儿，就叫"画蛇添足(zú)"。

五. 语法复习 Grammar Review

1. 汉语句子的六种基本成分 The six basic functional components of a Chinese sentence

The basic functional components of a Chinese sentence are the subject, the predicate, the object, the attributive, the adverbial, and the complement.

We have already learned that a noun, a pronoun, or a noun phrase can all function as the subject. In addition, a verbal phrase, an adjectival phrase, or a subject-predicate phrase may also serve as the subject. The predicate is usually composed of a verb, an adjective, a verbal phrase, or an adjectival phrase. A subject-predicate phrase or a nominal phrase can also serve as the predicate. The subject usually precedes the predicate. For example:

这些书都是新的。

他 来北京了。

马大为 头疼。

白的 漂亮。

现在 七点四十。

寄航空比海运贵。

贵一点儿 没关系。

我们去打球,好吗?

When the context is clear and unambiguous, the subject is often omitted. Sometimes the predicate can also be omitted. For example:

你带照片来了吗?

——(我)带来了。

谁有词典?

——我(有词典)。

The object is usually placed after the verb. We have learned that the object is usually composed of a noun, a pronoun, a nominal phrase, a verbal phrase, or a subject-predicate phrase. For example:

他有哥哥。

我不认识他。

买两张到前门的。

他喜欢吃烤鸭。

我觉得这件太长了。

Some verbs may have two objects. For example:

谁教你 汉语?

我问老师 一个问题。

The attributive is mainly used to modify a noun and must be placed before the element that it modifies. We have learned that an adjective, an adjectival phrase, a noun, or a pronoun often functions as the attributive. In addition, a verb, a verbal phrase, or a subject-predicate phrase can also serve as the attributive (refer to Lesson 14 in the Workbook for Volume I).

The adverbial is used to modify a verb, an adjective, an adverb, or a whole sentence. The adverbials that we have already learned are mainly composed of adverbs. In addition, time nouns, prepositional phrases, and adjectives can also be used as adverbials. For example:

他们<u>也</u>都看了这个京剧。

力波<u>一定</u>去。

你<u>今天</u>穿得很漂亮啊!

你<u>从那儿</u>拿一张表来。

咱们<u>快</u>走。

The complement is a sentence component placed after a verb or an adjective to give additional information about that verb or adjective. For example:

他来得<u>很早</u>。　　　　　　　　　(the complement of state)

年轻人(说)英语说得也<u>很流利</u>。

我们进<u>去</u>吧!　　　　　　　　　　(the directional complement)

你带照片<u>来</u>了吗?

这儿的书可以借<u>一个月</u>。　　　　　(the time-measure complement)

他(画)中国画已经画了<u>11年</u>了。

这件红的比那件绿的短<u>两公分</u>。　　(the complement of quantity)

我觉得这件小<u>一点儿</u>。

这件漂亮<u>极</u>了。　　　　　　　　　(the complement of degree)

这件比那件贵<u>多了</u>。

我听<u>懂</u>了,可是记<u>错</u>了。　　　　(the resultative complement)

2. 动词谓语句(1) Sentences with a verbal predicate (1)

The following is a summary of the kinds of sentences in which the verb is a major element of the predicate:

(1) Sentences with "是"

她<u>是</u>英国留学生。

这四本书<u>是</u>中文的。

(2) Sentences with "有"

我们系<u>有</u>三十五位老师。

他没有女朋友。

(3) Sentences without an object

我在北京生活。

(4) Sentences with a single object

他每天锻炼身体。

(5) Sentences with double objects

她送他一瓶酒。

我告诉你一件事儿。

(6) Sentences with a verb or a verbal phrase as the object

现在开始工作。

北京人爱吃火锅。

我会说一点儿汉语。

(7) Sentences with a subject-predicate phrase as the object

我不知道他是经理。

听说这两年上海发展得非常快。

(8) Sentences with serial verb phrases

他去商场买东西。

现在是不是坐电梯上楼去?

(9) Pivotal sentences

他请我吃饭。

妈妈不让她喝咖啡。

(10) The "把" sentence

我把这事儿忘了。

请把通知单给我。

他把护照拿来了。

六. 汉字　　Chinese Characters

1. 汉字的构字法(6) Methods of constructing Chinese characters (6)

The pictophonetic method (2): In this method, a character is formed by placing the component indicating the sound on the left side and the component indicating the meaning on the right side. For example: 放, 翻, 刚, 故, 和, 剧, 鸭, 瓶, 颜, 邮.

2. 认写基本汉字 Learn and write basic Chinese characters

(1) 丸 　 丿 九 丸

  wán pill   3 strokes

(2) 曲 　 丨 冂 曰 曲 曲

  qǔ melody   6 strokes

3. 认写课文中的汉字 Learn and wirte the Chinese characters appearing in the text

(1) 火锅 huǒguō（火鍋）

  锅 → 钅 + 口 + 内   12 strokes

(2) 因为 yīnwèi（因爲）

  因 → 囗 + 大   6 strokes

(3) 涮羊肉 shuànyángròu

  涮 → 氵 + 尸 + 巾 + 刂 11 strokes

  肉 → 冂 + 人 + 人   6 strokes

(4) 热 rè（熱）

  热 → 扌 + 丸 + 灬   10 strokes

(5) 郊区 jiāoqū（郊區）

  郊 → 交 + 阝   8 strokes

  区 → 匚 + 乂   4 strokes

(6) 或者 huòzhě

  或 → 戈 + 口 + 一   8 strokes

  （一 口 戓 或）

(7) 化妆 huàzhuāng（化妝）

  化 → 亻 + 匕   4 strokes

  妆 → 丬 + 女   6 strokes

(8) 民族 mínzú

族 → 方 + ㇉ + 矢　　　　　11 strokes

(9) 乐器 yuèqì（樂器）

器 → 口 + 口 + 犬 + 口 + 口　16 strokes

夫（chūnzìtóu）　一 = 三 夫 夫　　5 strokes

(10) 演奏 yǎnzòu

演 → 氵 + 宀 + 一 + 由 + 八　14 strokes

奏 → 夫 + 天　　　　　　　9 strokes

毌 guàn　乚 口 毌 毌　　　　4 strokes

　　(Note: pay attention to the difference between "毌" and "母".)

(11) 习惯 xíguàn（習慣）

惯 → 忄 + 毌 + 贝　　　　11 strokes

(12) 花儿 huār

花 → 艹 + 化　　　　　　7 strokes

(13) 照相机 zhàoxiàngjī（照相機）

相 → 木 + 目　　　　　　9 strokes

(14) 旁边 pángbiān（旁邊）

旁 → 产 + 方　　　　　　10 strokes

冊（biǎnzìlǐ）丨 冂 冃 冊 冊　5 strokes

(15) 篇 piān

篇 → 竹 + 户 + 冊　　　　15 strokes

(16) 文章 wénzhāng

章 → 立 + 早   11 strokes

小 (shùxīndǐ) 亅 丿 小 小   4 strokes

(17) 恭喜 gōngxǐ

恭 → 共 + 小   10 strokes

(18) 着急 zháojí（著急）

着 → 羊 + 目   11 strokes

急 → 勹 + ヨ + 心   9 strokes

夂 (yèzìlǐ) 丿 勹 夕 夂   4 strokes

(19) 《春江花月夜》《Chūn Jiāng Huā Yuè Yè》

春 → 夫 + 日   9 strokes

江 → 氵 + 工   6 strokes

夜 → 亠 + 亻 + 夂   8 strokes

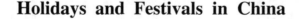

文化知识　　Cultural Notes

Holidays and Festivals in China

Besides National Day (October 1st) and International Labour Day (May 1st), which are the two major official holidays celebrated all over the country, there are many other traditional holidays and festivals in China.

The Spring Festival (Chinese New Year's Day) falls on the first day of the first month on the Chinese lunar calendar (usually in January or February of the solar calendar), and the day before it is Chinese New Year's Eve. The Han people and other ethnic minorities in China all celebrate the Spring Festival, with such activities as setting off firecrackers (now prohibited in some cities), pasting *chunlian* (couplets matching each other in sound and meaning, written on red paper) on the door, extending New Year's greetings to each other, and performing the *yangge* (literally, "rice seedling song") dance and the lion dance.

The fifteenth day of the first lunar month is the Yuanxiao Festival, also known as the Lantern Festival or Shang Yuan Festival. The special food for this festive day is called *yuanxiao*, a ball-shaped dumpling made of glutinous rice flour with sweet sesame or meat stuffing.

Qing Ming (Clear and Bright) Festival is on the fourth or fifth day of April. This is the time of year when people go out to the tombs and memorials to pay tribute to the dearly departed and national heroes.

Duan Wu or the Dragon Boat Festival is celebrated on the fifth day of the fifth lunar month (June of the solar calendar). This is a festival dedicated to the memory of Qu Yuan, the great poet-statesman from the state of Chu during the Warring States Period (475–221 BC). Legend has it that after Qu Yuan drowned himself in protest against the corrupt government of Chu's king, people feared that Qu Yuan's body might be eaten by the fish in the river. So they wrapped up glutinous rice with bamboo leaves, and taking these dumplings, they raced each other in their boats to the place where Qu Yuan had died. They threw the dumplings into the river to feed the fish, so as to keep Qu Yuan's body from harm. Later, the act of wrapping glutinous rice in bamboo leaves evolved into the tradition of preparing a special food called *zongzi* for this festival. The boat race to save Qu Yuan's body was the origin of the dragon boat race, which is held on this day, every year.

The Mid-Autumn Festival, which falls on the fifteenth day of the eighth lunar month (September of the solar calendar), is also known as Family Reunion Day. This is a time when the whole family enjoys getting together to look at the full moon, and to eat delicious moon cakes.

Sing a song

茉莉花

1= ♭E

江苏民歌

中速

好一朵茉莉 花，　　　好一朵茉 莉 花，
好一朵茉莉 花，　　　好一朵茉 莉 花，
好一朵茉莉 花，　　　好一朵茉 莉 花，

满　园　　花　开　　香也 香不过 它；
茉　莉　　花　开　　雪也 白不过 它；
满　园　　花　开　　比也 比不过 它；

我 有 心　采　一朵　戴，　看 花的 人儿 要
我 有 心　采　一朵　戴，　又 怕 旁人
我 有 心　采　一朵　戴，　又 怕 来年

将　我　　骂。　　　我 有 心　采　一朵
笑　　发　　话。
不　　发　　芽。

戴，又 怕 来年　不 发　芽。

The reporter, Lu Yuping, carries out an interview to find out how the Foreign Students' Soccer Team won over the Chinese College Students' Soccer Team. In this lesson, we will learn how to emphasize the time and location of past events, and the manner in which they have occurred, and also how to talk about directions and locations.

第二十一课 Lesson 21

我们的队员是从不同国家来的

一. 课文　　Text

（一）

陆雨平：听说上星期你们留学生队赢了一场足球比赛。我想写一篇文章，介绍一下留学生足球队的事儿。

丁力波：太好了。你是怎么知道的？

陆雨平：我是听你的同学说的。① 别忘了我是记者，我今天是来问你们问题的。你们留学生队是跟谁比赛的？

丁力波：我们队是跟中国大学生队比赛的。

陆雨平：你们是在哪儿比赛的？

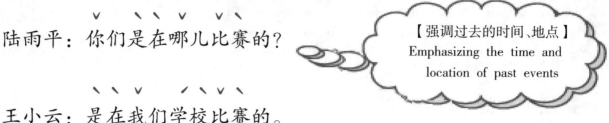

【强调过去的时间、地点】
Emphasizing the time and
location of past events

王小云：是在我们学校比赛的。

陆雨平：中国大学生队的水平比你们高吧？②

丁力波：他们的水平比我们高多了。

王小云：宋华说，大学生队的教练是从国家队来的。

陆雨平：他是什么时候从国家队下来的？

王小云：他是去年从国家队下来的。这位教练来了以后，大学生队

的水平提高得很快。③

丁力波：大学生队的10号踢得很好。左边的5号、右边的12号跑

得都很快。

陆雨平：你们留学生队呢？

丁力波：我们的队员是从不同国家来的，我们不常练习。

陆雨平：你们是怎么赢的？

【谈体育比赛】Talking about sports matches

丁力波：上半场0比0。下半场他们帮助我们进了一个球，是1比0赢的。④

生词 New Words

1. 队员	N	duìyuán	team member 我们的队员,有名的队员,年轻的队员,很多队员,老队员,新队员,一个队员
队	N	duì	team 你们队,我们队,中国队,留学生队,语言学院队
2. 不同	A	bùtóng	different 不同的人,不同的学生,不同时间,不同语言,不同岁数
3. 国家	N	guójiā	country 国家队,不同国家,我们国家,一个国家,哪个国家
4. 赢	V	yíng	to win 我赢,他赢,赢他们,赢了没有
5. 场	M	chǎng	match; set; (a measure word for sports, films, performances) 一场电影,上半场,下半场
6. 足球	N	zúqiú	soccer 足球队,足球队员,看足球,一场足球
足	N	zú	foot
球	N	qiú	ball 打球,看球,进了一个球
7. 比赛	N/V	bǐsài	match/to compete; to have a match 一场比赛,一场足球比赛,赢了一场比赛,比赛足球,跟留学生队比赛
赛	N/V	sài	race; match/to compete; to race 足球赛,看了一场足球赛
8. 同学	N	tóngxué	classmate; schoolmate 你的同学,女同学,男同学,新同学,老同学,同学们

*9. 记者	N	jìzhě	reporter　一个/位记者,别的记者,外国记者
10. 大学生	N	dàxuéshēng	university student; college student　大学生队,一个/位大学生,中国大学生
11. 学校	N	xuéxiào	school　我们学校,这个学校,有名的学校,学校办公室
12. 水平	N	shuǐpíng	level　大学生队的水平,普通话水平,汉语水平高,专业水平不高
13. 教练	N	jiàoliàn	coach　大学生队的教练,足球队的教练,那位教练
14. 去年	N	qùnián	last year　去年三月,去年圣诞节,去年开始,去年认识
*15. 以后	N	yǐhòu	after; afterwards　来了以后,走了以后,开学以后
16. 提高	V	tígāo	to improve; to increase　提高得很快,提高水平,提高房租
提	V	tí	to lift
17. 踢	V	tī	to kick　踢足球,踢球,踢得很好
18. 左边	N	zuǒbian	the left side　左边的队员,左边的书,队员左边,书左边,在学校左边
左	N	zuǒ	left
19. 右边	N	yòubian	the right side　右边的队员,右边的房子,我右边,在饭馆右边
右	N	yòu	right

陆雨平：我还要问问你们：你们去看大为租的房子了没有？房子在

　　　哪儿？

王小云：去了，房子在学校东边，⑤ 离学校不太远。⑥ 那儿叫花园小

区，大为住八号楼。

陆雨平：你们是怎么去的？

丁力波：我们是坐公共汽车去的。车站就在小区前边。下车以后先

往右拐，再往前走三分钟，就到八号楼了。⑦

陆雨平：那儿怎么样？

丁力波：很好。八号楼下边是一个小花园，左边有一个商店，商店旁

边是书店。右边是银行和邮局。大为的房子在八号楼九层，

上边还有六层。

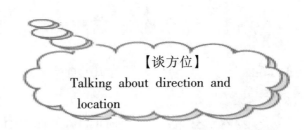

【谈方位】
Talking about direction and location

陆雨平：房子不大吧？

王小云：那套房子一共有 56 平方米。

丁力波：进门以后，左边是卫生间，右边是客厅。

学校　水平　提高　趣易

陆雨平：厨房在哪儿？

王小云：厨房在客厅北边，卧室在客厅东边。卧室外边有一个大阳台。

丁力波：记者先生，你问了很多问题，你也要写一篇文章介绍马大为租

的房子吧？

陆雨平：问问题是记者的

职业习惯啊。

| 卫生间 | 厨房 | 卧室 | 阳台 |
| 客厅 | | | |

生词 New Words

1. 东边	N	dōngbian	east side　东边的商场,学校东边,美术馆东边,在中国银行东边
东	N	dōng	east　往东走
2. 离	Prep	lí	away; off; from　离学校,离这儿,离那儿,离商店
3. 远	A	yuǎn	far　不远,很远,非常远,太远,离学院不太远
4. 花园小区	N	huāyuán xiǎoqū	garden district　叫花园小区,住花园小区
花园	N	huāyuán	garden　花园东边,花园里边,花园左边,大花园,一个漂亮的花园
区	N	qū	district; section; area　学院区,宿舍区

5.	车站	N	chēzhàn	bus stop
6.	前边	N	qiánbian	front; ahead　前边的公园,前边的人, 花园小区前边,图书馆前边,在宿舍前边
	前	N	qián	front; ahead; forward　往前走
7.	拐	V	guǎi	to turn　往右拐,往左拐,往东拐, 先往右拐
8.	下边	N	xiàbian	below; underneath　楼下边,床下边, 在书下边,下边的生词,下边的纸
	下	N	xià	down; under
9.	书店	N	shūdiàn	bookstore　外文书店
10.	上边	N	shàngbian	above; over; upward　上边的衣服, 上边的报,九层上边,邮局上边,在本 子上边
	上	N	shàng	upper; up　往上走
11.	平方米	M	píngfāngmǐ	square meter　56平方米,多少平 方米,有100平方米
	平方	M	píngfāng	square
	米	M	mǐ	meter 56米,多少米
12.	卫生间	N	wèishēngjiān	washroom; bathroom　一个卫生间, 一间卫生间,一间小卫生间
	卫生	N	wèishēng	hygiene; health
13.	客厅	N	kètīng	living room　一个客厅,一间客 厅,一间大客厅
14.	北边	N	běibian	north side 北边的房子,卫生间北边, 客厅北边,在花园小区北边
	北	N	běi	north　北楼,往北走,往北拐
15.	卧室	N	wòshì	bedroom　一个卧室,一间卧室, 一间新卧室
	卧	V	wò	to lie on one's back
16.	外边	N	wàibian	outside　去外边玩儿,去外边看看, 到外边走走
17.	阳台	N	yángtái	balcony　一个阳台,一个大阳台

1. 电影院	N	diànyǐngyuàn	cinema
2. 咖啡馆	N	kāfēiguǎn	coffee bar
3. 南边	N	nánbian	south (side)
4. 足球场	N	zúqiúchǎng	soccer field
5. 出差	V	chūchāi	to go on a business trip
6. 后边	N	hòubian	back; behind
7. 输	V	shū	to lose
8. 天堂	N	tiāntáng	heaven; paradise
9. 苏杭	PN	Sū Háng	Suzhou and Hangzhou
苏州	PN	Sūzhōu	Suzhou
杭州	PN	Hángzhōu	Hangzhou
10. 城市	N	chéngshì	city
11. 山水	N	shānshuǐ	landscape
山	N	shān	hill; mountain
12. 园林	N	yuánlín	garden; park
13. 修建	V	xiūjiàn	to build; to construct
14. 诗人	N	shīrén	poet
15. 设计	V	shèjì	to design
16. 建筑师	N	jiànzhùshī	architect

二. 注释　Notes

① 我是听你的同学说的。

"I heard it from your classmates."

Students in the same class or the same school call each other "同学"; for example: "他是我同学", "这是宋华同学". Teachers or other people also call students "同学"; for example: "同学们".

② 中国大学生队的水平比你们高吧？

"Isn't the level of the Chinese College Students' Team higher than yours?"

In addition to softening the tone in sentences expressing persuasion, a request, or an order, the modal particle "吧" can also be used in interrogative sentences to denote a tone of estimation or uncertainty. For example:

我是马大为，您是家美租房公司的经理吧？

今天是十九号吧？

你喜欢听音乐会吧？

③ 这位教练来了以后，大学生队的水平提高得很快。

"Ever since this coach arrived, the College Students' Team has improved rapidly."

The word "以后" refers to a time later than the present time or a specific moment. It functions in sentences as an adverbial modifier. Besides being used by itself, "以后" (as well as "以前", which we will study in the next lesson) can also be used together with nouns, verb phrases, subject-predicate phrases, and so on, to form phrases. For example: "新年以后，五年以后，开学以后". It not only can describe things in the past, but also things in the future. For example:

我认识你以后，汉语口语水平提高得很快。

以后我要跟你一起练习普通话。

④ 上半场 0 比 0。下半场他们帮助我们进了一个球，是 1 比 0 赢的。

"The score was 0 to 0 in the first half of the game. In the second half, they 'helped' us score a goal. Then it was 1 to 0, and we won."

The word "比" here indicates the score of the two competing sides or teams. One may use "几比几？" to ask about the score.

⑤ 房子在学校东边。

"The house is to the east of the school."

Chinese people are accustomed to using "东，西，南，北" to denote direction and location. For example: "学院东边，厨房西边，在医院北边". As well, "前，后，左，右" can also be used to denote direction and location. For example: "客厅前边，卧室左边，卫生间右边".

⑥ 离学校不太远。

"It's not too far from the school."

The preposition "离" often forms a prepositional phrase with a noun of place: "离 + PW". Placed before a verb or an adjective, it indicates distance. For example:

> 语言学院离王府井很远。

> 北京图书馆离中国银行不太远。

We have previously learned that: "在+PW" denotes the place where an action happens; "从+PW" denotes the starting point of an action; "往+PW" denotes the direction towards which an action moves.

⑦ 下车以后先往右拐,再往前走三分钟,就到八号楼了。

"After getting off the bus, turn right first, and walk straight ahead for three minutes, then you will arrive at building no. 8."

The adverb "再"(2) may indicate that an action starts after another action finishes (The adverb "先" is often inserted before the first verb to form the construction "先…再…"), or after a certain situation or time. For example:

> 我们上课以后先翻译生词,再复习课文。

> 看完电影再走吧。

三. 练习与运用 Drills and Practice

KEY SENTENCES
1. 我们的队员是从不同国家来的。
2. 你们是在哪儿比赛的?
3. 他是去年从国家队下来的。
4. 我们是坐公共汽车去的。
5. 房子离学校不太远。
6. 下车以后先往右拐,再往前走三分钟,就到八号楼了。
7. 八号楼下边是一个小花园,左边有一个商店。
8. 卧室在客厅东边,卧室外边有一个大阳台。
9. 房子不大吧?

1. 熟读下列短语 Master the following phrases

(1) 十分钟以后　　半小时以后　　三天以后　　一星期以后　　两个月以后
　　看了以后　　　写了以后　　　听了以后　　懂了以后
　　复习以后　　　考试以后　　　上课以后　　认识他以后　　回答问题以后
　　练习汉字以后　取了包裹以后　提高了水平以后

(2) 离商场　　离医院　　离宿舍　　离公司　　离邮局　　离北楼　　离南方
　　离广州很远　　　离王府井不远　　　离北京图书馆不太远
　　离中国美术馆非常远

(3) 九点钟再来　　　明天再交　　复习了课文再睡觉　　打了电话再去
　　翻译了句子再休息
　　先办证,再借书　　先买票,再参观　　先锻炼,再休息
　　先介绍汉字,再学习生词

(4) 是去年认识的　是新年寄的　是星期五晚上走的　是 1980 年 10 月 25 号出生的
　　是在海关取的　是在加拿大买的　是在家里写的　是在图书馆查的
　　是坐公共汽车去的　是用墨画的　是用民族乐器演奏的　是用英文说的

(5) 前边有一个公园　　左边有一个公司　　右边有一个商场　　上边还有两层
　　里边是厨房 外边是阳台 东边是宿舍 北边是邮局 下边就是大为的新房子
　　客厅在卧室北边　　　卫生间在阳台东边　　　花园小区在语言学院东边

(6) 中式衣服不便宜吧　　　他们队的水平不太高吧
　　您就是留学生队的教练吧

2. 句型替换 Pattern drills

(1) 她去西安了没有?

她去西安了。

她是什么时候去西安的?

她是昨天去西安的。

她先去西安,再去上海。

上海	上星期五	美国
美术馆	上午	王府井
学校	下午 3:00	银行
医院	上午 9:00	公司

（2）他是从哪儿来的？
　　　他是从<u>国家队</u>来的。
　　　他是跟谁一起来的？
　　　他是跟<u>教练</u>一起来的。

美国	他同学
加拿大	他弟弟
英国	一位记者
欧洲	一位画家

（3）他去<u>办公室</u>了没有？
　　　他去办公室了。
　　　他是怎么去的？
　　　他是<u>坐公共汽车</u>去的。

南方	坐火车
王府井	坐出租车
花园小区	开车
十楼	坐电梯

（4）他们是来<u>工作</u>的吧？
　　　他们不是来工作的，
　　　他们是来<u>旅行</u>的。

学习	参观
玩儿	比赛
找你	找宋华
学汉语	学音乐
借书	还书

（5）<u>卫生间</u>在<u>里边</u>吗？
　　　卫生间不在里边，在<u>外边</u>。

阳台	东边	北边
饭馆	上边	下边
客厅	前边	那儿
卧室	左边	右边

（6）<u>宿舍楼前边</u>有什么？
　　　楼前边有一个<u>花园</u>。
　　　这个花园大不大？
　　　这个花园不太大。

银行旁边	邮局
商店左边	书店
商场东边	医院
图书馆北边	饭馆

（7）学校里边有<u>邮局</u>吗?

有一个邮局。

请问邮局在哪儿?

邮局在<u>宿舍楼东边</u>。

离这儿远不远?

不太远。

银行	商店旁边
图书馆	办公楼左边
饭馆	花园北边
医院	汉语系前边

（8）学校东边是什么地方?

学校东边是<u>美术馆</u>。

前边	电影院(diànyǐngyuàn)
北边	咖啡馆(kāfēiguǎn)
南边(nánbian)	足球场(zúqiúchǎng)

3. 课堂活动 Classroom activity

As a reporter, interview your classmate or teacher about some specific thing that has happened in the past, using the construction "是…的". For example, Ms. Chen's mother was sick, so she went to Xi'an to visit her. Three days later, she returned to Beijing by train with her friend.

4. 会话练习 Conversation exercises

［谈论过去的时间、地点 Talking about the time and location of past events］

（1）A: 您的孩子今年几岁了?

B: 他今年 ＿＿＿＿＿＿＿。

A: 他是 ＿＿＿＿＿＿年出生的吧?

B: 对,他是 ＿＿＿＿＿＿＿＿＿ 的。

A: 他是在哪儿出生的?

B: 他是 ＿＿＿＿＿＿＿＿＿ 的。

（2）A: 你是什么时候到北京的? 怎么不先给我打个电话?

B: 我打电话了,你不在。我是 ＿＿＿＿＿＿＿＿ 到这儿的。

A: 你是怎么来的?

B: 我是坐火车来的。

A: 你是来旅行的吧?

B: 不是,我这次是来出差(chūchāi)的,只在这儿住三天。

A: 太短了! 晚上有时间吗? 到我家去玩儿,好吗?

B: 一定去。我是跟一位教授一起来的,我先打电话告诉他一下儿。

[谈方位 Talking about direction and location]

(1) A: 您是租房公司吗? 我想租一套50平方米的房子。

B: 我查一下。有,白石小区有一套55平方米的,在建国门北边。

A: 那很好,离我们公司不远。那儿怎么样?

B: 那儿很好:小区东边有一个大公园,前边不远就有一个大商场。小区
旁边就是公共汽车站。

A: 那儿 _____?

B: 有,医院在后边(hòubian)。医院旁边还有银行和邮局。

A: 房租是多少?

B: 每月两千五。

A: 房租有点儿贵。我们想想,再给您打电话。

(2) B: 这是六号楼十五层,上边还有三层。

A: 我想看看房子。

B: 请进。

A: 厨房在哪儿?

B: 厨房在右边,左边是客厅,客厅有26平方米。

A: 卧室呢?

B: 有两个卧室,都在客厅南边(nánbian)。大卧室外边还有一个阳台。

A: 这儿是卫生间吗? 卫生间小一点儿。

B: 这个卫生间是五平方米。

A: 好吧,我们先到别的楼看看。

[问路 Asking about direction]

(1) A: 请问,新邮局在哪儿?

   B: 对不起,我不住这儿,我也不知道。

   A: 麻烦您,这儿有一个新邮局吗?

   B: 有,在前边。中国银行的北边就是新邮局。

   A: 谢谢您。

   B: 不客气。

(2) A: 请问,去花园小区怎么走?

   B: 从这儿坐945路公共汽车,到花园路下车。下车以后先往前走,再往左拐,走10分钟就到了。

   A: 谢谢。

[谈体育比赛 Talking about sports matches]

   A: 昨天你去看足球赛了吗?

   B: 没有。谁跟谁赛?

   A: 咱们系足球队跟外语系队比赛。

   B: 咱们系队赢了吗?

   A: 输(shū)了!0比2。两个球都是下半场进的。

   B: 咱们系队怎么踢得这样糟糕?

5. 看图说话 Describe the following pictures

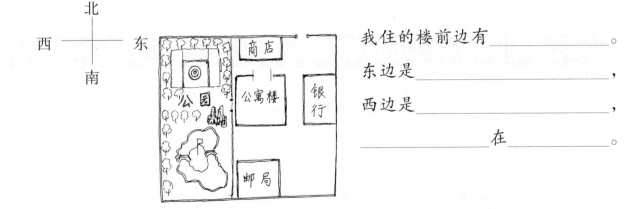

我住的楼前边有_____。

东边是_____,

西边是_____,

_____在_____。

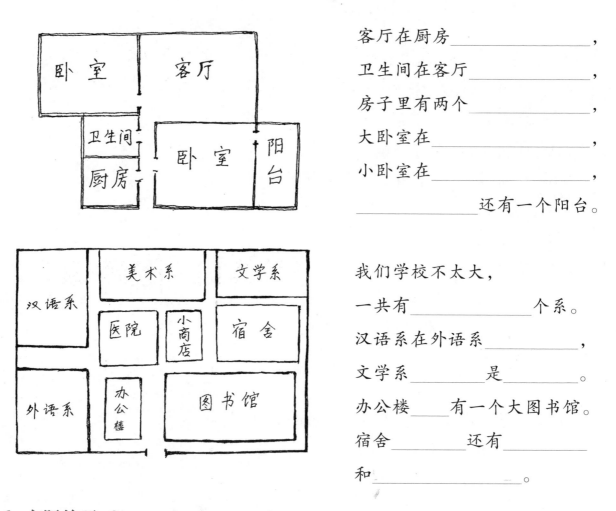

客厅在厨房＿＿＿＿＿＿＿，

卫生间在客厅＿＿＿＿＿＿＿，

房子里有两个＿＿＿＿＿＿＿，

大卧室在＿＿＿＿＿＿＿，

小卧室在＿＿＿＿＿＿＿，

＿＿＿＿＿＿＿还有一个阳台。

我们学校不太大，

一共有＿＿＿＿＿＿＿个系。

汉语系在外语系＿＿＿＿＿＿，

文学系＿＿＿＿是＿＿＿＿。

办公楼＿＿有一个大图书馆。

宿舍＿＿＿＿还有＿＿＿＿

和＿＿＿＿＿＿＿。

6. 交际练习 Communication practice

(1) You heard that one of your classmates went to Europe, so you inquire of the other students about the specific details concerning his or her departure.

(2) Inquire about the birthdays and birthplaces of at least 5 of your friends.

(3) You become acquainted with a new friend. You invite him or her to see your family as a guest. You describe to him or her the surroundings of the place where you live and the layout of your house.

四. 阅读和复述 Reading Comprehension and Paraphrasing

南方的花园

中国人常说："上有天堂(tiāntáng)，下有苏杭(Sū Háng)。"意思是：苏州和杭州这两个城市(chéngshì)跟天堂一样美。它们都在中国的南方，是中国南方的"花园"。它们的美在哪儿呢？——杭州的山水(shānshuǐ)和苏州的园林（yuánlín）。苏州的园林非常有名。那些园林是过去一些有钱人请人修建（xiūjiàn）的。园林里边有山、有水、有花儿，真是一幅非常美的山水画。中国的园林跟西方的园林很不一样。中国的园林好像是一幅中国画，是用水和墨画的；西方的园林好像是油画，是用油彩画的。因为中国的园林常常是画家和诗人（shīrén）设计（shèjì）的，西方的园林常常是建筑师（jiànzhùshī）设计的，所以它们的美很不同。

五. 语法　　Grammar

1. "是…的" 句 The construction "是…的"

The construction "是…的" can be used to emphasize the time and location of past events, and the manner in which they have occurred. The word "是" is placed before the part to be emphasized (sometimes it can be omitted), and the "的" is placed at the end of the sentence. The negative form is "不是…的".

Subject	"是"	Word(s) indicating time, place or manner	V	O	"的"
他	是	（去年	来）		的。
你们	是	在学院	比赛		的吗？
我们的队员	是	从不同国家	来		的。
你	是	怎么	知道	这件事儿	的？
我们	不是	坐出租车	去	大为家	的。

Some sentences with a verb as the predicate simply express that a certain thing has happened in the past. The meaning of this kind of sentence is different from that of a sentence with "是…的" as predicate. Compare the following:

他是去年来的。（emphasizes that the time when he came was last year）

去年他来了。（tells generally what happened last year）

The sentence with "是…的" can also be used to emphasize purpose, function, and origin. For example:

我今天是来问你们问题的。

我是听朋友说的。

-153-

gòu bian
(right sides)

2. 方位词 Location words
↑ *Not pronounced in tone*

The words "里边", "外边", "左边", "右边", "上边", "下边", "前边", "后边", "东边", "西边", "南边", and "北边" are all nouns expressing direction and location and can function as subject, object, and attributive. They can also be modified by attributives. For example:

里边有什么？

邮局在前边。

左边的床是我的。

图书馆外边有很多人。

Notes:

(1) When a location word functions as an attributive, the word "的" must be placed after it. For example: "上边的报，前边的花园". When a location word functions as a central word, "的" is not usually used before it. For example: "厨房里边，银行北边".

(2) The word "里边" cannot be used after the name of a country, a place or a workplace. For example, one may only say "在中国/北京", but we cannot say ⊗ "在中国/北京里边"; one may only say "我在中国银行工作", but we cannot say ⊗ "我在中国银行里边工作".

cannot be used together.

3. 表示存在的句子 Sentences indicating existance

We have learned that in order to indicate that a certain person or thing exists in a certain direction or location, the word "在" is often used as the main verb of the predicate. The subject of this kind of sentence is usually a person or thing that exists; the object is usually a noun or a phrase expressing direction or location.

↑ *IN/AT/ON*

S (Phrase indicating persons or things that exist)	V "在"	O (Phrase indicating location)
我	在	他右边。
大为的房子	在	八号楼九层吗？
厨房	不在	客厅的北边。

In order to indicate the meaning of "in a certain direction or location, there exists a certain person or thing", the words "有" or "是" are usually employed as the main verb of the predicate. The subject of this kind of sentence is usually a noun or a phrase expressing direction or location; the object is usually a person or thing that exists.

S (Phrase indicating location) place	V "有"/"是" Someone / something.	O (Phrase indicating persons or things that exist)
卧室外边	有	一个大阳台。
办公室里边	没有	老师。
前边 qián biān	有没有	一个小花园?
图书馆后边	是	英语系。
阳台东边 dong biān Yangbai	不是	卫生间。
你前边 qiánbiān	是	谁? shéi

Note: There are two differences between sentences that use "是" or "有" to indicate existence：

(1) A sentence with "有" only denotes what exists in a certain place, while a sentence with "是" not only indicates that a certain thing exists in a certain place, but also further specifies what that thing is.

(2) The object of a sentence indicating existence with "有" is usually a general reference, while the object of a sentence indicating existence with "是" is usually a specific reference. Therefore, we can say "图书馆前边有一个学院"；but we cannot say ⊗ "图书馆前边有我们学院". *有 indicates something* ∴ *Not definite* Instead, we should say "图书馆前边是我们学院" or "我们学院在图书馆前边".

六. 汉字　　Chinese Characters

1. 汉字的构字法(7) Methods of constructing Chinese characters (7)

The pictophonetic method (3): In this method, a character is formed by placing the component indicating meaning on the top, and the component indicating sound at the bottom. For example: 花, 寄, 蕉, 篇, 苹, 舍, 药.

2. 认写基本汉字 Learn and write basic Chinese characters

(1) 凡　　丿 几 凡

fán　　　　every　　　　　　　　　　　　　3 strokes

(2) 臣　　一 丁 丏 丏 丏 臣

chén　　　　official under a feudal ruler　　　　6 strokes

xian
先 ．．． 再 ．．． used to indicat sequence of actions.

先 ．．．, 再 ．．．
is ___, and then ___, and then ___ etc....

3. 认写课文中的汉字 Learn and write the Chinese characters appearing in the texts

(1) 不同 bùtóng

同 → 冂 ＋ 一 ＋ 口　　　　　　　6 strokes

(2) 赢 yíng（贏）

赢 → 亡 ＋ 口 ＋ 月 ＋ 贝 ＋ 凡　　　17 strokes

共 (sàizìyāo)　一 二 卡 卄 丗 丼 共　　7 strokes

(3) 比赛 bǐsài（比賽）

赛 → 宀 ＋ 共 ＋ 贝　　　　　　14 strokes

(4) 学校 xuéxiào（學校）

校 → 木 ＋ 交　　　　　　　　10 strokes

(5) 以后 yǐhòu（以後）

后 → 厂 ＋ 一 ＋ 口　　　　　　6 strokes

(6) 提高 tígāo

提 → 扌 ＋ 是　　　　　　　　12 strokes

(7) 踢 tī

踢 → 𧾷 ＋ 日 ＋ 勿　　　　　　15 strokes

(8) 左边 zuǒbian（左邊）

左 → 𠂇 ＋ 工　　　　　　　　5 strokes

(9) 右边 yòubian（右邊）

右 → 𠂇 ＋ 口　　　　　　　　5 strokes

(10) 离 lí（離）

离 → 亠 ＋ 凶 ＋ 禸　　　　　　10 strokes

(11) 远 yuǎn（遠）

远 → 元 + 辶   7 strokes

(12) 拐 guǎi

拐 → 扌 + 口 + 力   8 strokes

(13) 卫生间 wèishēngjiān（衛生間）

卫 → 卩 + 一   3 strokes

(14) 卧室 wòshì（臥室）

卧 → 臣 + 卜   8 strokes

(15) 阳台 yángtái（陽臺）

阳 → 阝 + 日   6 strokes

台 → 厶 + 口   5 strokes

文化知识   Cultural Notes

Sports in China

China has traditional sports such as martial arts, wrestling, qigong, and high-swinging. Among these, martial arts is also called "Chinese *gongfu*" by foreigners. The main function of Chinese martial arts is to improve one's health and increase one's strength.

Modern sports started very late in China, but developed very rapidly. China's first world record was established by the weight lifter, Chen Jingkai, in 1956. Table tennis, badminton, gymnastics, diving, and middle and long-distance races are China's strongest sports. In the World Championships of Table Tennis in 1982, China won all the first and second-place titles. In the 1980's, the Chinese Women's Volleyball Team won the championship five times in a row in the World Cup Competition and other international competitions. China achieved the worldwide third-place ranking at the 2000 Sydney Olympic Games, for both the number of gold medals they won and their total number of overall medals. Up to now, Chinese athletes have won 1317 world champions, setting 1026 world records.

In 2008, the twenty-nineth Olympic Games will be held in Beijing.

Did you know that in addition to the Beijing opera there are diverse regional operas, such as the Shaoxing opera? Do you know the renowned classical Chinese novel, Dream of the Red Chamber? In this chapter, Song Hua and Lin Na will tell you about these subjects. You will also learn how to comment on your past experiences, how to make an appointment with somebody, and how to express your opinions on various topics.

第二十二课 Lesson 22

你看过越剧没有

一. 课文　Text

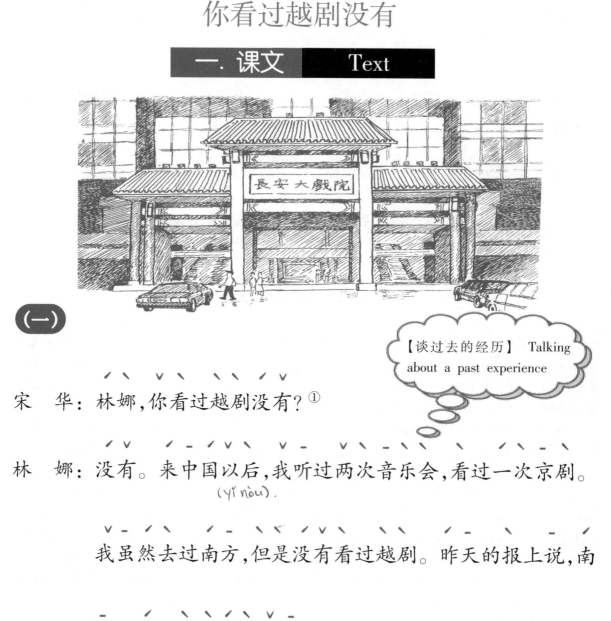

（一）

【谈过去的经历】 Talking about a past experience

宋　华：林娜，你看过越剧没有？①

林　娜：没有。来中国以后，我听过两次音乐会，看过一次京剧。

我虽然去过南方，但是没有看过越剧。昨天的报上说，南

方的一个越剧团到北京来了。②

宋　华：是啊，越剧是中国有名的地方戏。这个剧团是从上海来的，

现在在长安大戏院上演《红楼梦》。③

林　娜：上演《红楼梦》吗？太好了！我知道《红楼梦》是中国有名

的古典小说，我看过一遍，是用英文翻译的。

宋　华：你觉得这部小说怎么样？

林　娜：我觉得小说里的爱情故事非常感人。

宋　华：你想不想再看一次越剧的《红楼梦》？我有两张票。

林　娜：当然想看。是什么时候的票？

【约会】
Making an appointment or
a date with someone

宋　华：是明天晚上七点一刻的。座位很好，楼下五排八号和十号。

林　娜：我没去过长安大戏院。这个戏院在哪儿？

宋　华：我去过啊，长安大戏院离建国门不远，就在建国门的西边。

咱们一起打的去。

林　娜：好，明天见。

生词 New Words

1. 过	AsPt	guo	(indicating a past experience)　看过,听过,去过,写过,试过,踢过
2. 越剧	N	yuèjù	the Shaoxing opera　看过越剧,看过一次越剧,一场越剧,两张越剧票
剧	N	jù	opera; dramatic work; play
3. 虽然	Conj	suīrán	although; though
4. 但是	Conj	dànshì	but; whereas; yet
5. 剧团	N	jùtuán	opera troupe; theatrical group　越剧团,京剧团,一个剧团,南方的剧团
6. 地方戏	N	dìfāngxì	regional opera　有名的地方戏,地方戏剧团 (local)
戏	N	xì	drama; play; show　看戏,听戏,唱戏,南方的戏,一场戏　↳ same as jù
7. 上演	V	shàngyǎn	to stage a show; to perform　上演越剧,上演地方戏,上演京剧
演	V	yǎn	to act; to perform; to play　演戏,演电影,演大学生,演记者
8. 古典	A	gǔdiǎn	classical　古典音乐,古典乐曲,古典音乐会,古典文学
9. 小说	N	xiǎoshuō	novel; fiction　看小说,写小说,看过一遍小说,古典小说
*10. 遍	M	biàn	number of times (of action)　一遍,几遍,多少遍,看过一遍,听过一遍
11. 部	M	bù	(a measure word for films, works of literature)　一部小说,一部电影　diànyǐng + movie
12. 爱情	N	àiqíng	love　爱情小说,爱情戏,他们的爱情
13. 故事	N	gùshi	story; tale　爱情故事,留学生的故事,足球队的故事,租房子的故事,一个有意思的故事

我 wǒ zài shánghǎi dǎ guo liǎng cì dī.
yī/hē cí

14. 感人	A	gǎnrén	touching; moving　感人的故事,感人的爱情,非常感人,演得很感人,唱得很感人
15. 座位	N	zuòwèi	seat　好座位,有座位,一个座位
16. 排	N	pái	line; row　五排,八排,几排
17. 西边	N	xībian	west side　厨房西边,医院西边,在公园西边,西边的书店
18. 打的	VO	dǎdī	to take a taxi　一起打的,打的去,是打的来的
19. 见	V	jiàn	to see; to meet with　见过,再见,明天见,下星期见,什么时候见
20. 长安大戏院	PN	Cháng'ān Dà Xìyuàn	the Chang'an Theatre
戏院	N	xìyuàn	theatre
21.《红楼梦》	PN	《Hónglóu Mèng》	*Dream of the Red Chamber*　上演《红楼梦》,看一次越剧的《红楼梦》
梦	N	mèng	dream　做梦,好梦,一个梦,我的梦

（二）

【评价】Making comments

宋　华：你觉得越剧《红楼梦》怎么样？

林　娜：我从来没有看过这么感人的戏。④两个主角演得好极了。

我觉得越剧的音乐特别优美,越剧的风格跟京剧很不一样。

宋　华：你说得很对。你可能还不知道，很早以前京剧里没有女演员，都是男演员演女角色。越剧跟京剧不同，以前没有男演员，让女演员演男角色。所以越剧的风格跟京剧很不一样。

林　娜：听说中国地方戏的种类很多，每个地方都有吧？

宋　华：是啊，每种地方戏都有自己的风格，每个地方的人都习惯看自己的地方戏，但是京剧是全中国的，喜欢京剧的人特别多。

林　娜：中国京剧团两年以前到英国访问过，我跟爸爸妈妈一起去看过一次。他们都觉得京剧很美。

宋　华：很多外国朋友都喜欢中国京剧，一些外国留学生还到北京来学京剧。现在他们有的人会唱京剧，有的人还会演京剧。⑤

林　娜：我有一个朋友，也是英国留学生，他就会演京剧。

宋　华：我还从来没听过外国留学生唱越剧。你这么喜欢越剧的

音乐，应该学一学越剧。

林　娜：我虽然喜欢越剧音乐，可是我觉得唱越剧太难了。

宋　华：你的嗓子很好。你可以先多听听，再学唱。⑥

楼下　5排　8号　　　长安大戏院入场券

生词 New Words

1. 从来	Adv	cónglái	all along; always　从来没有看过，从来没有见过，从来没有演过，从来没有说过
2. 这么	Pr	zhème	so; such; like this　这么感人，这么有名，这么流利，这么容易，这么喜欢，这么放心，这么着急
3. 主角	N	zhǔjué	leading actor or actress　两个主角，电影主角，男主角，女主角
4. 特别	Adv	tèbié	extraordinary; especially; particularly　特别感人，特别高兴，特别远，特别愿意，特别喜欢，特别想

5.	优美	A	yōuměi	graceful; fine; exquisite; elegant 特别优美, 这么优美, 优美的音乐, 优美的故事
6.	风格	N	fēnggé	style; manner 越剧的风格, 小说的风格, 不同的风格
7.	以前	N	yǐqián	before; ago; previously; formerly 两年以前, 三天以前, 上课以前, 开学以前, 认识你以前
8.	演员	N	yǎnyuán	actor or actress; performer 越剧演员, 电影演员, 一位男演员
9.	角色	N	juésè	character; role 男角色, 女角色, 演一个角色, 电影角色
10.	种类	N	zhǒnglèi	kind; sort; type; variety 地方戏的种类, 语言的种类, 乐曲的种类, 不同的种类, 别的种类
	种	M	zhǒng	kind; sort; type 每种地方戏, 这种照相机, 一种乐器
11.	地方	N	dìfang	place; region 每个地方, 这个地方, 很多地方, 什么地方
12.	访问	V	fǎngwèn	to visit; to call on 访问过, 访问过一次, 访问英国, 访问上海, 访问中国京剧团, 访问老画家
13.	有的	Pr	yǒude	some 有的人, 有的学生, 有的演员, 有的剧团, 有的故事, 有的特别优美, 有的非常感人
14.	难	A	nán	difficult; hard 太难了, 特别难, 这么难, 难学, 难唱, 难演, 难极了

Handwritten annotations:
- 10. 种类 · 禾 | zhǒng → type of
- 12. ↳ +N = Sub → (can be N + 有的)
- 13. +N ≠ obj. ↳ Before or aft SUB.

1.	研究	V	yánjiū	to study; to discuss; to consider
2.	顿	M	dùn	(a measure word for meals)
3.	便饭	N	biànfàn	a simple meal
4.	太太	N	tàitai	wife; Mrs.
5.	不怎么样	IE	bù zěnmeyàng	not so good
6.	悲伤	A	bēishāng	sad; sorrow
7.	贾宝玉	PN	Jiǎ Bǎoyù	(name of the leading male character in *Dream of the Red Chamber*)
8.	聪明	A	cōngming	clever; bright
9.	林黛玉	PN	Lín Dàiyù	(name of the leading female character in *Dream of the Red Chamber*)
10.	诗	N	shī	poem; poetry
11.	相爱	V	xiāng'ài	to fall in love
12.	结婚	VO	jiéhūn	to get married
13.	骗	V	piàn	to cheat; to trick
14.	烧	V	shāo	to burn
15.	哭	V	kū	to cry; to weep
16.	死	V	sǐ	to die
17.	回忆	V	huíyì	to reminisce; to recollect; to recall
18.	离开	V	líkāi	to leave; to depart from

二. 注释   Notes

① 林娜, 你看过越剧没有?

"Lin Na, have you ever seen the Shaoxing opera?"

The Shaoxing opera is a regional opera from Zhejiang Province. It is derived from local folk songs, and is mainly popular in areas such as Jiangsu Province and Zhejiang Province, as well as in Shanghai. It is a well-known regional opera in China, characterized by sweet and elegant melodies.

② 昨天的报上说,南方的一个越剧团到北京来了。

"It was announced in yesterday's newspaper that a Shaoxing opera troupe from the south has come to Beijing."

When combined with a preceding noun, some location words such as "上边", "外边", and "里边", usually drop the character "边". For example: 报上，书上，头上，小说里，家里，楼里，系里.

When "上" follows a noun, it can indicate the literal, physical location of an object, for example, 头上，身(体)上; or the abstract, figurative location, i.e. in the area or scope of something, for example, 书上，报上.

③ 现在在长安大戏院上演《红楼梦》。

"*Dream of the Red Chamber* is now playing at the Chang'an Theatre."

Dream of the Red Chamber is one of the four most famous classical Chinese novels. This profound work depicts the rise and fall of the Jia, Wang, Shi, and Xue families; it is an encyclopaedic chronicle of late Chinese feudal society. The love story between the leading male character, Jia Baoyu, and the female character, Lin Daiyu, is the main plot of the novel.

④ 我从来没有看过这么感人的戏。

"I have never seen such a moving opera."

The demonstrative pronoun "这么", which in spoken Chinese is often pronounced "zème", denotes manner, status, method and degree. It usually modifies adjectives or verbs. In this sentence, it indicates a degree. Further examples are: 这么好的课本, 这么美的油画. In cases such as "这么写", "这么念", and "这么做", "这么" demonstrates the method.

⑤ 现在他们有的人会唱京剧,有的人还会演京剧。

"Now some of them can sing the Beijing opera, while some of them can perform it on stage."

When the pronoun "有的" functions as a modifier, it often refers to only a part of the group of people or objects that it modifies. It can be used individually or it can appear two or three times in consecutive clauses within a sentence. For example:

有的人喜欢看小说,有的人喜欢听音乐。

有的书是中文的,有的书是英文的,有的书是日文(Japanese)的。

If the noun which "有的" modifies appears in the previous sentence, it can be omitted in the following sentences starting with "有的". For example:

这些衣服有的太长,有的太短。

Note: A noun with "有的" as its modifier usually doesn't follow a verb as an object. For example, we do not normally say ⊗ "我不太喜欢有的地方戏", but rather "有的地方戏我不太喜欢".

⑥ 你可以先多听听,再学唱。

"You can first listen to it well, and then learn how to sing it."

In this Chinese sentence, the object "越剧" has been omitted. The complete sentence is:

你可以先多听听越剧,再学唱越剧。

三. 练习与运用　Drills and Practice

KEY SENTENCES
1. 你看过越剧没有?
2. 来中国以后,我听过两次音乐会,看过一次京剧。
3. 我从来没有看过这么感人的戏。
4. 我觉得小说里的爱情故事非常感人。
5. 你想不想再看一次越剧的《红楼梦》?
6. 我虽然去过南方,但是没有看过越剧。
7. 我虽然喜欢越剧音乐,可是我觉得唱越剧太难了。
8. 现在他们有的人会唱京剧,有的人还会演京剧。

1. 熟读下列短语 Master the following phrases

(1) 报上　书上　课本上　本子上　词典上　电影上　名片上　光盘上
　　照片上　护照上　借书证上　明信片上　包裹通知单上　你填的表上

(2) 没有去过　　没有学过　　没有送过　　没有拿过　　没有写过
　　从来没听说过　从来没进去过　从来没参加过　从来没打扫过
　　从来没见过他　从来没有访问过画家　从来没赢过足球比赛
　　从来没有穿过旗袍　　从来没有看过《红楼梦》

(3) 这么容易　这么难　这么热　这么冷　这么早　这么晚
　　这么快　　这么慢　这么新　　这么旧
　　这么放心　这么爱　这么习惯　这么着急　　这么愿意
　　这么喜欢　这么想
　　从来没有看过这么好的小说　　从来没翻译过这么难的句子
　　从来没听过这么优美的音乐

(4) 特别贵　特别便宜　特别多　特别少　特别年轻　特别长　特别短
　　特别愿意　特别喜欢　特别想　特别放心　特别习惯　特别着急

(5) 有的朋友　有的角色　有的同学　有的队员　有的司机　有的语言
　　有的专业　有的乐曲　有的文章　有的课本　有的中学　有的民族
　　有的职业　有的地方　有的时候
　　有的特别优美　有的非常流利　有的合适极了
　　有的锻炼身体　有的演奏民乐

(6) 回答过问题　开过车　唱过越剧　画过中国画　查过词典　借过书
　　上过课没有　　演过京剧没有　　坐过火车没有　　参观过兵马俑没有

(7) 听过一次　开过一次玩笑　去过一次西安　换过一次人民币
　　看过一遍　念过一遍课文　写过一遍汉字　听过一遍生词

(8) 虽然合适,但是太贵了　　　虽然有意思,可是特别难
　　虽然从来没去过英国,但是很喜欢英国文学
　　虽然从来没有学过京剧,可是觉得京剧的音乐特别优美

2. 句型替换 Pattern drills

(1) 你看过京剧吗?

我看过京剧。

你是在哪儿看京剧的?

我是在北京看京剧的。

学	汉语	美国
听	中国民乐	上海
吃	北京烤鸭	加拿大
喝	中国红葡萄酒	宋华家

(2) 你知道《红楼梦》吗?

我知道,我看过这部小说。

你是什么时候看的?

我是三年以前看的。

徐悲鸿	看	他画的马	来中国以后
兵马俑	参观	那个地方	去西安旅行的时候
《春江花月夜》	听	这个乐曲	来中国以前
建国门	去	那儿	取包裹的时候

(3) 你去过长安大戏院没有?

我没有去过,

我很想去。

学	太极拳
看	这部小说
用	这种照相机
演	戏

(4) 你以前访问过那位老画家没有?

我访问过(那位老画家)。

你访问过他几次?

我访问过他两次。

见	那位演员
找	那位经理
麻烦	那位师傅
问	张教授
帮助	你同学

(5) 这课 汉字你写过几遍了?

我写过两遍了,

我要再写一遍。

本	小说	看
个	乐曲	听
篇	课文	念
部	电影	看

(6) 剧院里有什么?

剧院里有中国大学生,
也有外国留学生。

包裹里	书	词典
书店里	大学课本	中学课本
楼上	卧室	卫生间
汉语课本里	故事	小说

(7) 过新年的时候你的同学们做什么?

有的人去看京剧,有的人去听音乐会。

过生日的时候	吃蛋糕	去吃寿面
过圣诞节的时候	旅行	回家
下午四点以后	踢足球	去打太极拳
星期天	看朋友	去商场买东西

(8) 今天天气这么不好,别去公园玩儿了。

虽然天气不好,可是我女朋友一定要去。

排队的人这么多	在这儿换钱	现在我就要用钱
衣服这么贵	在这儿买	衣服的样子好
他们队的水平这么高	跟他们比赛	我们应该试试
公共汽车这么多	打的	车上的人也多

3. 课堂活动 Classroom activity

A asks B a question, and B replies; then B asks C a question, and C replies; ....

(1) 林娜看过越剧没有?

(2) 来中国以后,林娜听过音乐会吗?

(3) 她听过几次音乐会?

(4) 来中国以前,林娜听说过京剧没有?

(5) 中国京剧团到英国访问过没有?

(6) 林娜在英国看过京剧吗?

(7) 来中国以后,林娜看过京剧没有?

（8）林娜看过小说《红楼梦》没有？

（9）她看过几遍？

（10）林娜看过中文的《红楼梦》没有？

（11）林娜以前去过长安大戏院没有？

（12）宋华去过吗？

（13）林娜去过中国南方没有？

（14）林娜看过越剧吗？

（15）宋华听过外国留学生唱越剧没有？

（16）你学习过中国美术吗？

（17）你以前看过中文小说没有？

（18）你听过中国地方戏没有？

（19）你买过中国音乐光盘没有？

（20）你听过《梁祝》没有？

4. 会话练习 Conversation exercises

[谈过去的经历 Talking about a past experience]

（1）A：你去过欧洲没有？

　　B：我去过三次。

　　A：你到过英国吗？

　　B：（虽然）我去过很多欧洲国家，可是我还没去过英国。

　　A：下次你到英国，一定给我打电话。

（2）A：你访问过那位老画家没有？

　　B：＿＿＿＿＿＿＿＿＿＿＿＿＿。

　　A：你是在哪儿访问他的？

　　B：＿＿＿＿＿＿＿＿＿＿＿＿＿。

　　A：＿＿＿＿＿＿＿＿＿＿＿＿＿？

　　B：我访问过他两次。

　　A：你来中国以前听说过他没有？

　　B：我很早以前就听说过他。

（3）A：啊，王明，你刚才去哪儿了？

B：我_____了。有事儿吗？

A：你老同学来找过你三次，你都不在。

B：糟糕，上星期四我给他打过一次电话，让他今天下午来我这儿，可是我把这事儿忘了。

A：你可以去他那儿找他。

B：不行，我从来没有去过他那儿，我不知道他住哪儿。

[找工作 Looking for a job]

（1）A：张先生，您想来我们公司工作，是吗？

B：是的。

A：你以前学过什么？

B：我的专业是_____，我还学习过_____。

A：张先生，您学过电脑没有？

B：我虽然没有正式学习过，但是我看过一些电脑的书，也用过电脑。

A：很好。请下星期五再来见我们一次。

（2）A：我的朋友很愿意来你们学院工作，她想在英语系工作两年。

B：_____？

A：不，她是美国人。

B：她以前做过什么工作？

A：她一年以前在美国一个大学教过语言课，去年到中国以后教过英语语法。

B：她会说汉语吗？

A：她会说一点儿汉语。大学的时候她学过汉语口语。

B：谢谢您的介绍，我们研究(yánjiū)一下儿以后再告诉您。

[约会 Making an appointment or a date with someone]

（1）A：你还没有来过我的新家呢，星期六晚上到我家来玩儿，吃顿

（dùn）便饭（biànfàn），好吗？

B：我很想来，可是这个星期六我有点事儿。

A：星期天怎么样？

B：那好，我一定来。几点？

A：＿＿＿＿＿＿＿＿。你太太（tàitai）能一起来吗？

B：我想没问题。

A：那太好了。

（2）A：（打电话）喂，请问田小姐在家吗？

B：我就是。您是哪一位？

A：＿＿＿＿＿＿＿＿。田小姐，你看过电影《爱情故事》吗？

B：没有看过，可是我听说过，好像是一部很好的电影。

A：是啊，大家都说这部电影好。你想不想看？

B：想看。什么时候演啊？

A：＿＿＿＿＿＿＿＿＿＿＿＿，不知道你有没有时间。

B：我看看。可以，明天晚上我没有事儿。

A：我已经买了两张电影票，座位是十二排一号和三号。

B：好极了！咱们怎么去？

A：咱们一起打的去吧。七点半我在你家东边的商场等你。

B：好，明天七点半见。

[评价 Making comments]

A：《爱情故事》这部电影太感人了，我已经看了两遍，以后还想再看一遍。你觉得怎么样？

B：我觉得不怎么样（bù zěnmeyàng）。

A：为什么？你知道吗，女主角和男主角都很有名。

B：演员虽然有名，但是这次他们演得不好。

A：我觉得这部电影的音乐特别优美。

B：可是这部电影的故事太没有意思，我也不喜欢它的风格。

5. 看图说话 Describe the following pictures

你吃过北京烤鸭没有？

我＿＿＿＿＿＿＿＿＿＿＿＿＿。

你＿＿＿＿＿＿＿＿＿＿＿＿＿？

我吃过九次北京烤鸭。

你们＿＿＿＿＿＿＿＿＿＿＿＿＿？

我们跟中国大学生队比赛过足球。

你们比赛过几次？

我们＿＿＿＿＿＿＿＿＿＿＿＿＿。

力波看过这篇文章没有？

他＿＿＿＿＿＿＿＿＿＿＿＿＿。

他看过几遍？

＿＿＿＿＿＿＿＿＿＿＿＿＿。

大为＿＿＿＿＿＿＿＿＿＿＿＿？

他复习过那篇课文。

＿＿＿＿＿＿＿＿＿＿＿＿＿？

＿＿＿＿＿＿＿＿＿三遍课文。

6. 交际练习 Communication practice

(1) Talk to your classmate about an interesting experience you had last week.

(2) You have bought two movie tickets; invite your friend to see the movie with you.

(3) After watching the movie, you discuss your thoughts about it with your friend. Comment on the plot, music, style, actors, performance, make-up, etc.

四. 阅读和复述 Reading Comprehension and Paraphrasing

《红楼梦》里的爱情故事

中国古典小说《红楼梦》里有一个优美、悲伤(bēishāng)的爱情故事。

故事里的男主角叫贾宝玉(Jiǎ Bǎoyù)，是在有钱人的家里出生的。他很漂亮，也很聪明(cōngming)。故事里的女主角是一个非常美的姑娘，叫林黛玉(Lín Dàiyù)，她从南方来到贾家生活。她比贾宝玉小一岁，看过很多书，写诗(shī)写得很好，还会画画儿。他们每天一起吃饭、看书，一起写诗、画画儿。贾宝玉很爱林黛玉，林黛玉也特别喜欢贾宝玉。可是贾宝玉的奶奶和爸爸妈妈都不愿意他们相爱(xiāng'ài)，他们一定要让他和别的姑娘结婚(jiéhūn)。贾宝玉不愿意，在他生病的时候，奶奶骗(piàn)他，让他跟别的姑娘结了婚。就在贾宝玉结婚的时候，林黛玉在自己的卧室里把她写给贾宝玉的诗都烧(shāo)了，也烧了他送给她的礼物。她哭(kū)了一天，就死(sǐ)了。林黛玉死了以后，贾宝玉到她的房子去过很多次，每次都悲伤极了。他回忆(huíyì)他们有过的每一次聚会，回忆他们有过的快乐。他不愿意和那个跟他结婚的姑娘一起生活。他离开(líkāi)了家。

五. 语法　　　　Grammar

1. 过去的经验或经历 Past experience

The aspect particle "过", which occurs immediately after a verb, denotes that an action took place in the past. It is often used to emphasize experience. Here are some more examples:

> 他来过北京，他知道怎么坐车去王府井。

> 我朋友足球踢得很好，他参加过很多比赛。

The negative form of "过" is "没(有)…过". For example:

> 没有来过，没有参加过.

The V/A-not-V/A question with "过" is "…过…没有". For example:

> 来过没有?

> 参加过比赛没有?

diàn yǐng
is mult-

V+了 (completion)

guo (did you?)
└ indicates past experience

guo≠了
└ guo must ALWAYS be after the v.

$$V + 过 + (O)$$

cí hé cí
离合词
seperate together

zōngni yifu
chinese style address.

从来
└always followed by -ve
从来没有

wǎng
to→
somewhere

Subject	Predicate				
	Adverbial	**V**	**"过"**	**O**	**"没有"**
她		看	过	越剧《红楼梦》。	
丁力波	在加拿大	学	过	中国画。	
我	没有	开 (drives)	过	车。	
他	从来 没有	用	过	电脑。	
你		唱	过	京剧	没有？
你	以前	去	过	中国美术馆	没有？

Nǐ   Hou zian   Xué   guo   Kaoshi chuangguo

Notes:

(1) "过" must be placed immediately after the verb. If the verbal predicate has an object, "过" always precedes the object. Therefore, one does not say: ⊗ "我看那部电影过", but rather "我看过那部电影".

(2) To indicate one's experience, "过" is normally placed after the second verb in a sentence with serial verb phrases. For example:

他去西安参观过兵马俑。

(It is incorrect to say：⊗他去过西安参观兵马俑。)

我们去花园小区看过大为的新房子。

(It is incorrect to say：⊗我们去过花园小区看大为的新房子。)

└ 2nd OR last V.

不过
└ v. informal way to say
dàn shì and
ké shi,
└ more formal.

2. 动量补语 The action-measure complement

The action-measure word "次" or "遍" is often combined with a numeral and placed after a verb as the action-measure complement to express the frequency of an action. In addition to signifying the number of times, "遍" also denotes the whole process of an action from beginning to end. For example:

cì   biàn

Both can be used interchangeably here.

我上星期六打扫过一次。→ indicates occurance /repitition of action.

这部小说我又看了两遍。→ stresses from beginning to end
→ indicates whole process of action

When the object of the verb is a noun, the action-measure complement should be placed before the object. When the object is expressed by a pronoun, the complement often comes after the object.

when O = place
you MUST use
cì

Subject	Predicate					
	Adverbial	V	"过"	O(Pr)	Nu + action-measure word	O(N)
林娜 丁力波 我 王小云	今天下午　又 以前 到学院以后	去 写 来 找	过 过 过 过	这儿 他	两次 一遍 三次。 几次?	上海。 课本上的汉字。

→ wrote then once again

Apart from indicating the frequency of an action, the action-measure complement "一下儿" is also used to indicate an action that is performed in a casual way, or that lasts for only a short while (refer to Note One in Lesson 7). Here are some examples: 介绍一下儿, 等一下儿.

↳ measure word (similar to 一次)

3. 虽然…但是/可是…　The construction "虽然…但是/可是…"

"虽然…但是/可是…", meaning "although", is used to link two contradictory statements. "虽然" may go either before or after the subject of the first clause, while "但是" (or "可是") is always placed at the beginning of the second clause. For example:

虽然他从来没有看过这部小说,但是他很早就听说过。

我虽然喜欢西方的油画,可是不会画油画。

"虽然" can also be omitted. For example:

他(虽然)学汉语的时间不长,但是学得很好。

六. 汉字　　Chinese Characters

1. 汉字的构字法(8) Methods of constructing Chinese characters (8)

The pictophonetic method (4): In this method, a character is formed by placing the component indicating the meaning at the bottom, and the component indicating the sound on the top. For example: 帮, 婆, 华, 照, 您, 愿.

2. 认写基本汉字 Learn and write basic Chinese characters

(1) 旦　　丶 冂 日 日 旦

dàn　　dawn; daybreak　　　　5 strokes

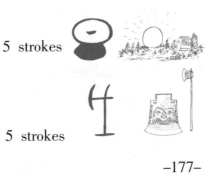

(2) 戊　　一 厂 戊 戊 戊

yuè　　battle-axe used in ancient China　　5 strokes

3. 认写课文中的汉字 Learn and write the Chinese characters appearing in the texts

(1) 越剧 yuèjù（越劇）

$$越 \longrightarrow 走 + 戊$$ 12 strokes

(2) 虽然 suīrán（雖然）

$$虽 \longrightarrow 口 + 虫$$ 9 strokes

(3) 但是 dànshì

$$但 \longrightarrow 亻 + 旦$$ 7 strokes

(4) 剧团 jùtuán（劇團）

$$团 \longrightarrow 囗 + 才$$ 6 strokes

(5) 地方戏 dìfāngxì（地方戲）

$$戏 \longrightarrow 又 + 戈$$ 6 strokes

(6) 遍 biàn

$$遍 \longrightarrow 户 + 冊 + 辶$$ 12 strokes

(7) 部 bù

$$部 \longrightarrow 立 + 口 + 阝$$ 10 strokes

(8) 爱情 àiqíng（愛情）

$$情 \longrightarrow 忄 + 青$$ 11 strokes

(9) 故事 gùshi

$$故 \longrightarrow 古 + 攵$$ 9 strokes

(10) 座位 zuòwèi

$$座 \longrightarrow 广 + 坐$$ 10 strokes

(11)《红楼梦》Hónglóu Mèng（紅樓夢）

梦 → 林 + 夕   11 strokes

(12) 主角 zhǔjué

角 → ⺈ + 用   7 strokes

(13) 特别 tèbié

特 → 牛 + 土 + 寸   10 strokes

(14) 优美 yōuměi（優美）

优 → 亻 + 尤   6 strokes

(15) 风格 fēnggé（風格）

格 → 木 + 夂 + 口   10 strokes

(16) 种类 zhǒnglèi（種類）

种 → 禾 + 中   9 strokes

类 → 米 + 大   9 strokes

(17) 访问 fǎngwèn（訪問）

访 → 讠 + 方   6 strokes

(18) 难 nán（難）

难 → 又 + 隹   10 strokes

| 文化知识 | Cultural Notes |

Classical Chinese Poetry, Prose, and Novels

Classical Chinese literature has a history as long as the literary histories of Greek, Arabic, and Sanskrit languages. Poetry is the most developed genre of classical Chinese literature.　The oldest collection of Chinese poetry, *The Book of Songs*, contains three hundred and five poems dating from the eleventh century B.C. to the sixth century B.C..　The golden age of Chinese poetry was during the Tang and Song dynasties. The poems of Qu Yuan, Li Bai, Du Fu, Bai Juyi, and Su Shi represent the highest achievements in this genre.

Chinese prose has a history just as long as poetry. The earliest prose consists of historical texts dating back to the eleventh century B.C.. These are followed by prose pieces representing various schools of thought.　During the Tang and Song dynasties, as well as in the Qing Dynasty, a great number of finely written prose pieces were produced.

Novels,　especially those written by known authors,　appeared fairly late in China. *The Romance of the Three Kingdoms, Journey to the West, Water Margin,* and *Dream of the Red Chamber* are the four most famous classical Chinese novels.

People in Beijing love to climb the Great Wall of China. Ding Libo and his friends climb the Great Wall with their teacher, Ms. Chen, once again before the holidays. You will tour the Great Wall with them and learn how to discuss plans, make suggestions, and talk about the scenery and the weather.

第二十三课 Lesson 23

我们爬上长城来了

一. 课文   Text

(一)

陈老师：要放假了，同学们有什么打算？

【谈计划】
Talking about plans

林　娜：有的同学去旅行，有的同学回家。

陈老师：小云，你呢？

王小云：我打算先去泰山，再回家看我爸爸妈妈。① 林娜，你去过

泰山没有？

林　娜：泰山我去过一次了。这次我想去海南岛旅行。
Hǎinán Dǎo (lǚ xíng) *travel.*

王小云：你跟宋华一起去吧？
(Sònghuá)

林　娜：是啊，去海南岛旅行就是他提出来的。②
Hǎinán Dǎo (lǚ xíng) jiù *tí chu* *(means)* *(put forwards).*

王小云：你们坐飞机去还是坐火车去？
Fēi jī *(airplane)* *huǒchē* *(train)*

林　娜：坐飞机去。机票已经买好了。力波呢？去不去泰山？
Fēi jī *(airplane)* *piào yǐ jīng* *(ticket) (already)* *Tài Shān*

王小云：去。他说他要从山下爬上去，再从山顶走下来。他还说，
shān pá *(hill) (climb)* *dǐng zǒu* *(the peak) (walk)*

先爬泰山，再去参观孔子教书的地方。③
(xiān) pá *(before) (climb).* *Kǒngzǐ jiāoshū dì fāng.* *(Confucious).* *(room)*

> 【提建议】
> Making suggestions

林　娜：对了，大为想去哪儿？④

王小云：小燕子建议大为也去海南岛。她说现在那儿天气好，气温
jiànyì *(make suggestion)* *Hǎinán dǎo* *qì wēn* *air temp.*

合适，能去游泳，还可以看优美的景色。现在北京是冬天，
hé shì *(suitable)* *yóu yǒng* *(swimming)* *(yōu měi) jǐngsè* *graceful (scenery)* *dōng tiān* *(winter).*

可是在海南岛还可以过夏天的生活，多有意思啊！⑤
Hǎinándǎo *xiàtiān shēnghuó (yǒu yì sī)* *(live) interesting.*

林　娜：小燕子是导游小姐，旅行的事儿她知道得很多，应该听她
dǎo yóu *lǚ xíng* *(tour guides) (travel)* *yīnggāi* *(should).*

的。大为可以跟我们一起去。
qǐ

王小云：大为还建议放假以前咱们一起去长城。陈老师，您能不能

跟我们一起去？

陈老师：行。我很愿意跟你们一起去爬一次长城。

生词 New Words

1.	爬	V	pá	to climb 爬上来,爬上去,爬一次
2.	放假	VO	fàngjià	to have a holiday or vacation 要放假了,开始放假,放假的时候,放假以前,放假以后
	假	N	jià	vacation; holiday 请假
3.	打算	N/V	dǎsuan	plan/to plan; to intend 我的打算,放假的打算,有什么打算,打算去看越剧,打算去旅行
4.	提	V	tí (→ tí chū)	to put forward; to raise 提出,提出来,提问题
5.	飞机	N	fēijī	airplane 坐飞机,开飞机,上飞机,下飞机
	飞	V	fēi	to fly 飞到北京,飞回加拿大
	机	N	jī	airplane
6.	山	N	shān	hill; mountain 高山,山上,山下,山里,爬山,爬上山来,爬上山去
7.	顶	N	dǐng	peak; tip 山顶,楼顶,头顶
8.	教书	VO	jiāoshū	to teach
9.	建议	V/N	jiànyì	to make suggestions/advice; suggestion 建议去爬山,建议坐飞机,提建议,有一个建议
10.	气温	N	qìwēn	air temperature 气温合适,气温不太高,气温这么高,气温怎么样,今天的气温,北京的气温
11.	景色	N	jǐngsè	scene; scenery; landscape 优美的景色,山顶的景色,看景色
	景	N	jǐng	view; scene 美景,全景,远景
	色	N	sè	scene
*12.	游泳	V	yóuyǒng	to swim 去游泳,打算游泳,建议游泳,游泳

-183-

			队，游泳教练
13. 冬天	N	dōngtiān	winter 在冬天，冬天的气温，冬天的景色，冬天的时候
14. 夏天	N	xiàtiān	summer 喜欢夏天，夏天的生活，夏天的天气，夏天的衣服
15. 导游	N	dǎoyóu	tour guide 导游小姐，导游先生，一位导游，女导游，男导游
导	V	dǎo	to guide; to lead
游	V	yóu	to travel
*16. 行	V	xíng	to be O.K.
17. 长城	PN	Chángchéng	the Great Wall 爬长城，看长城，参观长城，爬一次长城
18. 泰山	PN	Tàishān	Taishan Mountain 爬泰山，画泰山，去泰山，爬上泰山去
19. 海南岛	PN	Hǎinán Dǎo	Hainan Island 去海南岛旅行，海南岛的景色
20. 孔子	PN	Kǒngzǐ	Confucius
21. 小燕子	PN	Xiǎo Yànzi	(name of a Chinese tour guide)

王小云：陈老师、林娜，加油！ 快上来！
jiā yóu
(make an effort)

陈老师：力波、大为他们呢？⑥

王小云：他们已经爬上去了。咱们也快要到山顶了。
yǐ jīng pá   *shān dǐng*
(already) (climbed).   *(hill top).*

陈老师：别着急。我觉得有点儿累，林娜也累了，咱们就坐下来休

息一会儿吧。⑦先喝点儿水再往上爬。

林　娜：这儿的景色多美啊！长城好像一条龙。⑧看，下边都是

山，火车从山里开出来了。我要多拍些照片寄回家去。

王小云：你来过这儿吗？

林　娜：来过。是秋天来的。那时候长城的景色跟现在很不一样。

王小云：是啊。现在是冬天，今天还是阴天，要下雪了。

林　娜：在长城上看下雪，太美了。

【谈天气】
Talking about
the weather

陈老师：今天这儿的气温是零下十度。可是你们知道吗？广州今

天是零上二十度。

林　娜：中国真大。北方还是这么冷的冬天，可是春天已经到了

南方。你们看，力波怎么走下来了？

丁力波：喂，你们怎么还没上来？要帮忙吗？⑨

王小云：不用。你不用跑过来，我们自己能上去。陈老师，您休息好了吗？

陈老师：休息好了。小云，你帮我站起来……

林　娜：啊！我们爬上长城来了！

生词　New Words

1. 加油	VO	jiāyóu	to make an extra effort; to cheer sb. on 给我们加油,给男同学加油
加	V	jiā	to increase; to add
2. 累	A	lèi	tired　有点儿累,特别累,这么累,从来不累,觉得很累
3. 条	M	tiáo	strip; long narrow piece; (a measure word for objects like rivers, dragons, trousers) 一条狗
4. 龙	N	lóng	dragon　一条龙,好像龙,画龙,龙的故事
5. 拍	V	pāi	to pat; to beat; to take (a picture)　拍照片,拍一张照片,拍山顶的景色,给他们拍照片
6. 秋天	N	qiūtiān	autumn　在秋天,喜欢秋天,北京的秋天,秋天的天气
7. 阴天	N	yīntiān	cloudy sky; overcast sky　今天阴天,阴天的时候
8. 下雪	VO	xià xuě	to snow　要下雪了,可能下雪,下雪的天气
雪	N	xuě	snow　雪人,雪景,一场大雪
9. 零(下)	N	líng(xià)	zero（below zero）
10. 度	M	dù	degree (for temperature)　十度,零下五度,气温是多少度
11. 北方	N	běifāng	north　在北方,到北方,北方人,北方话
12. 春天	N	chūntiān	spring　春天到了,春天的时候,南方的春天,春天的气温

13.	帮忙	VO	bāngmáng	to help	要帮忙,不用帮忙,请帮(个)忙,常常帮忙
	帮	V	bāng	to help; to assist	请帮我一下,帮同学
14.	站	V	zhàn	to stand	
15.	起	V	qǐ	to rise; to get up	起来,起床,站起来,坐起来
16.	广州	PN	Guǎngzhōu	Guangzhou	

补充生词　Supplementary　Words

1.	天气预报	N	tiānqì yùbào	weather forecast
2.	晴天	N	qíngtiān	sunny sky
3.	中国民航	PN	Zhōngguó Mínháng	Civil Aviation Administration of China (CAAC)
4.	起飞	V	qǐfēi	to take off
5.	停车场	N	tíngchēchǎng	parking lot
6.	菜单	N	càidān	menu
7.	渴	A	kě	thirsty
8.	熊	N	xióng	bear
9.	害怕	V	hàipà	to be afraid
10.	棵	M	kē	(a measure word for trees, plants)
11.	树	N	shù	tree
12.	死	V	sǐ	to die
13.	装	V	zhuāng	to pretend to be sth./sb.
14.	动	V	dòng	to move
15.	危险	A	wēixiǎn	dangrous

二. 注释　Notes

① 我打算先去泰山,再回家看我爸爸妈妈。

"I plan to go to Taishan first, and then go home to see my parents."

Taishan is a famous mountain in Shandong Province. It is one of the great tourist attractions of China.　It is also known as the　"Eastern Mountain"　of China's five famous mountains.

② 是啊,去海南岛旅行就是他提出来的。

"That's right, it is his idea to join the tour to Hainan Island."

Hainan Island is part of Hainan Province in China.　Its tropical scenery attracts many tourists.

③ 他还说,先爬泰山,再去参观孔子教书的地方。

"He furthermore said that he would climb Taishan first, and then go to visit the place where Confucius used to teach."

Confucius was a famous philosopher and educator in the Spring and Autumn Period of ancient China.　He was the originator of Confucianism.　His philosophy and educational thoughts have influenced generations of Chinese people.

④ 对了,大为想去哪儿?

"By the way, where does Dawei like to go?"

"对了"　is used to insert something into a conversation or to start a new topic to attract somebody's attention.　It is commonly used to indicate that the speaker has suddenly remembered something or is going to correct or add to his previous comments.　For example:

对了,你刚才说你想买什么?

对了,他是昨天上午来的,不是昨天下午来的。

⑤ 多有意思啊!

"How interesting!"

"多+A/V+啊!"　is commonly used in exclamatory sentences that express strong feelings.　The adverb　"多"　is usually used as an adverbial in front of adjectives or certain verbs.　The modal particle　"啊"　is often used at the end of the sentence. For example:

她的汉字写得多漂亮啊!

《红楼梦》这部小说多感人啊!

我多喜欢长城的景色啊！

"太…了", which you have previously learned, is also a form of exclamatory sentence.

⑥ 力波、大为他们呢?

"Where are Libo and Dawei?"

"力波、大为他们" is an appositive phrase. "力波、大为" is equivalent to "他们". For example: 小云她们, 我们大家. "张介元教授" and "王经理", which you have previously studied, are both appositive phrases.

⑦ 我觉得有点儿累, 林娜也累了, 咱们就坐下来休息一会儿吧。

"I feel a little tired. Lin Na is tired, too. Let's sit down to rest for a while."

The adverb "就" (3) links the previous statement and its conclusion. For example:

爬上山以后, 他们都觉得有点儿累, 就坐下来休息。

王贵觉得很不好意思, 就问张才: "刚才它跟你说什么了?"

⑧ 长城好像一条龙。

"The Great Wall looks like a dragon."

The dragon is a magical creature in ancient Chinese mythology. It has a long body, scales, horns, and feet. It is able to walk, fly, swim, and command the clouds and the rain. As the feudal period came to an end, the dragon was no longer the symbol of the imperial emperor. However, Chinese people all over the world still see themselves as the "descendants of the dragon." Images of the dragon and "dragon culture" can be seen all over China.

⑨ 喂, 你们怎么还没上来? 要帮忙吗?

"Hi, why haven't you come up? Do you need help?"

Note the important difference between "帮忙" and "帮助": the verb "帮助" may be followed by an object (for example: 帮助我, 帮助他们); whereas "帮忙" cannot be followed by an object. For example, one must say, "要帮忙", "来帮忙", and not, ⊗ "帮忙我".

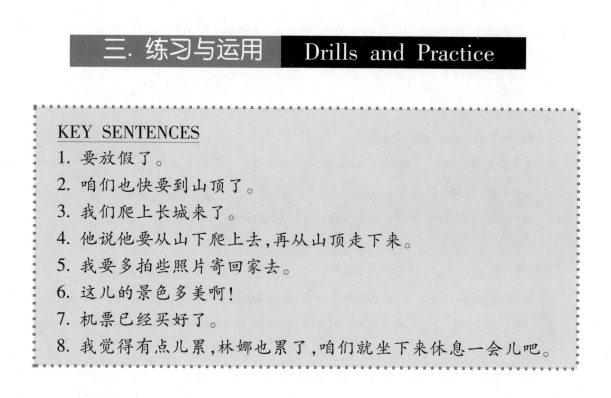

三. 练习与运用 Drills and Practice

KEY SENTENCES

1. 要放假了。
2. 咱们也快要到山顶了。
3. 我们爬上长城来了。
4. 他说他要从山下爬上去,再从山顶走下来。
5. 我要多拍些照片寄回家去。
6. 这儿的景色多美啊!
7. 机票已经买好了。
8. 我觉得有点儿累,林娜也累了,咱们就坐下来休息一会儿吧。

1. 熟读下列短语 Master the following phrases

(1) 有一个打算　有什么打算　说说你的打算
打算拍照片　打算游泳　打算爬山　打算去长城　打算踢足球
打算锻炼身体

(2) 建议去打工　建议多练习　建议听音乐会　建议访问老演员
建议去看越剧
提建议　有一个建议　好建议　新建议　合适的建议

(3) 写好汉字　画好画儿　复习好课文　做好练习　拍好照片
化好妆　填好表　办好借书证　借好书　打好电话
买好衣服　换好钱　租好房子

(4) 多好啊　多漂亮啊　多流利啊　多帅啊　多便宜啊　多合适啊
多热啊　多高啊　多远啊　多优美啊　多难啊　多累啊
多高兴啊　多可爱啊　多感人啊　多容易啊

(5) 林娜她们　陈老师他们　爸爸妈妈他们　姐姐她们

(6) 要开学了　要复习了　要考试了　要放假了　要过圣诞节了
快要上课了　快要开始了　快要开门了　快要爬上山顶了
快要到广州了

(7) 爬上来　走上去　坐下来　送下去　提出来　开出去　拐过来
　　游过去　站起来　爬上长城来　走下楼去　跑回学院来
　　寄回家去　提出问题来　送出国去
(8) 西安我去过　电影票买好了　太极拳学过　汉字写过一遍
　　生词念过两遍

2. 句型替换 Pattern drills

(1) 现在几点？
　　<u>七点五十</u>。
　　要<u>上课</u>了,快走吧。
　　等一下儿,我就来。

8:45	出发
9:10	上车
11:55	吃饭
4:20	去游泳
3:25	踢足球
5:12	拍照片

(2) 他们快要去<u>泰山</u>了吧？
　　他们<u>明天</u>就要去泰山了。
　　他们去过泰山没有？
　　他们没有去过。

来北京	下星期
去访问广州	下个月
来参观花园小区	星期五
到山顶	一会儿

(3) 谁从<u>长城上</u>　<u>走下来</u>了？
　　大为他们从长城上走下来了。

山下	爬上来
楼里	走出来
外边	走进来
前边	跑过来

(4) <u>宋华</u>他们呢？
　　他们<u>爬上</u>　<u>山</u>去了。

陈老师	走进	饭馆
你朋友	跑下	楼
你同学	住进	宿舍楼
你外婆	走回	家

(5) 他从邮局 寄出 一些照片去了吗?
他没有从邮局寄出一些照片去。

商场	买回	两件旗袍来
右边	踢进	一个球去
海关	取回	一个包裹来
老师那儿	拿回	本子去
楼下	拿上	一些书来
外边	带回	烤鸭来

(6) 机票已经买好了吗?
还没有买好呢。
买机票多难啊!

课文	复习	不容易
客厅	打扫	累
文章	写	难
饭	做	累

(7) 圣诞节 过得怎么样?
圣诞节过得很好。

那部小说	写	很感人
这部电影	拍	特别糟
衣服	洗	马马虎虎
那部乐曲	演奏	很优美
那条龙	画	很可爱

(8) 旅行的事儿她知道得多不多?
旅行的事儿她知道得不多。

汉语语法	考	好
生活口语	说	流利
学过的汉字	写	漂亮
老师的问题	回答	快
这一课的生词	用	对

3. 课堂活动 Classroom activity

Have a conversation with your classmate: A says he/she is planning to do something, and then B uses "可是要…了" to explain why this cannot be done. For example:

    A：我打算从现在开始在系办公室打工。

    B：可是要放假了。

4. 会话练习 Conversation exercises

[谈计划 Talking about plans]

(1) A：快要放假了,你有什么打算?

B：我打算＿＿＿＿＿＿＿＿＿＿＿＿＿＿。你呢?

A：去年我去过一次上海,今年我想先＿＿＿＿＿＿,再＿＿＿＿＿＿。

B：你打算在家里住多长时间?

A：我想住十天。

(2) A：要开学了!

B：是啊。＿＿＿＿＿＿＿＿＿＿＿?

A：上次我的汉语语法考得糟糕极了,我打算用一个星期的时间先复习一下。

B：你打算怎么复习?

A：我去图书馆借了＿＿＿＿＿＿＿＿,我想在这个星期看一遍。

B：要我帮忙吗?

A：你能帮助我当然好极了。

[提建议 Making suggestions]

(1) A：你要提高汉语水平,我有一个好建议。

B：什么好建议? 快说说。

A：我建议你放假的时候到北京去旅行一次,在那儿学习一个月汉语。

B：＿＿＿＿＿＿＿＿＿＿＿＿＿＿。

(2) A：新年你打算去哪儿?

B：我还没有想好呢。你帮我提提建议吧。

A：我打算去广州旅行,看看那儿的花儿。我建议你也＿＿＿＿＿＿。

B：太好了! 咱们一起去吧! 我特别喜欢花儿。

[谈天气 Talking about the weather]

(1) A：今天多冷啊,你听天气预报(tiānqì yùbào)了没有?

B：＿＿＿＿＿＿＿＿＿,天气预报说今天是阴天,中午以后还要下雪。

A：气温是多少？

B：气温是零下十二度。这儿的冬天你习惯吗？

A：这么冷,我有点儿不习惯,可是我很想看下雪的景色。

（2）A：今年夏天太热了！我每天都得去游泳。

B：是啊。我听说今年夏天的气温比去年高多了。

A：明天天气怎么样？

B：天气预报说明天上午是晴天(qíngtiān),可是下午是阴天。

A：太好了,阴天气温不会这么高了吧？

[买飞机票 Purchasing plane tickets]

A：先生,我要买两张去海南岛的飞机票。

B：您要哪一天的？

A：我要十二月十六号中国民航(Zhōngguó Mínháng)628次的,还有票吗？

B：还有。

A：请问飞机什么时候起飞(qǐfēi)？

B：＿＿＿＿＿＿＿＿＿。

A：谢谢你。

[去饭馆 Going to a restaurant]

（1）A：先生,请等一下儿。车不能开进王府井来。

B：好吧。我们走进去吃一点儿东西,请问停车场(tíngchēchǎng)在哪儿？

A：在东边,车得开过去。

（2）A：您好,两位请到楼上去,楼上有座位。

B：谢谢。大明,你今天累了,快坐下来吧。小姐,有菜单(càidān)吗？

A：有,我给您拿过来。

B：你想吃什么？

C：先来点儿水吧,我渴(kě)极了。

B：好。咱们吃火锅,怎么样?

C：没问题。小姐,我们吃涮羊肉。能不能快点儿?

A：行,一会儿就给您送上来。

5. 看图说话 Describe the following pictures

爬上去

走过来

跑下楼来

寄回英国去

6. 交际练习 Communication practice

(1) The summer holidays are coming soon. You and your friends discuss your individual plans for the summer.

(2) Give your classmate three different suggestions and try to convince him/her to take your advice.

(3) Talk about the weather in your city during each of the four seasons.

dào (arrive).
到

方食行
lǚ xíng.

大黑熊（xióng）跟你说什么了

很早以前，有两个年轻人，一个叫王贵，一个叫张才。王贵比张才大。因为他们常在一起玩儿，是很好的朋友，大家都说王贵、张才两个人就好像哥哥弟弟一样。

一天，他们上山去玩儿。爬上山以后，他们都觉得有点儿累，就坐下来休息。这时候，他们看见一个大黑熊走过来了。他们都很害怕（hàipà）。旁边有一棵（kē）大树（shù），王贵很快就爬上去了。张才不会爬树，非常着急。可是他听奶奶说过，熊不吃死（sǐ）人，他就装（zhuāng）死人。大黑熊在张才旁边走过来走过去，看他不动（dòng），它想这一定是个死人，就走了。王贵看见大黑熊走远了，就从树上爬下来，张才也站了起来。王贵觉得很不好意思，就问张才："刚才大黑熊跟你说什么了？"

张才有点儿不高兴，他说："大黑熊刚才跟我说：年轻人，我告诉你，在危险（wēixiǎn）的时候，就能知道谁是你的真朋友！"

五. 语法　　　　Grammar

1. 动作即将发生　An action that is going to take place in a short time

"要…了" indicates that an action or situation is going to take place soon. "就" or "快" can be used in front of "要" as an adverbial to indicate urgency. The subject can often be omitted in this type of sentence.

$$要 ＋ V／A （ ＋ O ） ＋ 了$$

Subject	Predicate				
	Adverbial	"要"	V/A	(O)	"了"
（天气）		要	开学		了。
	就 soon. zhào	要		热	了。
他们	明天　就	要	去	泰山	了。
我们	快	要	到 (arrives).	山顶	了。

indicates V. soon.　　来 come

This type of sentence is usually transformed into a question simply by adding "吗" at the end.　A negative response can be formed by using the negative adverb "没有" or "还没有呢".　For example:

-ve response

火车要开了吗?
——没有。

我们就要到海南岛了吗?
——还没有呢。

Notes:

（1）A time adverbial can be added in front of "要…了" or "就要…了". For example: "他们明天要走了" or "他们明天就要走了".　However, time adverbials cannot be added before "快要…了"; for example, one cannot say ⊗ "他们明天快要走了".

（2）"要…了" can be changed to "快…了", without changing the meaning of the sentence.　For example: "要放假了" = "快放假了".

2. 复合趋向补语 The complex directional complement

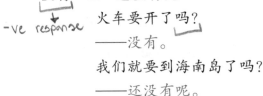

Directional verbs (上，下，进，出，回，过，起), followed by simple directional complements (来，去), can be used as complex directional complements to other verbs. This kind of directional complement indicates a certain compound direction of the action, and gives a more specific description of the action.　For example:

我从山上跑下去。

他们从外边走进来了。

Commonly used complex directional complements are:

	上	下	进	出	回	过	起
来	上来	下来	进来	出来	回来	过来	起来
去	上去	下去	进去	出去	回去	过去	✕

The basic meanings of these complex directional complements:

上来 —— to come up　　　　上去—— to go up

下来 —— to come down　　　下去—— to go down

进来 —— to come in　　　　进去—— to go in

出来 —— to come out　　　 出去—— to go out

[handwritten top margin:] V+ Compliment / if place/location is known / place btw V+ compliment

回来 —— to come back   回去 —— to go back

过来 —— to come over   过去 —— to go over

起来 —— to get up   ✗

The relation between the direction of the action and the speaker (or the topic being discussed), which is indicated by "来" and "去", is the same as in the case of a simple directional complement (see Lesson 16).

If an object is present after the verb with a complex directional complement, and the object is a word or phrase which indicates location or place, then the object must be placed before "来" or "去". For example:

我们爬上长城来了。

我要多拍些照片寄回家去。

[handwritten left margin:] # Record examples for 3*

[handwritten above heading:] 是 …… 的 / it was/is …… (do something)

3. 无标志被动句 Notional passive sentences *(unmarked passive)*

In some Chinese sentences, the subject of the sentence is itself an object of an action. Structurally, it is no different from a sentence in which the subject is the doer of the action, except that it is obviously a passive notion. The notional passive sentence may be used to emphasize the description of the object of the action. The subject of the sentence is usually a definite object. For example:

[handwritten left margin:] 1 SUB usually a specific obj. or thing / 2 Generally a straight forward statement (No +ve /-ve meaning)

越剧票已经买好了。   *[handwritten:]* S + bèi + O + U / 被

那部小说看过没有?

饭已经做好了,还没有拿进去。

旅行的事儿她知道得很多。

六. 汉字   Chinese Characters

1. 汉字的构字法 (9) Methods of constructing Chinese characters (9)

The pictophonetic method (5): In this method, a character is formed by placing the component indicating the meaning inside, and the component indcating the sound outside. For example: 问, 闷, 闻. There are very few characters of this type.

2. 认写基本汉字 Learn and write basic Chinese characters

(1) 山　　丨 山 山

　shān　　hill; mountain　　　　　　　3 strokes

(2) 飞（飛）乁 飞 飞

　fēi　　to fly　　　　　　　　　　3 strokes

(3) 义（義）丿 乂 义

　yì　　meaning　　　　　　　　　3 strokes

(4) 龙（龍）一 ナ 尢 龙 龙

　lóng　　dragon　　　　　　　　5 strokes

(5) 雨　　一 厂 冂 帀 雨 雨 雨 雨

　yǔ　　rain　　　　　　　　　　8 strokes

(6) 成　　一 厂 厈 成 成 成

　chéng　　to accomplish　　　　　6 strokes

3. 认写课文中的汉字 Learn and write the Chinese characters appearing in the texts

(1) 爬 pá

爬 → 爪 + 巴　　　　　　　　　8 strokes

叚 jiǎ　　一 丆 F F F F F 叚 叚

　(Pay attention to the difference from "段" duàn.)　9 strokes

(2) 放假 fàngjià

假 → 亻 + 叚　　　　　　　　　11 strokes

艹 (suànzìdǐ) 一 一 艹　　　　　3 strokes

(3) 打算 dǎsuan

算 → 竹 + 目 + 廾　　14 strokes

(4) 顶 dǐng（頂）

顶 → 丁 + 页　　8 strokes

(5) 建议 jiànyì（建議）

议 → 讠 + 义　　5 strokes

(6) 气温 qìwēn（氣溫）

温 → 氵 + 日 + 皿　　12 strokes

(7) 景色 jǐngsè

景 → 日 + 京　　12 strokes

(8) 游泳 yóuyǒng

泳 → 氵 + 永　　8 strokes

(9) 冬天 dōngtiān

冬 → 夂 + 冫　　5 strokes

(10) 夏天 xiàtiān

夏 → 一 + 自 + 夂　　10 strokes

(11) 导游 dǎoyóu（導遊）

导 → 巳 + 寸　　6 strokes

(12) 长城 chángchéng（長城）

城 → 土 + 成　　9 strokes

(13) 泰山 Tàishān

泰 → 夫 + 水　　10 strokes

鸟 (niǎozìtóu) ⟋ ⺈ ⺈ 鸟   4 strokes

(14) 海南岛 Hǎinándǎo （海南島）

岛 → 鸟 + 山   7 strokes

(15) 孔子 Kǒngzǐ

孔 → 子 + ㄥ   4 strokes

(16) 小燕子 Xiǎo Yànzi   16 strokes

燕 → 廿 + 口 + 扌 + 匕 + 灬

(In the ancient form of the character "燕 (swallow)", "廿" represents the head of the swallow; "口" represents the body; "北" is separated by "口" to indicate the wings; and the bottom four dots make up the tail.)

(17) 累 lèi

累 → 田 + 糸   11 strokes

(18) 条 tiáo （條）

条 → 夂 + 朩   7 strokes

(19) 拍 pāi

拍 → 扌 + 白   8 strokes

(20) 秋天 qiūtiān

秋 → 禾 + 火   9 strokes

(21) 阴天 yīntiān （陰天）

阴 → 阝 + 月   6 strokes

(22) 下雪 xià xuě

雪 → 雨 + ヨ   11 strokes

(23) 零(下) líng(xià)

零 → 雫 + 令　　　　　　　　　13 strokes

(24) 度 dù

度 → 广 + 廿 + 又　　　　　　　9 strokes

| 文化知识 | Cultural Notes |

Eastern and Western Regions of China

China is a huge country.　Its land area totals 9.6 million square kilometres, which makes it the third-largest country in the world,　behind only Russia and Canada.

Generally speaking, the western region of China is higher than the eastern region. Mountainous regions occupy over two-thirds of the total land area;　plains account for less than one-third and are mainly in the east.

Relatively speaking,　the geographical and climatic conditions are fairly good in the eastern region.　For historical reasons, the vast majority of the Chinese population live in the east.　China's agricultural, industrial, economic, and financial activities are also mostly concentrated in this area.　Therefore, the level of development in the east far surpasses that of the west.

China has just started to develop its western regions.　With its vast territory and abundance of resources, the west has a very promising future.

Xiaoyun and Libo go to the train station to pick up Xiaoyun's uncle. They find out from him that great changes have taken place in the lives of Shanghai farmers. In this lesson, you will learn how to talk about changing circumstances and actions in progress.

第二十四课 Lesson 24

你舅妈也开始用电脑了

一. 课文　Text

（一）

丁力波：小云,火车快到了吧?

王小云：从上海到北京的T23次八点四十分到,① 现在八点半,快到了。

丁力波：你舅舅是农民吗?

王小云：是。他过去是上海郊区的农民,现在当蔬菜公司的经理了。

丁力波：他来过北京吗？

王小云：他来过两次，可是我都不在。上次他来的时候，我正在南

【谈正在进行的动作】
Talking about an action in progress

方旅行呢。

丁力波：看，那个人正在问路呢。我们过去看看，那是不是你舅舅。

王小云：好像是吧。我十年以前见过他，这十年变化很大。不但

他不认识我了，而且我也可能不认识他了。

丁力波：可不。② 那时候你还是个小孩，现在是大姑娘了。

王小云：是啊，我舅舅也老了。那个人在看地图吗？

丁力波：他没在看地图，他好像在看照片。他向我们走过来了。③

王小云：他很像我舅舅。不错，是我舅舅。舅舅，您好！

舅　舅：小云！十年不见，你是大学生了。你今年上几年级了？

王小云：上大学三年级了。

【谈变化】
Talking about changes

舅　舅：有男朋友了吗？④

-204-

王小云：舅舅，这是我同学丁力波。他是加拿大留学生。

丁力波：您好，路上辛苦了。⑤ 快要下雨了，请上车吧！

生词 New Words

1. 舅妈	N	jiùmā	aunt (wife of mother's brother) 你舅妈，舅妈家，有舅妈，叫舅妈
2. 舅舅	N	jiùjiu	uncle (mother's brother) 你舅舅，是我舅舅，等舅舅，有两个舅舅
3. 农民	N	nóngmín	farmer; peasant 郊区的农民，一个农民
4. 当	V	dāng	to serve as; to be 当经理，当老师，当农民，当导游，当演员，当教练，当售货员，当司机，当教授，当医生

↳ followed by the title of the person.

5. 蔬菜	N	shūcài	vegetable 蔬菜公司，一些蔬菜，买一斤蔬菜，吃一点儿蔬菜
菜	N	cài	food; dish; vegetable 吃菜，买菜，做菜

General word for food.

6. 正在	Adv	zhèngzài	in the process of; in the middle of; (key word of a progressive construction) 正在南方旅行，正在等舅舅，正在上课，正在考试，正在爬山
在	Adv	zài	(used to indicate an action in progress) 在访问，在比赛，在化妆，在看照片，在等舅舅
7. 问路	VO	wèn lù	to ask directions (a route) 正在问路，在问路，去问路，应该问路 → can be seperated.

①问1l路 xià/guo
②向~wèn obj

8. 变化	N	biànhuà	change 变化很大，变化不多，有一个小变化
9. 不但	Conj	búdàn	not only
10. 而且	Conj	érqiě	but also; and also → informal
11. 可不	IE	kěbù	exactly; right; that's just the way it is /yes/correct

"Couldn't agree more"

12. 小孩	N	xiǎoháir	kid; child 是个小孩，有小孩，要小孩，一个小孩
13. 地图	N	dìtú	map 看地图，查地图，买地图，一张地图，中国地图
14. 向	Prep	xiàng	towards; to 向我们走过来，向他跑过去，向

15. 像	V	xiàng	to be alike; to take after 像我舅舅,很像那部电影的女主角,有点儿像售票员,不太像工作人员
16. 上	V	shàng	to be engaged in (work, study, etc.) at a fixed time 上中学
17. 年级	N	niánjí	grade 三年级,大学四年级,上一年级,二年级同学
18. 大学	N	dàxué	university; college 上大学,念大学,北京大学,一个大学,有名的大学,大学生活,大学的变化
19. 辛苦	A	xīnkǔ	hard; toilsome 路上辛苦了,特别辛苦,这么辛苦,辛苦极了
20. 下雨	VO	xià yǔ	to rain 要下雨了,可能下雨,下雨的天气
雨	N	yǔ	rain 一场大雨,下小雨

(二)

王小云:舅妈呢?怎么没有来?她说过要跟您一起来北京。

舅　舅:你舅妈在种温室蔬菜呢。她现在很忙,这次不来了。

王小云:现在你们种蔬菜的收入怎么样?

舅　舅:我们种温室蔬菜,收入比以前好多了。

【谈生活情况】
Talking about living conditions

王小云:家里的生活怎么样?⑥

舅　舅:生活还可以。⑦前年我们盖了一座两层的小楼,去年还买了一辆汽车。现在我们去别的城市也方便了。

丁力波：您的生活水平比城里人的还高。⑧

舅　舅：我们村吃的、穿的、住的都不比城里差。问题是我们农民的文化水平还比城里人的低一些。⑨

王小云：现在农民没有文化真不行。

舅　舅：你说得很对，农民也都要学习新技术。温室蔬菜是用电脑管理的。你舅妈也开始用电脑了。

王小云：今年我一定要去看看你们。

生词　New Words

1. 种	V	zhòng	to grow; to plant　种菜,种蔬菜,种花儿,正在种,打算种,建议种
2. 温室	N	wēnshì	greenhouse　温室蔬菜,郊区的温室,种温室蔬菜
温	A	wēn	warm　温水
3. 收入	N	shōurù	income; earnings　种蔬菜的收入,农民的收入,一些收入,主要收入,别的收入,提高收入
收	V	shōu	to accept; to receive
入	V	rù	to enter
4. 前年	N	qiánnián	the year before last year　前年的收入,前年的

				生活
5. 盖	V	gài		to build　盖楼,盖房子,盖温室,盖商店,盖宿舍,盖医院
6. 座	M	zuò		(a measure word for mountains, buildings and other similar immovable objects)　一座楼,一座山,一座两层的小楼,盖一座大楼
7. 辆	M	liàng		(a measure word for vehicles)　一辆车,一辆出租车,一辆公共汽车
8. 城市	N	chéngshì		city　城市的生活,城市里的人,一个大城市
城	N	chéng		city　城里,城外,去城里买东西
9. 方便	A	fāngbiàn		convenient　很(不)方便,不太方便,方便的时候
10. 村	N	cūn		village　村里,村里的农民,向村里走去
11. 文化	N	wénhuà		culture; education; literacy　中国文化,民族文化;文化水平,大学文化,有文化,没有文化,学文化
12. 低	A	dī		low　水平低,收入低,气温低,房租低
13. 技术	N	jìshù		technology; skill　新技术,电脑技术,有技术,要技术,学习技术,发展技术,提高技术水平
14. 管理	V	guǎnlǐ		to manage; to administer　用电脑管理,管理大学,管理银行,提高管理水平

补充生词　Supplementary Words

1. 暖和	A	nuǎnhuo		warm
2. 凉快	A	liángkuai		cool
3. 机场	N	jīchǎng		airport
4. 接(人)	V	jiē (rén)		to pick up (someone)
5. 行李	N	xíngli		baggage; luggage
6. 箱子	N	xiāngzi		box; case; trunk
7. 一路平安	IE	yílù píng'ān		to have a pleasant journey; *bon voyage*
8. 停	V	tíng		to stop; to cease
9. 爱人	N	àiren		husband or wife; spouse

10. 士兵	N	shìbīng	soldier
11. 将军	N	jiāngjūn	general
12. 站岗	VO	zhàngǎng	to stand guard
13. 冻	V	dòng	to freeze
14. 发抖	V	fādǒu	to shake; to tremble; to shiver
15. 生火	VO	shēnghuǒ	to make a fire
16. 正常	A	zhèngcháng	normal; regular
17. 声	N	shēng	sound; voice

二. 注释　Notes

① 从上海到北京的T23次八点四十分到。

"The T23 train from Shanghai to Beijing will arrive at 8:40."

In the construction "从…到…", "从" and "到" may be followed by words indicating either location or time to express distance or duration. For example:

从美国到中国很远。

从广州到海南岛不太远。

他从去年9月到今年6月在语言学院学习中国文学。

我每天从下午1点到3点去锻炼身体。

In Chinese, a train number is formed by adding "次" to a numeral. The initial "T" (read as "tè") precedes a train number to refer to an "express" (tèkuài) train. For example：T23次, T14次.

② 可不。

"Exactly!"

"可不" indicates one's agreement with what another person has said. It is interchangeable with "可不是". For example:

您有七十岁了吧？

——可不(是),今年五月就到七十岁了。

③ 他向我们走过来了。

"He is walking towards us."

The preposition "向" denotes the direction of an action. For example：向东看，向图书馆走去，向他问好.

④ 有男朋友了吗?

"Do you have a boyfriend?"

In China, when a senior family member, especially an elder relative, asks a younger member of the family about his/her age, occupation, income, family situation and marital status, it is not meant as an invasion of the privacy of the latter; rather it shows the elder's concern for the younger. Therefore such questions shouldn't be perceived as nosey or offensive. However, the latter sometimes need not give direct, exhaustive answers, either.

⑤ 您好,路上辛苦了。

"How are you? Did you have a good trip? (literally: You must have had a tiring journey.)"

"路上辛苦了" is a common expression used to greet and show concern for someone who has just returned from a trip. It is equivalent to expressions such as "一路辛苦"，"路上一定很辛苦吧?" or "辛苦了".

⑥ 家里的生活怎么样?

"How are living conditions at home?"

⑦ 生活还可以。

"Living conditions at home are not bad."

The family of Wang Xiaoyun's uncle lives in the outskirts of Shanghai, one of the most economically developed areas in China; therefore, his family's standard of living is fairly high. However, to be modest, he said "生活还可以".

⑧ 您的生活水平比城里人的还高。

"Your standard of living is even higher than that of city dwellers."

Here, the adverb "还" (3), found in the comparative sentence, is used to emphasize a further degree. For example:

今天比昨天还冷。　　　　（It was already very cold yesterday.）

您的生活水平比城里人的还高。（The city dwellers' standard of living is
　　　　　　　　　　　　　　　very high to begin with.）

⑨ 问题是我们农民的文化水平还比城里人的低一些。

"The problem is that the education level of we farmers is still a bit lower than that of city dwellers."

"文化水平" in this case refers to the standard of education.

三. 练习与运用　Drills and Practice

KEY SENTENCES
1. 我舅舅也老了。
2. 他现在当蔬菜公司的经理了。
3. 你舅妈也开始用电脑了。
4. 你是大学生了,今年上几年级了?
5. 看,那个人正在问路呢。
6. 你舅妈在种温室蔬菜呢。
7. 不但他不认识我了,而且我也可能不认识他了。
8. 从上海到北京的T23次八点四十分到。

1. 熟读下列短语 Master the following phrases

(1) 当演员　当教授　当售票员　当导游　当画家　当记者　当男主角
当出租车司机　当办公室工作人员　当商场售货员　当公司经理

(2) 从中国到欧洲　从前门到王府井　　从花园小区到长安大戏院
从东边到西边　从汉语系到英语系　从山顶到山下　从城里到村里
从阳台到客厅　从银行到邮局
从八点到十点　从上午到下午　从昨天到今天　从圣诞节到新年
从前年到去年　从春天到秋天　从去年冬天到今年夏天　从早到晚

(3) 向他走过去　向我们跑过来　向山顶爬去　向他学习　向她介绍

(4) 老了　热了　高了　难了　累了　低了　对了　　合适了　便宜了
上四年级了　上大学了　当教授了　租新房子了
是大学生了　是蔬菜公司经理了　是越剧团演员了
是有名的画家了　是足球队教练了

有女朋友了　　有孙女儿了　　有小孩了　　有变化了　　有电脑课了

(5) 在说　在想　在用　在喝　在找　在查词典　在看地图　在打电话
在打扫房子　　在买东西

正在听　正在唱　正在演　正在办　正在等人　正在练习汉字

在写呢　在画呢　在游泳呢　在上课呢　在问路呢　在爬山呢

正在念呢　　正在睡觉呢　　正在填表呢　　正在寄包裹呢

正在种蔬菜呢　　　正在拍照片呢

(6) 不但旧而且脏　不但对而且快　不但感人而且优美　不但年轻而且漂亮

不但喜欢音乐,而且喜欢美术　　不但学习汉语,而且学习中国文化

不但盖了新楼,而且买了汽车　　不但种温室蔬菜,而且用电脑管理

2. 句型替换 Pattern drills

(1) 现在是冬天了。

是啊,天气冷了。

春天	暖和(nuǎnhuo)
夏天	热
秋天	凉快(liángkuai)
十月	很舒服

(2) 已经两点了,怎么还不开始呢?

我们在等小燕子呢。

她有事儿,今天不来了。

出发	病了	去
开车	有点儿累	去参观
比赛	去郊区了	能来参加

(3) 他正在做什么?

他正在种蔬菜。

他跟谁一起种蔬菜?

他跟村里的农民一起种蔬菜。

看电视	他朋友
看球赛	他同学
听音乐	他舅舅
游泳	教练
拍照片	导游

(4) 他们在唱歌吗?

他们没在唱歌,他们在唱京剧呢。

(没有,他们唱京剧呢。)

比赛	练习
参观	工作
复习	写汉字
散步	打太极拳

(5) 他们正在哪儿<u>盖楼</u>呢？
他们正在<u>城里</u>盖楼呢。
你去过<u>他们那儿</u>吗？
我没有去过。

吃饭	饭馆里	那个饭馆
访问	村里	他们村
玩儿	花园里	那个花园
演奏	戏院里	那个戏院

(6) 你给她打电话的时候，她正在做什么呢？
我给她打电话的时候，她正在<u>看地图</u>呢。

去看她	睡觉
找车站	问路
到她家	给朋友写信
走进办公室	用电脑

(7) 你们下午从几点到几点上课？
我们从<u>两点</u>到<u>四点</u>上课。

办公	1:30	5:30
锻炼	4:00	6:00
参观	1:00	5:00
赛球	3:45	6:00

(8) 你弟弟上几年级了？
他上二年级了。
他<u>学习好</u>吗？
他不但学习好，而且<u>身体也很好</u>。

会打太极拳	会游泳
喜欢看电影	喜欢看戏
学习汉语	学习中国文化
常常踢足球	参加足球赛

3. 课堂活动 Classroom activity

A asks B a question and B replies; then B asks C a question, and C replies; ...
(1) T23次是从哪儿到哪儿的火车？
(2) 火车快到了吗？
(3) 小云的舅舅是上海人吗？
(4) 他现在是种蔬菜的农民吗？
(5) 他来过北京吗？
(6) 那个中年人正在做什么？

(7) 小云什么时候见过舅舅?

(8) 舅舅还认识小云吗? 小云呢?

(9) 舅舅有什么变化?

(10) 那个中年人在看地图吗?

(11) 小云今年上大学几年级了?

(12) 小云的舅妈来北京了吗?

(13) 她在做什么?

(14) 现在舅舅他们种蔬菜的收入怎么样?

(15) 舅舅家里的生活怎么样?

(16) 现在的温室蔬菜是用什么管理的?

(17) 舅妈有什么变化?

(18) (问你同学)你今年上几年级了?

4. 会话练习 Conversation exercises

[接人和送行 Picking someone up and seeing someone off]

(1) A: 请问,从北京来的飞机到了没有?

B: 快要到了,还有＿＿＿＿＿＿分钟。

A: 谢谢。

A: 啊,张先生,您来了。

C: 你好! 谢谢你来机场(jīchǎng)接(jiē)我。

A: 别客气,张先生。您的行李(xíngli)都到了吗?

C: 两个箱子(xiāngzi)都到了。

A: 您在这儿等一等,我去要出租车。

C: ＿＿＿＿＿＿＿＿＿＿＿。

(2) A: 雨平,我在这儿呢!

B: 小白! 怎么样? 路上辛苦吧?

A: 还可以。你等了很长时间了吧?

B: 可不,火车晚了半个小时。

A: 我也非常着急,想早点儿到北京。

B: 来,把箱子给我,我帮你拿。

(3) A：这次在＿＿＿＿＿＿的时间太短了，以后我一定再来。

B：我有时间也一定去北京看你。火车六点十分就要开了，上车吧。

A：好，我到了北京就给你打电话。

B：别忘了，我等你的电话。祝你一路平安(yílù píng'ān)！

A：谢谢。＿＿＿＿＿＿＿！

B：再见！

[谈变化 Talking about changes]

(1) A：糟糕，下雪了。

B：是吗？我们不能去长城了。

A：下雪的时候长城＿＿＿＿＿＿＿，我们应该去拍些照片。

B：可是外边真冷。

A：可不，到零下十度了。咱们等雪停(tíng)了再去吧。

(2) A：不下雨了吧？

B：还在下呢。但是雨小点儿了。

A：现在已经九点半了，我们该走了。

B：好吧。这儿的冬天真冷。

A：你不习惯吧？

B：开始我觉得太冷，现在已经有点儿习惯了。

[谈生活情况 Talking about living conditions]

A：王先生，好久不见！还在大学＿＿＿＿＿＿吗？

B：我前年就不当老师了，现在开了一家翻译公司。

A：啊，当经理了。收入一定不少吧？

B：还可以。公司跟大学很不一样，我开始不太习惯，现在＿＿＿＿＿了。

A：听说你买了新房子？

B：是去年刚买的，在建国门。有时间你和你爱人(àiren)到我家去坐坐。

A：好，有时间我们一定去。

5. 看图说话 Describe the following pictures

以前他不忙,现在他_____。

虽然现在刚到五月,但是天气已经_____。

去年他学习音乐,今年他____。

他以前是游泳队队员,可是现在他___。

看

考

6. 交际练习 Communication practice

(1) You go to the airport to see off a friend who is leaving for the United States. Then, you rush off to the train station to pick up your younger brother.

(2) Tell your classmate about the changes you have experienced in the last couple of years.

(3) Discuss your present living conditions, and then compare it to that of your close friends.

士兵(shìbīng)和将军(jiāngjūn)

一个冬天的晚上,天气非常冷,不但风很大,而且雪也很大。路上已经没有人了,可是有一个士兵正在外边站岗(zhàngǎng)。从下午到现在他还没有吃一点儿东西。他穿得又很少, 胳膊和腿都冻(dòng)得发抖(fādǒu)。

这时候,就在离他不远的客厅里,将军在喝酒呢。桌上有很多吃的、喝的,士兵还给他生了火(shēng le huǒ),客厅里非常暖和。将军喝了很多酒,觉得非常热,有点儿不舒服。他很不高兴,说:"已经十二月了,应该冷了,可是现在还这么热,天气真不正常(zhèngcháng)!"

外边站岗的士兵听到了这些话,就大声(shēng)说:"将军,您那儿的天气不正常,可是我这儿的天气很正常。您喜欢正常的天气,咱们就换一换地方,请您到外边来站一站吧。"

五. 语法　　　　Grammar

1. 情况的变化(1) Changed circumstances (1) → 了 always @ end of sentence. ↳ for the adj.

The particle "了" ② is employed at the end of a sentence to indicate changed circumstances or the emergence of some new situation or status. This usage of "了" frequently occurs in sentences with adjectival predicates, or sentences with "是" or "有" as the verb. For example:

① V + 了 + O (completion of action).
② V + O + 了 (completion of something must be in past)
③ 太 + adj + 了 (just to complete sentence)

你舅舅也老了。 → in past he was young but now becoming old.　（以前不老）

现在天气冷了。 （以前不冷）

雪大了。 （以前不大）

你是大学生了。 （以前不是）

我有男朋友了。 （以前没有）　Changes state. (past becoming present)

In sentences with verbal predicates, the particle "了" ② often emphatically confirms the completion or realization of some event or situation (refer to Lesson 15), sometimes it can also indicate changed circumstances. For example:

现在他当蔬菜公司的经理了。（以前没当）

现在天气很冷
↳ now temp is cold
(if 了 means it wasn't cold before).

念 读 看

你舅妈也开始用电脑了。 （以前没用）

（她）上大学二年级了。 （以前没上）

Also, in sentences with the negative adverb "不" preceding a verbal predicate, the particle "了" at the end of the sentence often indicates a change. For example:

她这次不来了。 （以前打算来）

他不认识我了。 （以前认识）

2. 动作的进行 The progressive aspect of an action

To indicate an action in progress, one may place either of the adverbs, "在" or "正在", before the verb or the "呢" at the end of the sentence. "正在" further emphasizes the progressive aspect of an action at a certain time. "在" or "正在" can also be used together with "呢".

$$正在／在 + V + O + （呢）$$

Subject	Predicate			
	Adv	**V**	**O**	**Pt**
你	在	做	什么？	
我	在	写	汉字。	
力波	（现在）正在	念	课文。	
林娜她们	正在	看	越剧《红楼梦》	呢。
你舅妈		种	温室蔬菜	呢。

"没有" itself can be used as the negative form of the progressive aspect. The structures "没在+V", or "没(有)+V" may also be used. For example:

他在看地图吗？

——没有，他在看照片。

——没有。

——他没在看地图，他在看照片。

——他没(有)看地图，他在看照片。

An action in progress may take place in the present, the past, or the future time. For example:

小云，你在写什么呢？ 我在写文章呢。 （ in the present ）

昨天下午他给我打电话的时候，我正在看报。 （ in the past ）

-218-

Oral test
in reg room.
16:00 - 16:15
oral exam.

Final
12/10
12:30 - 15:00
REN 2107.

下星期六晚上你去找他的时候,他一定在复习语法呢。 (in the future)

3. 不但…而且… The construction "不但…而且…"

"不但…而且…" generally occurs in complex progressive sentences. If the two clauses share the same subject (usually appearing in the the first clause), "不但" is usually placed after the subject. If each clause has its own subject, "不但" and "而且" are normally placed before their respective subjects. For example:

张教授不但是我的汉语老师,而且也是我的中国朋友。

我们不但盖了一座小楼,而且还买了一辆汽车。

好的 朋友 female friend.
好 朋友 girl friend

不但他不认识我了,而且我也可能不认识他了。

不但中国人喜欢《红楼梦》,而且外国人也很喜欢这部小说。

In the second clause, "而且" is often used together with the adverb "也" or "还".

→ not only
→ But also.
→ if @ begining of sentance.
there are 2 subs, in 1st clause.

六. 汉字　　Chinese Characters

---

1. 汉字的构字法(10) Methods of constructing Chinese characters (10)

The pictophonetic method (6): In this method, a character is formed by placing the component indicating the meaning outside, and the component indicating the sound inside. For example: 园, 房, 府, 厅, 进, 历, 座, 裹.

2. 认写基本汉字 Learn and write basic Chinese characters

(1) 农(農)　丶　一　ナ　ヤ　농　农

nóng　　　agriculture　　　　　　　6 strokes

(2) 而　　一　ア　产　丙　而　而

ér　　　and; as well as　　　　　　6 strokes

(3) 入　　ノ　入

rù　　　to enter　　　　　　　　2 strokes

(Pay attention to the difference between "入" and "人".)

3. 认写课文中的汉字 Learn and write the Chinese characters appearing in the texts

臼　ノ　ィ　ィ　臼　臼　臼
jiù　　　　　　　　　　　　　　　　　6 strokes

(1) 舅妈 jiùmā（舅媽）

舅 → 臼 ＋ 男　　　　　13 strokes

疋 (shūzìpáng)　ㄱ ＋ 止　　　　5 strokes

(2) 蔬菜 shūcài

蔬 → 艹 ＋ 疋 ＋ 疏　15 strokes
菜 → 艹 ＋ 采　　　　11 strokes

亦 (biànzìtóu)　　丶 亠 广 亣 亦 亦　6 strokes

(3) 变化 biànhuà（變化）

变 → 亦 ＋ 又　　　　8 strokes

(4) 小孩 xiǎoháir

孩 → 孑 ＋ 亥　　　　9 strokes

(5) 向 xiàng

向 → ノ ＋ 向　　　　6 strokes

(6) 年级 niánjí（年級）

级 → 纟 ＋ 及　　　　6 strokes

(7) 辛苦 xīnkǔ

辛 → 立 ＋ 十　　　　7 strokes
苦 → 艹 ＋ 古　　　　8 strokes

(8) 收入 shōurù

收 → 丩 ＋ 攵　　　　6 strokes

(9) 盖 gài（蓋）

盖 → 羊 + 皿   11 strokes

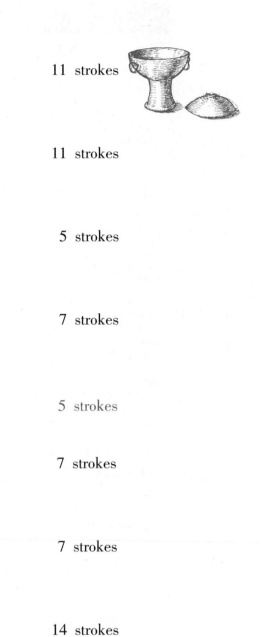

(10) 辆 liàng（輛）

辆 → 车 + 两   11 strokes

(11) 城市 chéngshì

市 → 亠 + 巾   5 strokes

(12) 村 cūn

村 → 木 + 寸   7 strokes

氏　ノ 𠂆 𠂇 氏 氏
dī   5 strokes

(13) 低 dī

低 → 亻 + 氐   7 strokes

(14) 技术 jìshù（技術）

技 → 扌 + 十 + 又   7 strokes

(15) 管理 guǎnlǐ

管 → ⺮ + 官   14 strokes

文化知识　　Cultural Notes

Administrative Divisions of China

Division	Place	Abbreviation	Administration Centre	Division	Place	Abbreviation	Administration Centre
Municipality Directly Under the Central Government	北京市 Běijīng Shì	京 Jīng	北京 Běijīng	Province	湖南省 Húnán Shěng	湘 Xiāng	长沙 Chángshā
	上海市 Shànghǎi Shì	沪 Hù	上海 Shànghǎi		广东省 Guǎngdōng Shěng	粤 Yuè	广州 Guǎngzhōu
	天津市 Tiānjīn Shì	津 Jīn	天津 Tiānjīn		海南省 Hǎinán Shěng	琼 Qióng	海口 Hǎikǒu
	重庆市 Chóngqìng Shì	渝 Yú	重庆 Chóngqìng		四川省 Sìchuān Shěng	川 Chuān	成都 Chéngdū
Province	河北省 Héběi Shěng	冀 Jì	石家庄 Shíjiāzhuāng		贵州省 Guìzhōu Shěng	黔 Qián	贵阳 Guìyáng
	山西省 Shānxī Shěng	晋 Jìn	太原 Tàiyuán		云南省 Yúnnán Shěng	滇 Diān	昆明 Kūnmíng
	辽宁省 Liáoníng Shěng	辽 Liáo	沈阳 Shěnyáng		陕西省 Shǎnxī Shěng	陕 Shǎn	西安 Xī'ān
	吉林省 Jílín Shěng	吉 Jí	长春 Chángchūn		甘肃省 Gānsù Shěng	甘 Gān	兰州 Lánzhōu
	黑龙江省 Hēilóngjiāng Shěng	黑 Hēi	哈尔滨 Hā'ěrbīn		青海省 Qīnghǎi Shěng	青 Qīng	西宁 Xīníng
	江苏省 Jiāngsū Shěng	苏 Sū	南京 Nánjīng		台湾省 Táiwān Shěng	台 Tái	台北 Táiběi
	浙江省 Zhèjiāng Shěng	浙 Zhè	杭州 Hángzhōu	Autonomous Region	内蒙古自治区 Nèiměnggǔ Zìzhìqū	内蒙古 Nèiměnggǔ	呼和浩特 Hūhéhàotè
	安徽省 Ānhuī Shěng	皖 Wǎn	合肥 Héféi		广西壮族自治区 Guǎngxī Zhuàngzú Zìzhìqū	桂 Guì	南宁 Nánníng
	福建省 Fújiàn Shěng	闽 Mǐn	福州 Fúzhōu		西藏自治区 Xīzàng Zìzhìqū	藏 Zàng	拉萨 Lāsà
	江西省 Jiāngxī Shěng	赣 Gàn	南昌 Nánchāng		宁夏回族自治区 Níngxià Huízú Zìzhìqū	宁 Níng	银川 Yínchuān
	山东省 Shāndōng Shěng	鲁 Lǔ	济南 Jǐnán		新疆维吾尔自治区 Xīnjiāng Wéiwú'ěr Zìzhìqū	新 Xīn	乌鲁木齐 Wūlǔmùqí
	河南省 Hénán Shěng	豫 Yù	郑州 Zhèngzhōu	Special Administrative District	香港特别行政区 Xiānggǎng Tèbié Xíngzhèngqū		香港 Xiānggǎng
	湖北省 Húběi Shěng	鄂 È	武汉 Wǔhàn		澳门特别行政区 Àomén Tèbié Xíngzhèngqū		澳门 Àomén

Sometimes, unpleasant incidents occur in our lives, like the time when Lin Na collided with a car on her bike, or when Dawei's bike was stolen. In this lesson, you will learn how to give an account of an incident; how to show your concern when you visit a patient; and how to make complaints in Chinese.

第二十五课 Lesson 25

司机开着车送我们到医院

一. 课文　　Text

（一）

王小云：宋华，你来帮我们一下，好吗？

宋　华：你们怎么了？① 现在你在哪儿？

王小云：林娜被撞伤了，正在第三医院检查呢。②

宋　华：她伤了哪儿了？伤得重吗？

王小云：还没有检查完呢。你带点儿钱来。

宋　华：好的，你们等着，我马上就来。

（在第三医院）

宋　华：林娜，你怎么样？伤得重不重？

林　娜：伤得不太重。我的胳膊被撞伤了，右腿也有点儿疼。

宋　华：你是怎么被撞伤的？

林　娜：怎么说呢？③下午我和小云看完电影，骑着自行车回学

院。我们说着、笑着，往右拐的时候没有注意，撞到了车

上。那辆车停在路(旁)边，司机正在从车上拿东西。

宋　华：你们是怎么到医院来的？④

林　娜：那位司机看到我被撞伤了，就马上开着车送我们到医院。

宋　华：那位司机真不错。

林　娜：我们带的钱不多，医药费都是他帮我们交的。他还给了我

一张名片。

宋　华：真应该谢谢那位司机，明天我去把钱还他。刚才我还以为

你被汽车撞了。⑤

林　娜：还好，汽车被我撞了。⑥如果我被汽车撞了，就糟糕了。

生词　New Words

1. 着	Pt	zhe	(indicating the continuous aspect)　说着，笑着，等着，开着车，带着花儿，穿着旗袍
2. 送	V	sòng	to take someone somewhere; to see someone off　送我回家，开着车送我们到医院，送我到门外(边)，送我到火车站
3. 被	Prep	bèi	by (used to indicate the passive voice)　被问，被踢，被访问，被罚款
4. 撞	V	zhuàng	to knock; to collide　被车撞，撞车，撞人
5. 伤	V	shāng	to hurt; to wound　被撞伤，撞伤人
6. 第	Pref	dì	(for ordinal numbers)　第一，第十二，第二十五课，第三医院
7. 检查	V	jiǎnchá	to examine　检查身体，检查电脑，检查汽车，检查练习

8. 重	A	zhòng	serious; heavy 伤重,伤不重;衣服很重,包裹不重,工作不重
9. 完	V	wán	to finish; to run out of 看完电影,做完练习,用完钱,吃完饭
10. 马上	Adv	mǎshàng	right away; immediately 马上就来,马上去,马上看完,马上出发
11. 胳膊	N	gēbo	arm 胳膊被撞伤,胳膊疼
12. 腿	N	tuǐ	leg 撞伤腿,腿有点儿疼
13. 骑	V	qí	to ride 骑马,骑车
14. 自行车	N	zìxíngchē	bicycle 骑自行车,买自行车,骑着自行车回学院
15. 笑	V	xiào	to laugh; to smile 笑着,笑着说,别笑了,喜欢笑,大笑
16. 注意	V	zhùyì	to pay attention to 没有注意,注意语法,注意听,注意看
17 停	V	tíng	to stop; to park 停在路旁边,停车,停课
18. 医药费	N	yīyàofèi	medical expenses 交医药费
19. 以为	V	yǐwéi	to think (with more subjectivity) 我以为,别以为,都以为
20. 如果	Conj	rúguǒ	if

（二）

陆雨平：大为,林娜宿舍的门开着,她躺着看电视呢。

林　娜：啊,陆雨平、大为,快进来。

【问候病人】
Visiting a patient

马大为：林娜,你怎么样? 好点儿了吗?⑦

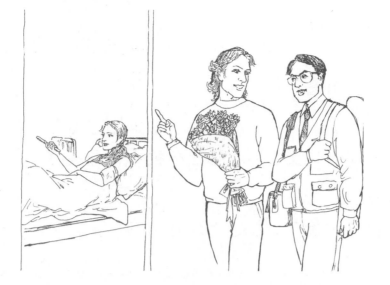

林　娜：好多了。你们这么忙，还带着花儿来看我，谢谢你们。这

束花儿真漂亮，放在桌(子)上吧。

马大为：检查的结果怎么样？

林　娜：医生说没有大的问题，他让我躺在床上休息休息。大为，

你把电视关了吧，咱们说会儿话。

【抱怨】
Making complaints

陆雨平：现在胳膊还疼不疼？

林　娜：不疼了。可是胳膊这么弯着，写字很不方便。上星期我汉字

没有考好，现在又撞伤了胳膊，真倒霉！⑧这两天都是坏消息。

马大为：别着急，我有一个好消息。

林　娜：什么好消息？

马大为：上星期六晚上，我的自行车被小偷偷走了。

林　娜：自行车被偷了，这是什么好消息？

马大为：你听着，来你这儿以前，派出所给我打了一个电话，让我去一下。⑨

林　娜：你去派出所做什么？

马大为：小偷被抓到了，我丢的车也找到了，现在在派出所呢。你说，这是不是好消息？

林　娜：是个好消息。

陆雨平：真应该祝贺你！

生词　New Words

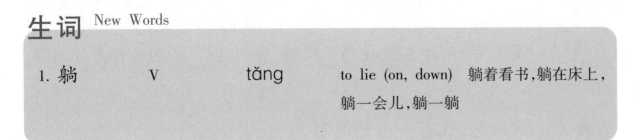

1. 躺	V	tǎng	to lie (on, down) 躺着看书,躺在床上,躺一会儿,躺一躺

2. 电视				...,买电视,用电视,
				...花儿
				...放花儿,放东西,
				...床上,放在包裹里
			...desk	一张桌子,桌子上,放在桌
				上
			result;outcome	检查的结果,考试的
				结果,比赛的结果
7.		guān	to close; to turn off	关门,关电视
8. 弯		wān	to bend	弯着胳膊,弯着腿,弯着
				身体
9. 倒霉	A	dǎoméi	bad luck	真倒霉,特别倒霉,倒霉极了
10. 坏	A	huài	bad;broken	坏苹果,电视坏了,自行车
				坏了,撞坏,考坏,用坏
11. 消息	N	xiāoxi	news	好消息,一个坏消息,有消息,
				没有消息,听到消息,看到消息
12. 小偷	N	xiǎotōu	thief	一个小偷,被小偷偷走
偷	V	tōu	to steal	偷钱,偷东西,偷汽车,偷电视,
				偷自行车
13. 派出所	N	pàichūsuǒ	police substation	去派出所
14. 抓	V	zhuā	to clutch; to catch; to arrest	小偷
				被抓到,抓住,抓小偷
15. 丢	V	diū	to lose	丢钱,丢东西,丢自行车,丢汽
				车,丢电视

补充生词 Supplementary Words

1. 型号	N	xínghào	model; type
2. 补	V	bǔ	to mend; to patch; remediation
3. 信用卡	N	xìnyòngkǎ	credit card
4. 挂失	VO	guàshī	to report the loss of something
5. 项链	N	xiàngliàn	necklace
6. 警车	N	jǐngchē	police car; police van
7. 手机	N	shǒujī	cell phone
8. 突然	A	tūrán	sudden/suddenly
9. 刀	N	dāo	knife
10. 警察	N	jǐngchá	policeman
11. 吓	V	xià	to scare; to frighten
12. 手	N	shǒu	hand
13. 掉	V	diào	to drop; to fall
14. 地上	N	dìshang	ground; floor

二. 注释　Notes

① 你们怎么了?

"What's happened to you?"

"怎么了" is used here to ask about what has happened to somebody or something, in the case where the speaker does not yet know. For example:

他怎么了? 今天没有来上课。

你的车怎么了?

——昨天被撞坏了。

② 林娜被撞伤了,正在第三医院检查呢。

"Lin Na ran into a car and hurt herself. She is now undergoing a medical examination at Hospital No. 3."

One can turn a cardinal number into an ordinal number by putting the prefix "第" before it. For example: "第一课", "第三医院", "第十天", "第十五个月". Sometimes, a cardinal number can be used as an ordinal number without "第". "一楼", "四〇二号", and "二年级" are examples which we have learned in previous lessons.

③ 怎么说呢？

"How should I put it?"

It means "it's not easy to explain".

④ 你们是怎么到医院来的？

"How did you come to the hospital?"

The constructions "到+PW+来/去" and "来/去+PW" have the same basic meaning. For example："到学院来"(="来学院"), "到上海去"(="去上海").

⑤ 刚才我还以为你被汽车撞了。

"Just now I thought that you had been knocked down by a car."

The word "以为" has the same meaning as "想", but is often used to show that one's initial assumption has turned out to be different from the fact. For example:

我以为他不会来,可是他已经来了。

快下雪了,我还以为今天是好天气。

⑥ 还好,汽车被我撞了。

"Fortunately, I was the one who struck the car."

Here, "还好" means "fortunately". For example:

还好,排队的人不多。

还好,我们没有坐错车。

⑦ 你怎么样？ 好点儿了吗？

"How are you? Are you feeling better?"

This is an expression that one would use to ask a patient about his/her condition.

⑧ 上星期我汉字没有考好,现在又撞伤了胳膊,真倒霉!

"Last week I did badly in the Chinese character test, and now I have hurt my arm. What bad luck!"

The adverb "又"(2), used here in the sense of "furthermore／in addition", indicates that an event is not a repetition of the previous one, but is an additional occurrence. For example:

他昨天去了王府井,又看了电影。

司机送林娜到医院,又帮她交了医药费。

⑨ 来你这儿以前,派出所给我打了一个电话,让我去一下。

"Before I came here, I got a call from the police substation, telling me to go over there."

"派出所" *(police substations)* are police stations operating at the grass-roots level in Chinese communities, which manage residence cards and ensure public security within a neighbourhood.

三. 练习与运用　Drills and Practice

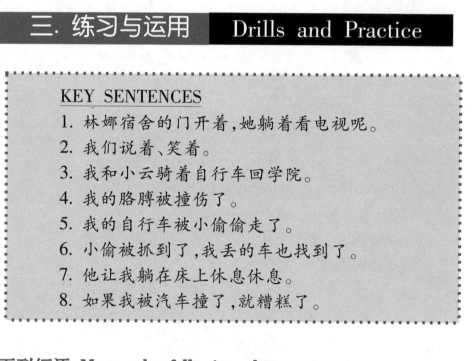

KEY SENTENCES
1. 林娜宿舍的门开着,她躺着看电视呢。
2. 我们说着、笑着。
3. 我和小云骑着自行车回学院。
4. 我的胳膊被撞伤了。
5. 我的自行车被小偷偷走了。
6. 小偷被抓到了,我丢的车也找到了。
7. 他让我躺在床上休息休息。
8. 如果我被汽车撞了,就糟糕了。

1. 熟读下列短语 Master the following phrases
(1) 听着　写着　笑着　用着　住着　想着　放着　等着　试着

　　注意着　　发展着　　变化着

　　说着话　睡着觉　排着队　打着电话　拍着照片　踢着足球

开着汽车　　唱着越剧　　种着蔬菜　　盖着大楼

门开着　　商场开着　　电视开着　　电脑关着　　车停着　　香蕉放着

坐着说话　　躺着休息　　骑着车去学校　　带着花儿看朋友

穿着旗袍参加聚会　　看着课文回答问题

(2) 被介绍　　被罚款　　被检查　　被访问　　被忘了

被(自行车)撞伤　　被(小偷)偷走　　被(大为)记错　　被(人)借去

被(同学)拿走　　被(农民)请去　　被(大家)吃完

(3) 第一次　　第二天　　第二十五课　　第三遍　　第一部电影　　第一本小说

第二语言　　第一外语　　第一件事儿　　第五篇文章　　第四场戏

(4) 到学校去　　到书店去　　到饭馆去　　到郊区去　　到派出所去

到城里去　　到长城去　　到北方去

(5) 看到山　　见到小云　　抓到小偷　　拿到借书证　　买到中药　　找到导游

租到房子　　学习到第二十课　　送到医院　　撞到汽车上

上到四年级　　翻译到晚上　　睡到十点　　放假放到九月　　游泳游到中午

(6) 躺在床上　　站在阳台上　　坐在客厅里　　睡在卧室里　　住在郊区

排在前边　　停在楼前　　放在桌上　　写在本子上　　画在纸上

种在温室里

(7) 打完电话　　喝完咖啡　　复习完生词　　回答完问题　　检查完身体

办完借书证　　办完事儿　　拍坏了照片　　穿坏了衣服　　用坏了乐器

2. 句型替换 Pattern drills

(1) 他拿着什么？
他拿着照相机。

穿	一件新衬衫
洗	衣服
吃	寿面
带	书和本子

(2) 宿舍的门开着没有？
宿舍的门没开着，
我把它关了。

| 汽车的门 |
| 卫生间的门 |
| 办公室的电脑 |
| 客厅里的电视 |

（3）他们在做什么呢？
　　他们在<u>站着</u> 说话呢。

坐着	演奏乐器
等着	买音乐会票
笑着	拍照片
看着书	回答问题
喝着咖啡	听音乐

（4）你的<u>自行车</u>在吗？
　　不在。我的自行车被我同学<u>借走</u>了。

照相机	拿去
练习本子	拿错
汽车	开走
词典	丢

（5）<u>胳膊</u>被<u>撞伤</u>了没有？
　　胳膊没有被撞伤。

头	撞疼
腿	撞坏
球	踢进
钱	偷去
他	罚款

（6）他们听到<u>这个消息</u>没有？
　　他们听到这个消息了。

复习	第二十三课
买	那套西服
拿	包裹通知单
见	那位演员
爬	山顶
拍	长城的景色

（7）<u>那束花儿</u>你放在哪儿了？
　　我放在<u>桌(子)</u>上了。

那些生词	写	本子上
那张明信片	放	书里
那件中式衣服	放	客厅
那些音乐光盘	放	办公室
你的车	停	楼前

（8）他们<u>看完那个电影</u>了没有？
　　他们没有看完那个电影。

吃	饭
学	这本书
赛	足球
参观	美术馆
办	护照
交	医药费

3. 课堂活动 Classroom activity

This game is to be played by two groups of students. The students in Group A make up ten conditional clauses using "如果", and the students in Group B are required to complete the sentences by making up ten corresponding clauses with "就". The scoring method is as follows: if Group B gives the correct answer, it gets one point; if it gives an incorrect answer and Group A can provide the correct one, then Group A gets the point. When the game is over, the two groups reverse roles and play it again, using the same scoring method. The group that gets the higher score wins.

4. 会话练习 Conversation exercises

[叙述事情的经过 Talking about an incident]

（1）A：先生，我的自行车不见了。

　　B：你的自行车是什么型号(xínghào)的？

　　A：是飞龙黑色男车。

　　B：车号是多少？

　　A：060809742。

　　B：是什么时候丢的？

　　A：昨天下午。

　　B：你的自行车是在哪儿放着的？

　　A：在图书馆前边放着的。下午两点，我骑车到图书馆以后，车就放在那儿。四点钟我从图书馆出来，自行车就不见了。

　　B：你先等着。如果有消息，我们马上告诉你。

（2）A：老先生，您看到一个小男孩跑过来没有？

　　B：什么样儿的小男孩？

A：他穿着一件红衬衫，手里拿着一个小球。他是跟我们一起来公园玩儿的，刚才我们说着话，没有注意，他就不见了。

B：红衬衫？刚才我看到一个穿着红衬衫的小男孩，他往东边跑过去了。你们快去看看。

A：谢谢。

[问候病人 Visiting a patient]

A：听说你住院了，大家都不放心，让我们来看看你。

B：你们学习这么忙，还跑来看我，真谢谢你们。

A：你好点儿了吗？

B：好多了，已经不发烧了，头也不太疼了。

C：吃东西怎么样？

B：还是不太想吃东西，这儿的饭我也不习惯。

A：睡觉还好吗？

B：很好。可是我不愿意这么躺着，我想早点儿回学校去。现在咱们该学第二十四课了吧？

C：第二十四课已经学完了，这个星期正在学第二十五课。你别着急，以后我们帮你补(bǔ)这两课。

A：我们该走了，你好好休息吧。

[抱怨 Making complaints]

A：真倒霉！

B：怎么了？

A：我的钱包被小偷偷走了。

B：丢了多少钱？

A：五百块人民币，还有三百美元。学生证、借书证和信用卡(xìnyòngkǎ)也都丢了。

B：真糟糕！你得马上到银行挂失(guàshī)，还得到办公室去办新证。

5. 看图说话 Describe the following pictures

练习"着"

练习"着"

练习"被"

练习"被"

6. 交际练习 Communication practice

（1）Your teacher fell ill and was hospitalized. What should you say to her when you go to visit?

（2）You rode your bike and knocked down an elderly person. What should you do?

（3）Your notebook computer was stolen from your room. How do you report it to the police substation?

四. 阅读和复述 Reading Comprehension and Paraphrasing

张大力的故事

　　昨天是张大力女儿的生日，他给女儿的礼物是一条很漂亮的项链 (xiàngliàn)。他知道女儿喜欢看越剧,还买了两张晚上的越剧票。

　　他们在饭馆吃了饭以后,就去看戏。回家的时候,已经很晚了。天气不好,开始下雪了,路上的人也少了。他们骑着自行车往右拐的时候,一个人从旁边走出来,问他们:"请问,这儿有没有派出所?"大力告诉他:"没有。派出所离这儿很远。" 那个人又问："现在哪儿可以叫一辆警车（jǐngchē）来？"大力回答说："可以打110电话。"

"你有没有手机（shǒujī）？"那个人又问。

大力说："没有。"

张大力正在想，那个人为什么要问他这些问题，突然（tūrán），那个人拿出刀（dāo）来，对大力说："对不起，把你们的项链和钱都给我！"

张大力笑着说："你忘了问一个问题了。我告诉你，这儿虽然没有派出所，可是有一个老警察（jǐngchá），他抓过九十八个像你这样的人，马上要抓第九十九个。"

"老警察在哪儿？"那人问。

"在这儿！我就是！"

那个人被吓（xià）坏了，手（shǒu）里的刀也掉（diào）在地上（dì shang）。他被大力送到了派出所。

guǎn (closed).
关

| 五. 语法 | Grammar |

1. 动作或状态的持续 The continuous aspect of an action or a state

The aspect particle "着" is placed directly after a verb to express the continuous aspect of an action or a state.   For example: └Emphasize something in a certain state.

zhàn
站
(to stand).

我们说着、笑着。

林娜宿舍的门开着。

胳膊这么弯着。

她穿着红的旗袍。

When used in a sentence with serial verb phrases,   in addition to emphasizing that the two actions in the sentence are happening simultaneously,   the construction "V+着 (+O)"   also frequently indicates the manner of the action expressed by the second verb.   For example:

我们骑着自行车回学院。

他笑着说："应该祝贺你！"   ┌ Thing you want to say

你们还带着花儿来看我。   └ main vb.

SUB+ V₁ + 着 +O₁ +V₂ +O₂

The negative form of this construction is "没(有)+V+着", and its V/A–not–V/A question form is "V+着+没有". For example：

> 电视开着没有？
>
> ——电视没有开着。
>
> 你带着护照没有？
>
> ——我没带着护照。
>
> 他没有躺着看电视，他坐着看电视呢。

The construction "V+着" is frequently used with words such as "在"，"正在"，and "呢". For example：

> 林娜躺着看电视呢。
>
> 他正在打着电话呢。
>
> 他在开着车呢。

Note that complements should not be used after the "V+着" construction. We cannot say ⊗ "他写着汉字写十分钟", for example.

2. "被"字句 The "被" sentence

Besides the notional passive sentences, there is another kind of passive sentence with the preposition "被" (often replaced by "叫" or "让" in spoken Chinese), which is used to introduce the agent of an action, or to emphasize that the subject of the sentence is the recipient of an action.

S(receiver)+"被"+O(agent)+V+other element

(handwritten: if obvious O can be omitted)

Subject (receiver)	"被"	O (agent) *(or action Vb.)*	V	Other elements
我的自行车	被	小偷	偷	走了。
那本小说	被	我同学	借	去了。
那套西服	被	人	买	走了没有？
她的新照相机	让 ràng	她弟弟	撞	坏了。
小偷	叫 jiào	谁	抓	到了？

(handwritten under 让/叫: same meaning but informal)

(handwritten under last row: now is caught but not before)

If there is no need to introduce the agent of an action, "被" can be placed directly before the verb; however, this is not true with "叫" or "让" in spoken Chinese. For example:

> 我的胳膊被撞伤了。
>
> 自行车被偷了。

(handwritten notes:)
both emphasized
but only O₁ is emphasized in bèi structure.
S + V + O
S₁ + 把 + O₁ + V + elements.
S₂ (O₁) + 被 + O₂ (S₁) + V + elements.

—239—

Note that a negative adverb or an optative verb must be placed before "被" ("叫", "让"). For example:

这本小说没有被借走。(We cannot say：⊗这本小说被没有借走。)

那套西服明天会被人买走。(We cannot say：⊗那套西服明天被人会买走。)

→ indicates successful completion of action.

3. 结果补语"到"、"在" The resultative complements "到" and "在"

The verb "到" is often used as a resultative complement to express that an action has attained its objective. For example:

小偷被抓到了,我丢的车也找到了。

你去买那本词典了没有？

——我去买了,可是我没有买到。 *→ I went to buy it but didn't successfully buy it.*

"到" can also be used to show that an action has ended in a certain place (with a noun or noun phrase of place used as the object), or that it has continued up to a certain time (with a noun or noun phrase of time used as the object). For example:

她撞到了车上。 *在 before V. = state that is static.*

我们学到第二十五课了。 *V. 在 = occuring as a change of position.*

他晚上写汉字常常写到十点。

"在" is often used as a resultative complement to indicate that a person or an object has come to be at a certain place (with a noun or noun phrase of place used as the object) as a result of the action. For example:

他让我躺在床上休息休息。

那位司机的车停在路边。

花儿放在桌子上。

他住在二楼。

4. 如果…就… The conditional construction "如果…就…"

The first clause introduced by the conjunction "如果" presents a condition, and the second clause denotes the result that is brought about by the first clause. The adverb "就" (3) in the second clause often indicates a conclusion derived from the conditional clause. The word "如果" in the first clause may be omitted. For example:

如果明天天气不好,我们就不去了。

如果有问题,你就打电话找我。

(如果)你昨天来,你就看见他了。

第 一 = 1st (not 1)

六. 汉字 　　Chinese Characters

1. 区分同音字 Differentiating homophones

There are only over 1300 meaningful phonetic syllables with tones in the common speech of modern Chinese, but there are 3500 Chinese characters in common use. As a result, it is not unusual that some characters may have the same pronunciation. For example, the characters "游，邮，油" that we have learned before are all pronounced yóu, and they are distinguished from one another only by their written forms. Therefore, when we study homophonetic characters, we must learn to distinguish them by comparing them in terms of form, meaning and word combinations. For example, "导游" cannot be written as "导油" or "导邮", and "游泳" cannot be written as "油泳" or "邮泳".

2. 认写基本汉字 Learn and write basic Chinese characters

(1) 壬　　 丿 二 千 壬

　　 rén 　　　the ninth of the ten Heavenly Stems　　　4 strokes

(Pay attention to the difference between "壬" and "王".)

(2) 束　　 一 厂 一 口 由 束 束

　　 shù 　　　bunch (of flowers)　　　7 strokes

("木" indicates the firewood, and "口" indicates the
　　rope which bundles the firewood.)

3. 认写课文中的汉字 Learn and write the Chinese characters appearing in the texts

(1) 被 bèi

被 → 衤 + 皮　　　　　　　　10 strokes

(2) 撞 zhuàng

撞 → 扌 + 立 + 里　　　　　　15 strokes

(3) 伤 shāng（傷）

伤 → 亻 + 𠂉 + 力　　　　　　6 strokes

(4) 第 dì

第 → 竹 + 弓 + 丨 + 丿　　　　　　11 strokes

(5) 检查 jiǎnchá（檢查）

检 → 木 + 佥　　　　　　　　　　　11 strokes

(6) 完 wán

完 → 宀 + 元　　　　　　　　　　　7 strokes

(7) 胳膊 gēbo

胳 → 月 + 夂 + 口　　　　　　　　　10 strokes

膊 → 月 + 甫 + 寸　　　　　　　　　14 strokes

(8) 腿 tuǐ（腿）

腿 → 月 + 艮 + 辶　　　　　　　　　13 strokes

(9) 骑 qí（騎）

骑 → 马 + 大 + 可　　　　　　　　　11 strokes

(10) 注意 zhùyì

注 → 氵 + 主　　　　　　　　　　　8 strokes

(11) 停 tíng

停 → 亻 + 亠 + 口 + 冖 + 丁　　11 strokes

(12) 如果 rúguǒ

如 → 女 + 口　　　　　　　　　　　6 strokes

(13) 躺 tǎng

躺 → 身 + 屵 + 冋　　　　　　　　　15 strokes

(14) 电视 diànshì（電視）

视 → 礻 + 见　　　　　　　　　　　8 strokes

(15) 桌子 zhuōzi

桌 → 卓 + 木　　　　　　　　　　　10 strokes

(16) 结果 jiéguǒ（結果）

结 → 纟 + 士 + 口　　　　　　　　9 strokes

(17) 弯 wān（彎）

弯 → 亦 + 弓　　　　　　　　　　　9 strokes

(18) 倒霉 dǎoméi（倒楣）

倒 → 亻 + 到　　　　　　　　　　　10 strokes
霉 → 雨 + 每　　　　　　　　　　　15 strokes

(19) 坏 huài（壞）

坏 → 土 + 不　　　　　　　　　　　7 strokes

(20) 消息 xiāoxi

消 → 氵 + 丷 + 月　　　　　　　　10 strokes

(21) 小偷 xiǎotōu

偷 → 亻 + 人 + 一 + 月 + 刂　11 strokes

(22) 派出所 pàichūsuǒ

派 → 氵 + 厂 + ㇄　　　　　　　　9 strokes

(23) 抓 zhuā

抓 → 扌 + 爪　　　　　　　　　　　7 strokes

(24) 丢 diū

丢 → 丿 + 去　　　　　　　　　　　6 strokes

(Pay attention to the first stroke which is a left falling stroke, not a
   horizontal one.)

Our leading characters are reviewing their achievements in studying Chinese during the past year. We will also review and summarize the main contents that we have studied in Volume Two.

第二十六课 Lesson 26 （复习 Review）

你快要成"中国通"了

一. 课文　　Text

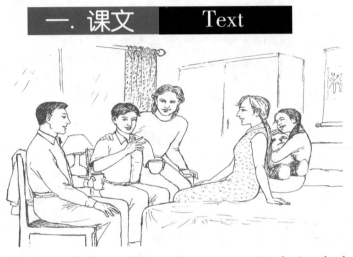

宋　华：林娜,你来中国已经快一年了吧? 你不但学习了汉语,而且

还认识了很多中国朋友, 中国的情况又知道得不少,你快

要成"中国通"了。

林　娜：哪里,哪里,"中国通"真不敢当,还差得远呢。① 说实在的,

我越来越喜欢中国文化了。② 中国从南到北,从东到西,每

个地方都有自己的特点。③

宋　华：历史博物馆正在举办"2002——中国"展览，那儿有很多图片，有的是我们见过的，有的是我们没见过的。你对中国文化这么感兴趣，我建议你去看看。④

林　娜：好极了，我一定去。今天我们有一个结业聚会，力波他们快要来了。你把这个消息告诉他们，我想他们也一定会非常感兴趣。

宋　华：好啊。林娜，你还记得吗？刚来的时候你说过，如果每天都让你吃中餐，你就会饿死。现在你不但喜欢吃中餐，而且还学会了做中国菜。

林　娜：可不，现在如果一天不吃中餐，我就会觉得有点儿不舒服。

（丁力波、马大为进宿舍）

马大为：你们在聊什么呢？去哪儿吃中餐？我也去。

宋　华：我们在说,你们这些老外快成"中国通"了。⑤ 力波当然就

不用说了。⑥

【回忆往事】
Recalling past events

丁力波：因为我妈妈是中国人,所以我早就有点儿中国化了。林娜

爱穿旗袍,爱吃中国菜,还喜欢看越剧、听中国民乐,好像

也有点儿中国化了。

林　娜：我是到北京以后才开始中国化的。⑦

马大为：我看这很容易,像有的留学生那样,找个中国姑娘做妻

子。⑧ 你找个长得帅的中国小伙子做丈夫,每天在一起生

活,就可以中国化了。

林　娜：别开玩笑。说真的,我现在觉得汉语语法不太难,可是汉

字很难。

马大为：声调也不容易,我常常说错。

-246-

宋　华：你们在中国才学习了一年，汉语水平就提高得这么快，主
要是因为你们学习都很努力。

【谈语言学习】
Talking about language studies

丁力波：这儿的老师教得特别认真，朋友们对我们也非常热情，常
常帮助我们学汉语，所以我们进步很快。

林　娜：一年的学习时间太短了。我虽然已经能听懂中国人说的
一些话，可是自己说汉语还说得不太流利，明年我还要来
中国学习。

马大为：林娜，老师和同学们都在等着我们呢，⑨ 我们走吧。

丁力波：好，明年再"中国化"吧！

林　娜：宋华，明天你陪我去参观"2002——中国"展览，好吗？

宋　华：好，明天见！

林　娜：不见不散！⑩

生词 New Words

1. 成	V	chéng	to become　成妈妈了,成教授了,成大学生了,成主角了
2. 中国通	N	zhōngguótōng	an expert of China　成中国通了,一位中国通,西方的中国通
3. 情况	N	qíngkuàng	situation　中国的情况,学校的情况,这种情况,情况怎么样
4. 实在	A/Adv	shízài	honest/truly; really　说实在的,实在便宜,实在辛苦,实在不敢当
5. 越来越	IE	yuè lái yuè	more and more　越来越喜欢,越来越习惯,越来越提高,越来越方便
6. 南	N	nán	south　从南到北
7. 特点	N	tèdiǎn	characteristic; feature　有特点,自己的特点,一个特点,不少特点
8. 历史	N	lìshǐ	history　历史故事,中国历史,感人的历史
9. 博物馆	N	bówùguǎn	museum　历史博物馆,文化博物馆,美术博物馆,一座博物馆
10. 举办	V	jǔbàn	to conduct; to hold　举办音乐会,举办足球比赛
11. 展览	N	zhǎnlǎn	exhibition; show　举办展览,参观展览,看展览,"2002——中国"展览,油画展览,一个展览
12. 图片	N	túpiàn	photograph; picture　展览图片,历史图片,很多图片,一张图片
13. 对	Prep	duì	to　对中国文化,对汉字,对力波说,对他笑
14. 感兴趣	IE	gǎn xìngqù	to be interested in sth.　非常感兴趣,对中国文化感兴趣,对汉字感兴趣,越来越感兴趣

感	V	gǎn	to feel; to sense
兴趣	N	xìngqù	interest　有兴趣,有点儿兴趣,没有兴趣,提高兴趣,有很大的兴趣
15. 结业	VO	jiéyè	to complete a course　结业聚会,快要结业了,结业的时候
16. 记得	V	jìde	to remember; to retain　还记得,不记得他的名字,记得以前的朋友,记得中学生活
17. 中餐	N	zhōngcān	Chinese food (meal)　吃中餐,习惯中餐,越来越喜欢中餐
18. 饿	A	è	hungry　很饿,有点儿饿,越来越饿,饿极了
19. 死	V	sǐ	to die　饿死,忙死,疼死,累死
20. 菜	N	cài	dish; vegetable　中国菜,南方菜,做菜,吃菜,买菜,种菜
21. 聊	V	liáo	to chat 聊什么,聊家里的事儿,聊学校的情况,聊中国历史,喜欢聊,愿意聊
22. 老外	N	lǎowài	foreigner　这些老外,一个老外,像老外,成老外了
23. 中国化	V	zhōngguóhuà	to make Chinese in quality or characteristics; Sinicize 有点儿中国化,越来越中国化
化	V	huà	to change; to turn　绿化,美化,老化,西方化
24. 才	Adv	cái	just　才开始,才举办,才学习一年,才聊了一会儿
25. 那样	Pr	nàyàng	such; so; like that　像留学生那样,像中国通那样,像导游那样介绍

26.	妻子	N	qīzi	wife	做妻子,有妻子,他妻子,当妻子了
27.	小伙子	N	xiǎohuǒzi	young man	中国小伙子,帅小伙子,一个小伙子
28.	丈夫	N	zhàngfu	husband	做丈夫,她丈夫,当丈夫了
29.	声调	N	shēngdiào	tone	汉语的声调,听声调,练习声调,注意声调,四个声调
30.	努力	A	nǔlì	to make great effort; to endeavor; to exert oneself	努力学习,努力工作,努力练习声调,越来越努力
31.	认真	A	rènzhēn	earnest; serious	非常认真,越来越认真,教得很认真,认真学习
32.	热情	A	rèqíng	warm; warmhearted; enthusiastic	很热情,那样热情,热情多了
33.	进步	N/V	jìnbù	progress; advancement/to make progress	进步很快,进步不太大,有进步,有一点儿进步
34.	明年	N	míngnián	next year	明年举办,明年结业,明年考试,明年再来
35.	陪	V	péi	to accompany	陪我去参观,陪妻子去买东西,陪丈夫参观
36.	不见不散	IE	bú jiàn bú sàn	don't leave unless we meet	
	散	V	sàn	to break up; to disperse	

补充生词 Supplementary Words

1.	了解	V	liǎojiě	to understand; to realize
2.	熟悉	V	shúxī	to be familiar with
3.	见面	VO	jiànmiàn	to meet; to see
4.	毕业	VO	bìyè	to graduate; to finish school
5.	离开	V	líkāi	to leave; to depart from
6.	经验	N	jīngyàn	experience

7. 方法	N	fāngfǎ	method	
8. 准备	N/V	zhǔnbèi	preparation/to prepare; to get ready	
9. 艺术	N	yìshù	art	
10. 请客	VO	qǐngkè	to feast; to treat sb. to sth. (a meal)	
11. 客人	N	kèrén	guest	
12. 意思	N	yìsi	meaning	
13. 句	M	jù	sentence	

二. 注释　　Notes

① 还差得远呢。

"I'm still not that good yet."

This is an expression of modesty that Chinese people often use when being praised. One can also say: "哪里,我还差得很多". Nowadays, Chinese people may also sometimes use "谢谢" to respond to others' compliments.

② 说实在的,我越来越喜欢中国文化了。

"Honestly speaking, I'm becoming more and more fond of Chinese culture."

The phrase "说实在的" is a commonly used expression that reveals the subjective attitude of the speaker in a conversation. The phrase "说真的" has the same meaning.

The phrase "越来越" expresses change in the degree of things with the progression of time. For example:

课文越来越有意思了。

他汉语说得越来越流利。

③ 中国从南到北,从东到西,每个地方都有自己的特点。

"From the south to the north, from the east to the west, every place in China has its own characteristics."

④ 你对中国文化这么感兴趣,我建议你去看看。

"Since you are so interested in Chinese culture, I suggest that you go and take a look."

The object of the preposition "对" often indicates the target of an action. The prepositional phrase "对+NP" is often used as an adverbial in a sentence. For example:

宋华对她说:"你怎么了?"

他对我笑笑,就走了。

老师对我们很热情。

他对中国画很感兴趣。

⑤ 我们在说,你们这些老外快成"中国通"了。

"We are talking about the fact that you foreigners are becoming experts on China."

The word "老外" is a casual, yet friendly way of addressing foreigners in spoken Chinese.

⑥ 力波当然就不用说了。

"Libo is certainly one of them."

The phrase "不用说" means "certainly, needless to say." It indicates that a reason is very clear, and that the listener also understands this. For example:

星期二公园里人这么多,星期天就不用说了。

他刚来的时候汉字就写得很好,现在就不用说了。

⑦ 我是到北京以后才开始中国化的。

"I didn't begin to become Sinicized until I arrived in Beijing."

The adverb "才" is contrary to "就", and is often used to express that things happen later, slowly, or with difficulty. For example:

他六点才来。　　　　　　　　(我五点半就来了。)

这个故事我听了三遍才听懂。　(他听了一遍就听懂了。)

我等了半个小时,才上公共汽车。(他等了两分钟就上车了。)

It can also express a small quantity or a short time. For example:

他一个人翻译了三篇文章,我们两个人才翻译了一篇。

你们在中国才一年。　　　　　　(我已经在中国三年了。)

⑧ 像有的留学生那样,找个中国姑娘做妻子。

"Just do what some foreign students do: find a Chinese girl to be your wife."

⑨ 老师和同学们都在等着我们呢。

"The teacher and classmates are all waiting for us."

In sentences expressing that an action is going on, the aspect particle "着" sometimes may be used after verbs. For example:

她正在看着电视呢。

我去找他的时候，他做着练习呢。

⑩ 不见不散！

"Don't leave unless we meet!"

This expression is commonly used to emphasize that one must meet with the other (i.e. one must wait until the other arrives) when setting up a rendezvous. The listener can also respond with this same expression.

三. 练习与运用 Drills and Practice

KEY SENTENCES

1. 说实在的，我越来越喜欢中国文化了。
2. 你对中国文化这么感兴趣，我建议你去看看。
3. 哪里，哪里，"中国通"真不敢当，还差得远呢。
4. 我是到北京以后才开始中国化的。
5. 你们在中国才学习了一年，汉语水平就提高得这么快。
6. 力波当然就不用说了。
7. 像有的留学生那样，找个中国姑娘做妻子。
8. 老师和同学们都在等着我们呢。

1. 熟读下列短语 Master the following phrases

(1) 成中国通了　　成大学教授了　　成有名的画家了　　成电影演员了

(2) 越来越认真　　越来越努力　　越来越热情　　　　越来越便宜

越来越习惯　　越来越感兴趣　　越来越喜欢中国文化

越来越注意汉语声调　　　　越来越习惯吃中餐

（3）很感兴趣　　　　特别感兴趣　　　　　越来越感兴趣

对汉字感兴趣　　对西方音乐感兴趣　　对英国足球也感兴趣

对中国历史一定感兴趣　　　　　　对这部爱情小说非常感兴趣

（4）才五分钟　　才三天　　才一个月　　才两块钱　　才三点

才看了一遍　　才去过一次

（5）也记得　　还记得　　不记得　　只记得　　都记得　　一定记得

记得什么时候　　　记得在哪儿　　　记得这座城市的历史

记得我们结业的时候　　　记得上大学三年级的时候

（6）学会课文　　学会游泳　　学会管理　　学会做中国菜　　学会骑自行车

（7）像小伙子那样　　像导游那样　　像记者那样　　像我们的朋友那样

像一位中国通那样

（8）如果好就买　　如果合适就要　　如果喜欢就拿　　如果方便就来

如果累就休息　　如果你对文化感兴趣,就应该去看看那个展览

如果你想学好汉语,就应该去中国

2. 句型替换 Pattern drills

（1）你是什么时候<u>开始学汉语</u>的？
　　我是<u>大学三年级</u>才开始学汉语的。
　　<u>他大学一年级就开始学汉语</u>了。

出发	下午五点	下午三点
去泰山	去年	前年
参观图片展览	今天上午	上星期
认识她	三年以前	五年以前

（2）这<u>篇课文</u>难不难？
　　很难,我<u>看</u>了三遍才<u>看懂</u>。
　　我觉得很容易,我<u>看</u>了一遍就
　　<u>看懂</u>了。

(个)故事	听	听懂
(些)汉字	写	写对
(个)声调	练	练会
(课的)语法	复习	复习好

(3) 为什么他声调 念得不太对？
他来北京才两个月。

车	开	好	学开车
汉字	写	漂亮	学中文
英语	说	流利	到英国

(4) 你喜欢这个博物馆吗？
我非常喜欢，
我对中国历史很感兴趣。

（幅）画儿	西方油画
（部）电影	爱情故事
（个）乐曲	民族音乐
（本）小说	城里情况

(5) 你觉得你们经理怎么样？
他对工作人员非常热情。

工作	努力
技术	了解(liǎojiě)
汇率	注意
管理	马虎

(6) 他为什么明年还要来这儿？
他对这儿的生活越来越喜欢了。

天气	习惯
文化	熟悉(shúxī)
变化	感兴趣

3. 课堂活动 Classroom activity

A game to build up a sequence of sentences on the topic of "talking about Chinese language studies": The whole class is divided into two groups. The teacher starts the game with Group A by saying: "我们大家学习汉语". After that, students in Group A must continue to make up sentences, one after the other, so that the word at the beginning of each sentence is the same as the last word in the previous sentence. For example: "我们大家学习汉语。""汉语是中国人说的语言。""语言学院有很多好老师。"… Group B then takes their turn at the game. At the end, calculate the number of correct sentences made by each group to see who wins.

4. 会话练习 Conversation exercises

[回忆往事 Recalling past events]

(1) A: 你是王平吧？

B: 是你啊！田元！咱们已经十年没有见面(jiànmiàn)了吧？

A: 是啊,老同学,你现在在哪儿工作？

B: 我从美国回来以后,在一家公司工作。

A: 你是什么时候去美国的？

B: 我是1990年去美国的。你是86年大学毕业(bìyè)的吧？

A: 不,我是 ＿＿＿＿＿＿ 的。毕业以后,我去南方了。

(2) A: 你还记得那次结业聚会吗？

B: 当然记得。那是在夏天,我们快要离开(líkāi)学校了。

A: 聚会好像是在宋华家。

B: 不对。你记错了,是在 ＿＿＿＿。

A: 对,是在陈老师家。她丈夫给大家做了很多菜。

B: 我记得林娜还唱了越剧。

[谈语言学习 Talking about language studies]

(1) A: 咱们汉语学习了一年了,今天大家在一起聊一聊,说说自己的经验
(jīngyàn)。

B: 我先说吧。我觉得汉语语法不太难,汉字很难。

C: 如果有好的学习方法(fāngfǎ),汉字也不太难。说实在的,我觉得口
语不容易。这次考试我口语考得非常糟糕。

B: 口语要多练习、多说。我有一个中国朋友,他每天下午都跟我练习一
个小时的口语。

(2) A: 快要考试了。你准备(zhǔnbèi)得怎么样？

B: 我有点儿不放心,因为我每次语法都考得不好。

A: 我想这次你们一定会考得很好。你们学习很努力,进步很快。如果认
真复习,不会有问题的。

B: 老师,我有一些语法上的问题,可以请您帮助我吗?

A: 可以。星期三下午我有时间,你到办公室来找我吧。

B: 好。谢谢老师。

5. 看图说话 Describe the following pictures

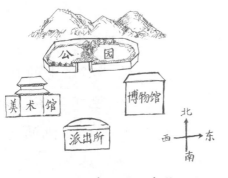

"有、是、在"

"被"

"了"

"正在、着"

6. 交际练习 Communication practice

(1) You and your classmates have been studying Chinese for one year. Talk about your own experience of studying the language.

(2) In a high school reunion party, you meet many good friends from the past. You all recall and talk about your lives and studies in high school.

四. 阅读和复述 Reading Comprehension and Paraphrasing

说话的艺术(yìshù)

说话也是一种艺术。我有一个朋友,他就不会说话。

一天,他在饭馆里请客(qǐngkè)。他一共请了四位客人(kèrén),来了三位,有一位还没有来。他等得有点儿着急了,就说:"你看,该来的没来!"有一位客人听了,很不高兴。他想:"该来的没来——我是不该来的了?"他走出餐厅去,对工作人员说:"如果他们找我,你就告诉他们不用等我了。"

　　过了一会儿,工作人员走进来问:"先生,您要的菜都准备好了,现在拿上来吗？"

　　"别忙,我们在等人呢。"我朋友问:"刚才出去的那位先生怎么还不回来？"工作人员说:"他已经走了。"我朋友非常着急,说:"不该走的走了！"

　　这时候还有两位客人在那儿等着。有一位很不高兴,他想:"不该走的走了,意思(yìsi)是该走的还没走,好,我是该走的,我现在就走!"他站起来,没有说一句(jù)话就离开了饭馆。

　　只有一位客人在那儿了。我朋友还在问自己:"他们怎么都走了？"这位客人说:"您刚才说该来的没来,不该走的走了,他们觉得自己是不该在这儿的了,所以他们都走了。以后您说话要注意点儿。"

　　"以后我一定注意。"我朋友说,"可是我说的不是他们啊!""什么？你说的是我啊?！"这位客人也走了。

五. 语法复习　　Grammar Review

1. 动词谓语句(2) Sentences with a verbal predicate (2)

(11)"是…的"句 Sentences with "是…的"

　　　　他是 2001 年来我们学院的。

　　　　我们是在上海认识的。

　　　　我朋友不是坐火车来的,是坐飞机来的。

　　　　力波是来学习美术的。

(12)表示存在的句子 Sentences indicating existance

　　　　邮局的旁边是什么地方？

　　　　楼后边有一个小花园。

　　　　厨房不在客厅右边。

（13）无标志被动句 Notional passive sentences

飞机票买好了没有？

兵马俑参观过一次。

（14）被动句 Passive sentences

那本小说被借走了。

自行车被我同学骑走了。

门让人撞坏了。

2. 动作的态 The aspects of an action

（1）动作或事情的完成 Completion or realization of an action or event

他去书店买了两本书。

他借了我的电脑。

她去上海了。

林娜买了旗袍了。

（2）情况的变化 Changed circumstances

天气越来越冷了。

他是教授了。

她有男朋友了。

小云的舅舅当公司的经理了。

她舅妈也开始用电脑了。

我弟弟上中学三年级了。

老师今天不来了。

（3）动作的持续 The continuous aspect of an action or a state

他们聊着过去的事儿。

我们带着花儿去她家。

宿舍门开着。

他穿着一件中式衣服。

书在桌上放着。

（4）过去的经验或经历 Past experience

        林娜以前看过《红楼梦》。

        他从来没有骑过自行车。

（5）动作即将发生 An action that is going to take place in a short time

        要开学了。

        他们明天就要考试了。

        火车快到广州了。

（6）动作的进行 The progressive aspect of an action

        他正在做什么？

        我在看电视呢。

        我去他家的时候，他正在画画儿。

        她在喝着咖啡呢。

3. 几种补语（1）Various kinds of complements（1）

（1）情态补语 The complement of state

        你来得真早。

        他们（说）普通话说得不太好。

（2）程度补语 The complement of degree

        今天冷极了。

        这部电影比那部好多了。

（3）趋向补语 The directional complement

        她出来了没有？

        我们先上楼去。

        你带没（有）带照片来？

        他们已经走下去了。

        我们爬上长城来了。

        他从邮局取回包裹来了。

（4）结果补语 The resultative complement

        我听懂了，可是记错了。

        请写上你的名字。

        他还没有看完这本小说呢。

        这篇文章已经写好了。

你买到那本词典没有?

老师住在二楼。

这张照片拍坏了。

(5) 数量补语 The complement of quantity

这件衣服比那件贵 50 块钱。

我比他小两岁。

这件衬衫太大,有小一点儿的吗?

(6) 时量补语 The time-measure complement

他在这儿工作了半年。

你(写)汉字写了多长时间?

我(学)汉语已经学了六年了。

她听了半个小时的音乐。

(7) 动量补语 The action-measure complement

他去过两次海南岛。

这部小说我又看了一遍。

老师让他念了两遍课文。

六. 汉字　Chinese Characters

1. 区分形近字　Discriminating characters with similar forms

Many Chinese characters have similar forms. To distinguish them, one must compare the shape, number, and combination of strokes, and position of components in each character.　For example:

(1) 儿——几　石——右　刀——力　入——人

(2) 犬——太　王——壬　土——士　夫——天

(3) 练——炼　孩——该　第——弟　泰——奏

(4) 放——访　明——朋　错——借　请——情

2. 认写基本汉字 Learn and write basic Chinese characters

(1) 史　　丶 ⼝ ⼝ 史 史

shǐ　　history　　　　　　　　　　　　5 strokes

(2) 歹　　（一 ＋ 夕）

dǎi　　evil　　　　　　　　　　　　　4 strokes

(Pay attention to the difference between "歹" and "夕".)

(3) 丈　　一 ナ 丈

zhàng　　unit of length　　　　　　　3 strokes

(Pay attention to the difference between "丈" and "文".)

(4) 夫　　一 二 ヺ 夫

fū　　husband　　　　　　　　　　　　4 strokes

(Pay attention to the difference between "夫" and "天".)

3. 认写课文中的汉字 Learn and write the Chinese characters appearing in the text

(1) 情况 qíngkuàng（情況）

况 → 冫 ＋ ⼝ ＋ 儿　　　　　7 strokes

(2) 历史 lìshǐ（歷史）

历 → 厂 ＋ 力　　　　　　　　4 strokes

(3) 博物馆 bówùguǎn（博物館）

博 → 十 ＋ 甫 ＋ 寸　　　　12 strokes

(4) 举办 jǔbàn（舉辦）

举 → 兴 ＋ 扌　　　　　　　　9 strokes

⺌(jiānzìtóu) 丨 丨丨 ⺌ ⺌ ⺌ 　　　　5 strokes

(5) 展览 zhǎnlǎn（展覽）
览 → ⺌ + 见　　　　9 strokes

(6) 感兴趣 gǎn xìngqù（感興趣）
趣 → 走 + 耳 + 又　　　　15 strokes

(7) 饿 è（餓）
饿 → 饣 + 我　　　　10 strokes

(8) 死 sǐ
死 → 歹 + 匕　　　　6 strokes

(9) 聊 liáo
聊 → 耳 + 卯　　　　11 strokes

⺕ (qīzìyāo) 乛 彐 彐 ⺕　　　　4 strokes

(10) 妻子 qīzi
妻 → 一 + ⺕ + 女　　　　8 strokes

(11) 小伙子 xiǎohuǒzi（小夥子）
伙 → 亻 + 火　　　　6 strokes

尸 (shēngzìdǐ) 乛 尸 尸 尸　　　　4 strokes

(12) 声调 shēngdiào（聲調）
声 → 士 + 尸　　　　7 strokes
调 → 讠 + 冂 + 土 + 口　　　　10 strokes

(13) 努力 nǔlì
努 → 女 + 又 + 力　　　　7 strokes

(14) 陪 péi
陪 → 阝 + 立 + 口　　　　10 strokes

Dynasties in China

The Title of a Dynasty	Years
五帝 (Wǔdì) Five Lords	Around the 26th century B.C. to around the end of the 22nd century or the beginning of the 21st century B.C.
夏 (Xià) Xia Dynasty	Around the end of the 22nd century or the beginning of the 21st century B.C. to around the 17th century B.C.
商 (Shāng) Shang Dynasty	Around the beginning of the 17th century B.C. to around the 11th century B.C.
周 (Zhōu) Zhou Dynasty	Around the 11th century B.C. to 256 B.C.
秦 (Qín) Qin Dynasty	221 B.C. to 206 B.C.
汉 (Hàn) Han Dynasty	206 B.C. to 220 A.D.
三国 (Sānguó) Three Kingdoms	220 to 280
晋 (Jìn) Jin Dynasty	265 to 420
南北朝 (Nán-Běi Cháo) Northern and Southern Dynasties	420 to 589
隋 (Suí) Sui Dynasty	581 to 618
唐 (Táng) Tang Dynasty	618 to 907
五代 (Wǔdài) Five Dynasties	907 to 960

The Title of a Dynasty	Years
宋　（Sòng） Song Dynasty	960　to　1279
元　（Yuán） Yuan Dynasty	1206　to　1368
明　（Míng） Ming Dynasty	1368　to　1644
清　（Qīng） Qing Dynasty	1616　to　1911

After having studied 26 lessons, you should have mastered over 800 new words, about 700 Chinese characters, and 197 key sentence patterns. You have studied Chinese phonetics, vocabulary, grammar, and Chinese characters at the beginner's level. You have also gained some knowledge of Chinese culture. Now, you should be able to converse about daily life in Chinese and read simple Chinese texts.

This is a good beginning. The next four volumes of the *New Practical Chinese Reader* will help you to communicate more freely in Chinese and to further understand the Chinese culture. Besides, you must be eager to learn the further adventures of our characters in China in the coming year.

她去上海了

（一）

林　　娜：力波，你來得真早。

丁力波：剛才銀行人少，不用排隊。林娜，你今天穿得很漂亮啊。

林　　娜：是嗎？我來銀行換錢，下午我還要去王府井買東西。

丁力波：今天一英鎊換多少人民幣？

林　　娜：一英鎊換十一塊五毛七分人民幣。明天我要去上海旅行，得用人民幣。

丁力波：什麼？明天你要去上海嗎？你剛從西安回北京，你真喜歡旅行！在西安玩兒得好不好？

林　　娜：我玩兒得非常好。

丁力波：吃得怎麼樣？

林　　娜：吃得還可以。這次住得不太好。

丁力波：你參觀兵馬俑了沒有？

林　　娜：我參觀兵馬俑了。我還買了很多明信片，你到我那兒去看看吧。

丁力波：好啊。我也很想去西安旅行，你給我介紹介紹吧。看，該你了。

林　　娜：小姐，我想用英鎊換人民幣。這是五百英鎊。

工作人員：好，給您五千七百八十五塊人民幣。請數一數。

（二）

馬大爲：林娜，早！好久不見，你回英國了嗎？

林　　娜：我沒有回英國，我去上海了。昨天剛回北京。

馬大爲：剛才宋華來了。他也問我，林娜去哪兒了？

林　　娜：我給宋華寫信了，他怎麼不知道？他現在在哪兒？

馬大爲：他回宿舍了。上海怎麼樣？聽說這兩年上海發展得非常快，是不是？

林　　娜：是啊，上海很大，也非常漂亮。那兒銀行多，商場也多，我很喜歡上海。

馬大爲：上海東西貴不貴？

林　　娜：東西不太貴。上海人做衣服做得真好，我買了很多件。

馬大爲：上海人喜歡說上海話，他們普通話說得怎麼樣？

林　　娜：他們普通話說得很好，年輕人英語說得也很流利。

馬大爲：你學沒學上海話？

林　　娜：學了。我會說"阿拉勿懂"。

馬大爲：你說什麼？我不懂。

林　　娜：這就是上海話的"我不懂"。

我把這事儿忘了

（一）

宋　　華：這是北京圖書館。我們進去吧。

丁 力 波：這個圖書館真大。

宋　　華：辦公室在三樓,我們上樓去,先把借書證辦了。

丁 力 波：今天就可以借書嗎?

宋　　華：可以,一會兒下來借書。……
　　　　　三樓到了。我看看,是這個辦公室。

丁 力 波：先生,我想辦借書證。

工作人員：您帶照片來了嗎?

丁 力 波：帶來了。

工作人員：請先填一張表。

宋　　華：力波,你從那兒拿一張表來。我告訴你怎麼填。

丁 力 波：我漢字寫得太慢,你來填吧。

宋　　華：不行。現在你在中國生活,你應該自己填表。

丁 力 波：好吧,我自己寫。"姓名"?

宋　　華："丁力波"。

丁 力 波："性別"寫什麼?

宋　　華：自己看。

丁 力 波：自——己——看? 啊,性別應該寫"男"。"職業"呢?

宋　　華：寫"學生"。好了。你把這張表和照片交了,一會兒那位先生就給你借書證了。

（二）

宋　　華：我們借書證辦了多長時間?

丁 力 波：辦了十五分鐘,辦得真快。

宋　　華：今天辦證的人不多。力波,聽説你們上星期考試了,你考得怎麼樣?

丁 力 波：我口語考得不錯,可是翻譯考得不太好,語法也有很多問題。我想借新的
　　　　　漢語課本看看。

宋　　華：現在我們就去借書,我們從這兒出去。我得先把上次借的書還了。

丁 力 波：這兒的書可以借多長時間?

宋　　華：可以借一個月。
　　　　　先生,我還書。

工作人員：好。……您的書過期了,您得交罰款。

宋　　華：真對不起,這個月太忙,我把這事兒忘了。罰多少錢?

工作人員：一本書過期一天罰兩毛,您借了四本書,過了十天,應該交八塊錢。

宋　　華：給您八塊。請問漢語課本在哪兒?

工作人員：那兒有電腦,您可以先查查。

丁 力 波：有外國人學漢語的新課本嗎?

工作人員：有。您找一找《新實用漢語課本》。

第十七课 Lesson 17

這件旗袍比那件漂亮

（一）

丁力波：小雲，哪兒賣中式衣服？

王小雲：你不知道嗎？你來北京多長時間了？

丁力波：我來北京半年了。可是你在北京已經二十年了，你是北京人，你當然比我知道得多。

王小雲：你說得對。現在北京的商店和商場多極了，大商場的東西比小商店的东西貴，可是小商店的東西不一定比大商場的差。你爲什麼現在想買中式衣服？

丁力波：從下星期開始，我要學太極拳，我得穿一套中式衣服。

王小雲：好極了！你穿中式衣服一定很帥。你喜歡什麼顏色的，黑的還是紅的？

丁力波：我喜歡白的。

王小雲：我也喜歡白的，白的漂亮。你想買好的還是買便宜的？

丁力波：我不要太貴的，也不要太便宜的。你說該去哪兒買？

王小雲：去王府井吧。那兒東西多，可能貴一點兒。

丁力波：貴一點兒沒關係。我們下午就去吧，我還想去公園走走。

（二）

宋　華：兩個小時過去了，你要的衣服還沒買。

林　娜：誰說我沒有買？我已經買了襯衫了。

宋　華：你要的旗袍呢？

林　娜：剛才看的旗袍都不錯，我真想都買了。

宋　華：我們還有時間，可以再多看看。這件綠的怎麼樣？

林　娜：啊，這件漂亮極了，顏色、樣子都比剛才看的旗袍好。

售貨員：您可以試一試。

林　娜：好。我覺得這件大點兒，是不是？

售貨員：我給您換一件小的。這件是三十八號，比那件小兩號。您再拿去試試吧。

林　娜：這件比那件合適，宋華，你看怎麼樣？

宋　華：我覺得這件太短了。

售貨員：對，您比我高，得穿長點兒的，我再給您找找。有了，這件紅的比那件綠的長兩公分。您再試一試這件。

林　娜：小姐，太麻煩您了，真不好意思。這件很合適。

宋　華：這件紅旗袍比那件綠的漂亮。

林　娜：可是也貴多了。

宋　華：比那件貴多少？

林　娜：貴九十塊錢。

宋　華：絲綢的當然貴一點兒。

林　娜：好吧，我就買這件。宋華，現在該去買你的了。你穿多大號的？想不想試試那套西服？

第十八课 Lesson 18

我听懂了,可是記錯了

(一)

馬大爲： 小姐,我要寄這個包裹。

工作人員： 好,我看一下。

馬大爲： 這些書都是新的。這四本書是中文的,那兩本書是英文的。這本大詞典是舊的……

工作人員： 好了,請包好。

馬大爲： 對不起,這是我剛學的課文,我想練習練習。

工作人員： 您漢語說得很流利。您要往哪兒寄?

馬大爲： 美國。

工作人員： 您寄航空還是海運?

馬大爲： 寄航空比海運貴,可是比海運快多了。寄航空吧。

工作人員： 郵費是一百零六塊。請在這兒寫上您的名字。

馬大爲： 小姐,我還要取一個包裹。

工作人員： 請把包裹通知單給我。對不起,您的包裹不在我們郵局取,您得去海關取。

馬大爲： 請問,海關在哪兒?

工作人員： 在建國門。別忘了把您的護照帶去。

馬大爲： 謝謝。

工作人員： 不客氣。

(二)

丁力波： 大爲,現在該去海關辦你的事兒了。從這兒怎麼去海關?

馬大爲： 海關在……我想想,叫什麼門。

丁力波： 看,這兒有八〇三路公共汽車,經過前門。

馬大爲： 對,好像是前門吧。車來了,咱們先上去。

售票員： 請大家往裏走。下一站,前門。下車的乘客請拿好自己的東西;剛上車的請買票。

馬大爲： 小姐,請問海關是不是在前門?

售票員： 海關是在建國門,不是在前門。

丁力波： 我們坐錯車了。

售票員： 沒關係,您可以在前門下車,在那兒換地鐵到建國門。

馬大爲： 沒有坐錯? 好極了! 買兩張到前門的。

售票員： 一塊一張。您這是五塊,找您三塊。請拿好票。

丁力波： 大爲,你說昨天郵局的工作人員告訴你了,你聽懂了沒有?

馬大爲： 我聽懂了,可是記錯了。

丁力波： 我得查一查:你把護照帶來了嗎?

馬大爲： 當然帶來了,你放心吧!

丁力波： 包裹通知單呢?

馬大爲： 糟糕,我把包裹通知單忘了。

第十九课 Lesson 19

中國畫跟油畫不一樣

丁力波：咱們來早了，美術館還沒有開門呢。

林　娜：來早了比來晚了好。今天我一定要參觀一個上午。

丁力波：你真喜歡中國畫！

林　娜：是啊，我非常喜歡徐悲鴻畫的馬。

丁力波：我跟你一樣，也很喜歡中國畫。從我十歲開始，媽媽就教我畫中國畫。你說說，我中國畫畫了多少年了？

林　娜：啊，已經畫了十一年了！我真不知道您還是一位"老畫家"。

丁力波：不敢當。我爸爸跟我媽媽一樣喜歡中國畫，可是他自己不會畫。我爸爸也有很多愛好，他喜歡唱中國京劇。現在他在家還常常唱京劇。

林　娜：他唱得怎麼樣？

丁力波：他唱京劇跟我畫中國畫一樣，馬馬虎虎。

林　娜：我想買一幅中國畫。大畫家畫的一定很貴，是不是？

丁力波：徐悲鴻畫的馬當然貴極了。我認識一位"老畫家"，他畫的馬不貴。

林　娜：這位老畫家是誰？

丁力波：是丁力波啊！我可以把我畫好的馬送你。

丁力波：咱們已經看了一個半小時的畫兒了，二樓的還沒有看呢。現在是不是坐電梯上樓去？

林　娜：好吧。力波，你覺得中國畫跟油畫一樣不一樣？

丁力波：當然一樣，都是畫兒啊。

林　娜：別開玩笑。

丁力波：我沒有開玩笑，我是說中國畫跟油畫一樣美。

林　娜：你說說哪兒不一樣？

丁力波：你找對人了，我來告訴你吧。中國畫和油畫用的材料不一樣。

林　娜：怎麼不一樣？

丁力波：中國畫用紙，油畫常常用布；中國畫主要用墨和水畫，油畫一定要用油彩畫。

林　娜：對，還有別的嗎？

丁力波：油畫沒有空白，中國畫常常有空白。你看這幅徐悲鴻的畫兒：畫家只畫了一匹馬，沒有畫別的。

林　娜：可是我們覺得還有別的東西。讓我們來想像一下：那匹馬往咱們這兒跑來了。我覺得它跑得非常快，好像還有風。

丁力波：對了。這就跟齊白石畫的蝦一樣，它們游來游去，真可愛！你看，畫家畫水了嗎？

林　娜：沒畫，可是我覺得有水。

丁力波：中國畫是不是跟油畫很不一樣？

林　娜：謝謝你的介紹。可是我還想看看"老畫家"畫的馬怎麼樣。

過新年

王小雲：中午咱們都去宋華家吃火鍋,他爸爸媽媽要我們跟他們一起過新年。

林　娜：在北京過新年一定很有意思。小雲,爲什麼北京很多飯館都有火鍋? 是不是因爲現在天氣冷,所以北京人常吃火鍋?

王小雲：不是。北京人就愛吃火鍋,主要是涮羊肉,天氣熱的時候也吃。北京的涮羊肉跟北京烤鴨一樣有名。

林　娜：過新年的時候北京人都吃涮羊肉嗎?

王小雲：不一定。

林　娜：你說說北京人怎麼過新年。

王小雲：跟西方人一樣,很多人去旅行。也可能開車去郊區玩兒,或者去鍛煉身體。

林　娜：晚上常常做些什麼?

王小雲：晚上看京劇、聽音樂會或者跟朋友聚會。我說林娜,快點兒吧! 你化妝化了半個小時了。咱們得早點兒走。

林　娜：一會兒就好。今天晚上咱們還要去聽音樂會,所以得正式一點兒。

王小雲：你知道嗎? 今天晚上聽中國民樂,它跟西方音樂很不一樣。

林　娜：我知道,中國民樂主要是用民族樂器演奏的中國音樂。剛來的時候我不太習慣聽民樂,可是現在我很愛聽。

王小雲：你喜歡《春江花月夜》嗎?

林　娜：啊,《春江花月夜》美極了。我已經買了這個樂曲的光盤,今天還要再買一些,給我朋友寄去。咱們怎麼去宋華家? 坐出租車還是坐公共汽車?

王小雲：今天路上的車一定很多。出租車比公共汽車快多了,坐出租車吧。

林　娜：咱們還沒有買禮物呢。送花兒是西方人的習慣,我們參加聚會的時候也可以帶吃的、喝的。中國人去朋友家的時候送什麼?

王小雲：過去常送一些吃的、喝的或者用的,現在的年輕人跟西方人一樣,也常送花兒。

林　娜：咱們買些花兒,再帶些吃的吧。

王小雲：好。別忘了把照相機帶去。

林　娜：我的照相機呢?

王小雲：在電話旁邊。

林　娜：大爲和力波怎麼不給咱們打個電話?

王小雲：我不知道大爲能不能去,因爲他要跟女朋友一起去旅行。力波一定去,他說要從這兒出發。

林　娜：再等一等他吧。

王小雲：好。咱們把陸雨平也叫去,讓他寫一篇文章,介紹留學生在中國怎麼過新年。

　　　　　　　　＊　＊　＊

丁力波：小雲,林娜,新年好! 恭喜恭喜!

林　娜：恭喜你! 大爲呢?

丁力波：大爲昨天晚上就坐火車去南方了。

王小雲：你又來晚了。

丁力波：真不好意思。二位小姐別著急,出租車已經來了。

王小雲：你把出租車叫來了,太好了。咱們快走。

林　娜：你給宋華帶什麼禮物去?

丁力波：今年是馬年,我又畫了一匹馬。你們看,畫得怎麼樣?

我們的隊員是從不同國家來的

（一）

陸雨平：聽說上星期你們留學生隊贏了一場足球比賽。我想寫一篇文章,介紹一下留學生足球隊的事兒。

丁力波：太好了。你是怎麼知道的?

陸雨平：我是聽你的同學說的。別忘了我是記者,我今天是來問你們問題的。你們留學生隊是跟誰比賽的?

丁力波：我們隊是跟中國大學生隊比賽的。

陸雨平：你們是在哪兒比賽的?

王小雲：是在我們學校比賽的。

陸雨平：中國大學生隊的水平比你們高吧?

丁力波：他們的水平比我們高多了。

王小雲：宋華說,大學生隊的教練是從國家隊來的。

陸雨平：他是什麼時候從國家隊下來的?

王小雲：他是去年從國家隊下來的。這位教練來了以後,大學生隊的水平提高得很快。

丁力波：大學生隊的十號踢得很好。左邊的五號、右邊的十二號跑得都很快。

陸雨平：你們留學生隊呢?

丁力波：我們的隊員是從不同國家來的,我們不常練習。

陸雨平：你們是怎麼贏的?

丁力波：上半場零比零。下半場他們幫助我們進了一個球,是一比零贏的。

（二）

陸雨平：我還要問問你們：你們去看大爲租的房子了沒有? 房子在哪兒?

王小雲：去了,房子在學校東邊,離學校不太遠。那兒叫花園小區,大爲住八號樓。

陸雨平：你們是怎麼去的?

丁力波：我們是坐公共汽車去的。車站就在小區前邊。下車以後先往右拐,再往前走三分鐘,就到八號樓了。

陸雨平：那兒怎麼樣?

丁力波：很好。八號樓下邊是一個小花園,左邊有一個商店,商店旁邊是書店。右邊是銀行和郵局。大爲的房子在八號樓九層,上邊還有六層。

陸雨平：房子不大吧?

王小雲：那套房子一共有五十六平方米。

丁力波：進門以後,左邊是衛生間,右邊是客廳。

陸雨平：廚房在哪兒?

王小雲：廚房在客廳北邊,臥室在客廳東邊。臥室外邊有一個大陽臺。

丁力波：記者先生,你問了很多問題,你也要寫一篇文章介紹馬大爲租的房子吧?

陸雨平：問問題是記者的職業習慣啊。

你看過越劇沒有

（一）

宋　華：林娜,你看過越劇沒有?

林　娜：沒有。來中國以後,我聽過兩次音樂會,看過一次京劇。我雖然去過南方,但是沒有看過越劇。昨天的報上說,南方的一個越劇團到北京來了。

宋　華：是啊,越劇是中國有名的地方戲。這個劇團是從上海來的,現在在長安大戲院上演《紅樓夢》。

林　娜：上演《紅樓夢》嗎? 太好了! 我知道《紅樓夢》是中國有名的古典小說,我看過一遍,是用英文翻譯的。

宋　華：你覺得這部小說怎么樣?

林　娜：我覺得小說裏的愛情故事非常感人。

宋　華：你想不想再看一次越劇的《紅樓夢》? 我有兩張票。

林　娜：當然想看。是什麼時候的票?

宋　華：是明天晚上七點一刻的。座位很好,樓下五排八號和十號。

林　娜：我沒去過長安大戲院。這個戲院在哪兒?

宋　華：我去過啊,長安大戲院離建國門不遠,就在建國門的西邊。咱們一起打的去。

林　娜：好,明天見。

（二）

宋　華：你覺得越劇《紅樓夢》怎麼樣?

林　娜：我從來沒有看過這麼感人的戲。兩個主角演得好極了。我覺得越劇的音樂特別優美,越劇的風格跟京劇很不一樣。

宋　華：你說得很對。你可能還不知道,很早以前京劇裏沒有女演員,都是男演員演女角色。越劇跟京劇不同,以前沒有男演員,讓女演員演男角色。所以越劇的風格跟京劇很不一樣。

林　娜：聽說中國地方戲的種類很多,每個地方都有吧?

宋　華：是啊,每種地方戲都有自己的風格,每個地方的人都習慣看自己的地方戲。但是京劇是全中國的,喜歡京劇的人特別多。

林　娜：中國京劇團兩年以前到英國訪問過,我跟爸爸媽媽一起去看過一次。他們都覺得京劇很美。

宋　華：很多外國朋友都喜歡中國京劇,一些外國留學生還到北京來學京劇。現在他們有的人會唱京劇,有的人還會演京劇。

林　娜：我有一個朋友,也是英國留學生,他就會演京劇。

宋　華：我還從來沒聽過外國留學生唱越劇。你這麼喜歡越劇的音樂,應該學一學越劇。

林　娜：我雖然喜歡越劇音樂,可是我覺得唱越劇太難了。

宋　華：你的嗓子很好。你可以先多聽聽,再學唱。

我們爬上長城來了

（一）

陳老師：要放假了，同學們有什麼打算？

林　娜：有的同學去旅行，有的同學回家。

陳老師：小雲，你呢？

王小雲：我打算先去泰山，再回家看我爸爸媽媽。林娜，你去過泰山沒有？

林　娜：泰山我去過一次了。這次我想去海南島旅行。

王小雲：你跟宋華一起去吧？

林　娜：是啊，去海南島旅行就是他提出來的。

王小雲：你們坐飛機去還是坐火車去？

林　娜：坐飛機去。機票已經買好了。力波呢？去不去泰山？

王小雲：去。他說他要從山下爬上去，再從山頂走下來。他還說，先爬泰山，再去參觀孔子教書的地方。

林　娜：對了，大爲想去哪兒？

王小雲：小燕子建議大爲也去海南島。她說現在那兒天氣好，氣溫合適，能去游泳，還可以看優美的景色。現在北京是冬天，可是在海南島還可以過夏天的生活，多有意思啊！

林　娜：小燕子是導遊小姐，旅行的事兒她知道得很多，應該聽她的。大爲可以跟我們一起去。

王小雲：大爲還建議放假以前咱們一起去長城。陳老師，您能不能跟我們一起去？

陳老師：行。我很願意跟你們一起去爬一次長城。

（二）

王小雲：陳老師、林娜，加油！快上來！

陳老師：力波、大爲他們呢？

王小雲：他們已經爬上去了。咱們也快要到山頂了。

陳老師：別著急。我覺得有點兒累，林娜也累了，咱們就坐下來休息一會兒吧。先喝點兒水再往上爬。

林　娜：這兒的景色多美啊！長城好像一條龍。看，下邊都是山，火車從山裏開出來了。我要多拍些照片寄回家去。

王小雲：你來過這兒嗎？

林　娜：來過。是秋天來的。那時候長城的景色跟現在很不一樣。

王小雲：是啊。現在是冬天，今天還是陰天，要下雪了。

林　娜：在長城上看下雪，太美了。

陳老師：今天這兒的氣溫是零下十度。可是你們知道嗎？廣州今天是零上二十度。

林　娜：中國真大。北方還是這麼冷的冬天，可是春天已經到了南方。你們看，力波怎麼走下來了？

丁力波：喂，你們怎麼還沒上來？要幫忙嗎？

王小雲：不用。你不用跑過來，我們自己能上去。陳老師，您休息好了嗎？

陳老師：休息好了。小雲，你幫我站起來……

林　娜：啊！我們爬上長城來了！

你舅媽也開始用電腦了

（一）

丁力波：小雲，火車快到了吧？

王小雲：從上海到北京的T23次八點四十分到，現在八點半，快到了。

丁力波：你舅舅是農民嗎？

王小雲：是。他過去是上海郊區的農民，現在當蔬菜公司的經理了。

丁力波：他來過北京嗎？

王小雲：他來過兩次，可是我都不在。上次他來的時候，我正在南方旅行呢。

丁力波：看，那個人正在問路呢。我們過去看看，那是不是你舅舅。

王小雲：好像是吧。我十年以前見過他，這十年變化很大。不但他不認識我了，而且我也可能不認識他了。

丁力波：可不。那時候你還是個小孩，現在是大姑娘了。

王小雲：是啊，我舅舅也老了。那個人在看地圖嗎？

丁力波：他沒在看地圖，他好像在看照片。他向我們走過來了。

王小雲：他很像我舅舅。不錯，是我舅舅。舅舅，您好！

舅　舅：小雲！十年不見，你是大學生了。你今年上幾年級了？

王小雲：上大學三年級了。

舅　舅：有男朋友了嗎？

王小雲：舅舅，這是我同學丁力波。他是加拿大留學生。

丁力波：您好，路上辛苦了。快要下雨了，請上車吧！

（二）

王小雲：舅媽呢？怎麼沒有來？她說過要跟您一起來北京。

舅　舅：你舅媽在種溫室蔬菜呢。她現在很忙，這次不來了。

王小雲：現在你們種蔬菜的收入怎,麼樣？

舅　舅：我們種溫室蔬菜，收入比以前好多了。

王小雲：家裏的生活怎麼樣？

舅　舅：生活還可以。前年我們蓋了一座兩層的小樓，去年還買了一輛汽車。現在我們去別的城市也方便了。

丁力波：您的生活水平比城裏人的還高。

舅　舅：我們村吃的、穿的、住的都不比城裏差。問題是我們農民的文化水平還比城裏人的低一些。

王小雲：現在農民沒有文化真不行。

舅　舅：你說得很對，農民也都要學習新技術。溫室蔬菜是用電腦管理的。你舅媽也開始用電腦了。

王小雲：今年我一定要去看看你們。

司机開着車送我們到醫院

（一）

王小雲：宋華,你來幫我們一下,好嗎?
宋　華：你們怎麼了? 現在你在哪兒?
王小雲：林娜被撞傷了,正在第三醫院檢查呢。
宋　華：她傷了哪兒了? 傷得重嗎?
王小雲：還沒有檢查完呢。你帶點兒錢來。
宋　華：好的,你們等着,我馬上就來。
（在第三醫院）
宋　華：林娜,你怎麼樣? 傷得重不重?
林　娜：傷得不太重。我的胳膊被撞傷了,右腿也有點兒疼。
宋　華：你是怎麼被撞傷的?
林　娜：怎麼説呢? 下午我和小雲看完電影,騎著自行車回學院。我們説著、笑著,往右拐的時候沒有注意,撞到了車上。那輛車停在路(旁)邊,司機正在從車上拿東西。
宋　華：你們是怎麼到醫院來的?
林　娜：那位司機看到我被撞傷了,就馬上開著車送我們到醫院。
宋　華：那位司機真不錯。
林　娜：我們帶的錢不多,醫藥費都是他幫我們交的。他還給了我一張名片。
宋　華：真應該謝謝那位司機,明天我去把錢還他。剛才我還以爲你被汽車撞了。
林　娜：還好,汽車被我撞了。如果我被汽車撞了,就糟糕了。

（二）

陸雨平：大爲,林娜宿舍的門開著,她躺著看電視呢。
林　娜：啊,陸雨平、大爲,快進來。
馬大爲：林娜,你怎麼樣? 好點兒了嗎?
林　娜：好多了。你們這麼忙,還帶著花兒來看我,謝謝你們。這束花兒真漂亮,放在桌(子)上吧。
馬大爲：檢查的結果怎麼樣?
林　娜：醫生説沒有大的問題,他讓我躺在床上休息休息。大爲,你把電視關了吧,咱們説會兒話。
陸雨平：現在胳膊還疼不疼?
林　娜：不疼了。可是胳膊這麼彎著,寫字很不方便。上星期我漢字沒有考好,現在又撞傷了胳膊,真倒楣! 這兩天都是壞消息。
馬大爲：別著急,我有一個好消息。
林　娜：什麼好消息?
馬大爲：上星期六晚上,我的自行車被小偷偷走了。
林　娜：自行車被偷了,這是什麼好消息?
馬大爲：你聽著,來你這兒以前,派出所給我打了一個電話,讓我去一下。
林　娜：你去派出所做什麼?
馬大爲：小偷被抓到了,我丟的車也找到了,現在在派出所呢。你説,這是不是好消息?
林　娜：是個好消息。
陸雨平：真應該祝賀你!

第二十六课 Lesson 26

你快要成"中國通"了

宋　華：林娜,你来中國已經快一年了吧。你不但學習了漢語,而且還認識了很多中國朋友,中國的情況又知道得不少,你快要成"中國通"了。

林　娜：哪里,哪里,"中國通"真不敢當,還差得遠呢。說實在的,我越來越喜歡中國文化了。中國從南到北,從東到西,每個地方都有自己的特點。

宋　華：歷史博物館正在舉辦"2002——中國"展覽,那兒有很多圖片,有的是我們見過的,有的是我們沒見過的。你對中國文化這麽感興趣,我建議你去看看。

林　娜：好極了,我一定去。今天我們有一個結業聚會,力波他們快要來了。你把這個消息告訴他們,我想他們也一定會非常感興趣。

宋　華：好啊。林娜,你還記得嗎? 剛來的時候,你說過,如果每天都讓你吃中餐,你就會餓死。現在你不但喜歡吃中餐,而且還學會了做中國菜。

林　娜：可不,現在如果一天不吃中餐,我就會覺得有點兒不舒服。

(丁力波、馬大爲進宿舍)

馬大爲：你們在聊什麽呢? 去哪兒吃中餐? 我也去。

宋　華：我們在說,你們這些老外快成"中國通"了。力波當然就不用說了。

丁力波：因爲我媽媽是中國人,所以我早就有點兒中國化了。林娜愛穿旗袍,愛吃中國菜,還喜歡看越劇、聽中國民樂,好像也有點兒中國化了。

林　娜：我是到北京以後才開始中國化的。

馬大爲：我看這很容易,像有的留學生那樣,找個中國姑娘做妻子。你找個長得帥的中國小夥子做丈夫,每天在一起生活,就可以中國化了。

林　娜：別開玩笑。說真的,我現在覺得漢語語法不太難,可是漢字很難。

馬大爲：聲調也不容易,我常常說錯。

宋　華：你們在中國才學習了一年,漢語水平就提高得這麽快,主要是因爲你們學習都很努力。

丁力波：這兒的老師教得特別認真,朋友們對我們也非常熱情,常常幫助我們學漢語,所以我們進步很快。

林　娜：一年的學習時間太短了。我雖然已經能聽懂中國人說的一些話,可是自己說漢語還說得不太流利,明年我還要來中國學習。

馬大爲：林娜,老師和同學們都在等著我們呢,我們走吧。

丁力波：好,明年再中國化吧!

林　娜：宋華,明天你陪我去參觀"2002——中國"展覽,好嗎?

宋　華：好,明天見!

林　娜：不見不散!

语法术语缩略形式一览表
Abbreviations for Grammar Terms

Abbreviation	*Grammar Terms in English*	*Grammar Terms in Chinese*	*Grammar Terms in Pinyin*
A	*Adjective*	形容词	xíngróngcí
Adv	*Adverb*	副词	fùcí
AsPt	*Aspect Particle*	动态助词	dòngtài zhùcí
Conj	*Conjunction*	连词	liáncí
IE	*Idiom Expression*	习惯用语	xíguàn yòngyǔ
Int	*Interjection*	叹词	tàncí
M	*Measure Word*	量词	liàngcí
MdPt	*Modal Particle*	语气助词	yǔqì zhùcí
N	*Noun*	名词	míngcí
NP	*Noun Phrase*	名词短语	míngcí duǎnyǔ
Nu	*Numeral*	数词	shùcí
O	*Object*	宾语	bīnyǔ
Ono	*Onomatopoeia*	象声词	xiàngshēngcí
OpV	*Optative Verb*	能愿动词	néngyuàn dòngcí
Pt	*Particle*	助词	zhùcí
PN	*Proper Noun*	专有名词	zhuānyǒu míngcí
Pr	*Pronoun*	代词	dàicí
Pref	*Prefix*	词头	cítóu
Prep	*Preposition*	介词	jiècí
PW	*Place Word*	地点词	dìdiǎncí
QPt	*Question Particle*	疑问助词	yíwèn zhùcí
QPr	*Question Pronoun*	疑问代词	yíwèn dàicí
S	*Subject*	主语	zhǔyǔ
StPt	*Structural Particle*	结构助词	jiégòu zhùcí
Suf	*Suffix*	词尾	cíwěi
TW	*Time Word*	时间词	shíjiāncí
V	*Verb*	动词	dòngcí
VC	*Verb plus Complement*	动补式动词	dòngbǔshì dòngcí
VO	*Verb plus Object*	动宾式动词	dòngbīnshì dòngcí
VP	*Verbal Phrase*	动词短语	dòngcí duǎnyǔ

生词索引(简繁对照)
Vocabulary Index
(Simplified Script with Traditional Version)

词条	繁体	词性	拼音	英译	课号

A

爱	爱	(V)	ài	to love	20
爱好	爱好	(N/V)	àihào	hobby/ to like	19
爱情	爱情	(N)	àiqíng	love	22

B

把	把	(Prep)	bǎ	(denoting the disposal of sth.)	16
白	白	(A)	bái	white	17
办公室	辦公室	(N)	bàngōngshì	office	16
帮	幫	(V)	bāng	to help; to assist	23
帮忙	幫忙	(V)	bāngmáng	to help	23
包	包	(V)	bāo	to wrap	18
包裹	包裹	(N)	bāoguǒ	parcel; package	18
北边	北邊	(N)	běibian	north side	21
北方	北方	(N)	běifāng	north	23
被	被	(Pr)	bèi	by (used to indicate the passive voice)	25
比	比	(Prep)	bǐ	than(indicating comparision)	17
比赛	比賽	(N/V)	bǐsài	match/to compete; to have a match	21
遍	遍	(M)	biàn	number of times (of action)	22
变化	變化	(N)	biànhuà	change	24
表	表	(N)	biǎo	form; table; list	16
别	别	(Adv)	bié	don't	18
别的	别的	(Pr)	biéde	other	19
兵马俑	兵馬俑	(N)	bīngmǎyǒng	(ceremonial clay statues of warriors and horses which are buried with the dead)	15
博物馆	博物館	(N)	bówùguǎn	museum	26
不错	不錯	(A)	búcuò	not bad	16
不但	不但	(Conj)	búdàn	not only	24
不敢当	不敢當	(IE)	bù gǎndāng	I really don't deserve this	19
不见不散	不見不散	(IE)	bú jiàn bú sàn	don't leave unless we meet	26
不同	不同	(A)	bùtóng	different	21
不行	不行	(V)	bùxíng	not be allowed; won't do	16
布	布	(N)	bù	cloth	19
部	部	(M)	bù	(a measure word for films, works of literature)	22

C

才	才	(Adv)	cái	just	26
材料	材料	(N)	cáiliào	material	19
菜	菜	(N)	cài	dish; vegetable	26
参观	參觀	(V)	cānguān	to visit (a place)	15
查	查	(V)	chá	to check; to look up	16

差	差	(A)	chà	not up to standard; poor; bad	17
长	長	(A)	cháng	long	16
长安大戏院	長安大戲院	(PN)	Cháng'ān Dà Xìyuàn	the Chang'an Theatre	22
长城	長城	(PN)	Chángchéng	the Great Wall	23
场	場	(M)	chǎng	match; set; (a measure word for sports, films, performances)	21
唱	唱	(V)	chàng	to sing	19
车	車	(N)	chē	vehicle	18
车站	車站	(N)	chēzhàn	bus stop	21
衬衫	襯衫	(N)	chènshān	shirt	17
成	成	(V)	chéng	to become	26
城	城	(N)	chéng	city	24
乘客	乘客	(N)	chéngkè	passenger	18
城市	城市	(N)	chéngshì	city	24
出	出	(V)	chū	to go or come out	16
出发	出發	(V)	chūfā	to set out; to start off	20
出租车	出租車	(N)	chūzūchē	taxi; cab	20
《春江花月夜》	《春江花月夜》	(PN)	《Chūn Jiāng Huā Yuè Yè》	(a famous, traditional Chinese music composition)	20
春天	春天	(N)	chūntiān	spring	23
词典	詞典	(N)	cídiǎn	dictionary	18
次	次	(M)	cì	(measure word for actions)	15
从	從	(Prep)	cóng	from	15
从来	從來	(Adv)	cónglái	all along; always	22
村	村	(N)	cūn	village	24
错	錯	(A)	cuò	wrong; erroneous	18

D

打的	打的	(VO)	dǎdī	to take a taxi	22
打算	打算	(V/N)	dǎsuan	to plan; to intend / plan	23
大家	大家	(Pr)	dàjiā	all; everybody	18
大学	大學	(N)	dàxué	university; college	24
大学生	大學生	(N)	dàxuéshēng	university student; college student	21
带	帶	(V)	dài	to bring	16
但是	但是	(Conj)	dànshì	but; whereas; yet	22
当	當	(V)	dāng	to serve as; to be	24
导游	導游	(N)	dǎoyóu	tour guide	23
倒霉	倒霉	(A)	dǎoméi	bad luck	25
得	得	(StPt)	de	(structural particle)	15
得	得	(V)	děi	to need; must; to have to	15
低	低	(A)	dī	low	24
地方	地方	(N)	dìfang	place; region	22
地方戏	地方戲	(N)	dìfāngxì	regional opera	22
地铁	地鐵	(N)	dìtiě	underground railway; subway	18
地图	地圖	(N)	dìtú	map	24
第	第	(Pref)	dì	(for ordinal numbers)	25
电脑	電腦	(N)	diànnǎo	computer	16
电视	電視	(N)	diànshì	TV	25
电梯	電梯	(N)	diàntī	elevator	19
顶	頂	(N)	dǐng	peak; tip	23
丢	丢	(V)	diū	to lose	25
东边	東邊	(N)	dōngbian	east side	21
冬天	冬天	(N)	dōngtiān	winter	23

懂	懂	（V ）	dǒng	to understand	15
度	度	（M ）	dù	degree（for temperature）	23
短	短	（A ）	duǎn	short	17
对	對	（Prep）	duì	to	26
队	隊	（N ）	duì	team	21
队员	隊員	（N ）	duìyuán	team member	21

E

饿	餓	（A ）	è	hungry	26
而且	而且	（Conj）	érqiě	but also；and also	24

F

发展	發展	（V ）	fāzhǎn	to develop	15
罚	罰	（V ）	fá	to punish；to penalize	16
罚款	罰款	（VO/N）	fákuǎn	to impose a fine or forfeit／fine	16
翻译	翻譯	（V ）	fānyì	to translate；to interpret	16
饭馆	飯館	（N ）	fànguǎn	restaurant	20
方便	方便	（A ）	fāngbiàn	convenient	24
访问	訪問	（V ）	fǎngwèn	to visit；to call on	22
放	放	（V ）	fàng	to put；to place	25
放假	放假	（VO ）	fàngjià	to have a holiday or vacation	23
放心	放心	（VO ）	fàngxīn	to set one's mind at rest；to be at ease；to feel relieved	18
飞机	飛機	（N ）	fēijī	airplane	23
非常	非常	（Adv ）	fēicháng	very；extremely；highly	15
风	風	（N ）	fēng	wind	19
风格	風格	（N ）	fēnggé	style；manner	22
幅	幅	（M ）	fú	（measure word for painting, cloth, etc.）	19

G

该	該	（V ）	gāi	to be sb.'s turn to do sth.	15
盖	蓋	（V ）	gài	to build	24
感人	感人	（A ）	gǎnrén	touching；moving	22
感兴趣	感興趣	（IE ）	gǎn xìngqù	to be interested in sth.	26
刚	剛	（Adv ）	gāng	just；only a short while ago	15
高	高	（A ）	gāo	high；tall	17
胳膊	胳膊	（N ）	gēbo	arm	25
公分	公分	（N ）	gōngfēn	centimeter	17
公共汽车	公共汽車	（N ）	gōnggòngqìchē	bus	18
恭喜	恭喜	（IE ）	gōngxǐ	congratulations	20
公园	公園	（N ）	gōngyuán	park	17
工作人员	工作人員	（N ）	gōngzuò rényuán	working personnel；staff member	15
古典	古典	（A ）	gǔdiǎn	classical	22
故事	故事	（N ）	gùshi	story；tale	22
拐	拐	（V ）	guǎi	to turn	21
关	關	（V ）	guān	to close；to turn off	25
管理	管理	（V ）	guǎnlǐ	to manage；to administer	24
广州	廣州	（PN ）	Guǎngzhōu	Guangzhou	23
国家	國家	（N ）	guójiā	country	21
过	過	（V ）	guò	to pass	16
过期	過期	（VO ）	guòqī	to be overdue	16
过去	過去	（V ）	guòqù	to pass	17

| 过去 | 過去 | (N) | guòqù | in or of the past | 20 |
| 过 | 過 | (AsPt) | guo | (indicating a past experience) | 22 |

H

海关	海關	(N)	hǎiguān	customhouse; customs	18
海南岛	海南島	(PN)	Hǎinán Dǎo	Hainan Island	23
海运	海運	(N)	hǎiyùn	sea transportation; ocean shipping; ocean freight	18
航空	航空	(N)	hángkōng	aviation	18
好久不见	好久不見	(IE)	hǎojiǔ bújiàn	haven't seen (sb.) for a very long time	15
好像	好像	(V)	hǎoxiàng	to seem; to be like	18
合适	合適	(A)	héshì	suitable; appropriate; right	17
黑	黑	(A)	hēi	black	17
红	紅	(A)	hóng	red	17
《红楼梦》	《紅樓夢》	(PN)	《Hónglóu Mèng》	*Dream of the Red Chamber*	22
护照	護照	(N)	hùzhào	passport	18
花儿	花兒	(N)	huār	flower	20
花园	花園	(N)	huāyuán	garden	21
花园小区	花園小區	(N)	huāyuán xiǎoqū	garden district	21
化	化	(Aff)	huà	to change	20
画	畫	(V)	huà	to paint	19
话	話	(N)	huà	dialect; language	15
画家	畫家	(N)	huàjiā	painter; artist	19
画儿	畫兒	(N)	huàr	painting	19
化妆	化妝	(VO)	huàzhuāng	to put on makeup	20
坏	壞	(A)	huài	bad; broken	25
还	還	(V)	huán	to give back; to return	16
换	換	(V)	huàn	to exchange; to change	15
火车	火車	(N)	huǒchē	train	20
火锅	火鍋	(N)	huǒguō	hotpot	20
或者	或者	(Conj)	huòzhě	or	20

J

机	機	(N)	jī	airplane	23
极(了)	(極)了	(Adv)	jí(le)	extremely	17
记	記	(V)	jì	to remember	18
记得	記得	(V)	jìde	to remember; to retain	26
技术	技術	(N)	jìshù	technology; skill	24
记者	記者	(N)	jìzhě	reporter	21
加油	加油	(VO)	jiāyóu	to make an extra effort; to cheer sb. on	23
检查	檢查	(V)	jiǎnchá	to examine	25
见	見	(V)	jiàn	to see; to meet with	22
建国门	建國門	(PN)	Jiànguó Mén	Jianguo Men (a place in Beijing)	18
建议	建議	(V/N)	jiànyì	to make suggestions/advice; suggestion	23
交	交	(V)	jiāo	to hand in; to hand over; to pay (the rent, etc.)	16
郊区	郊區	(N)	jiāoqū	suburb; outskirts	20
教书	教書	(VO)	jiāoshū	to teach	23
教练	教練	(N)	jiàoliàn	coach	21
结果	結果	(N)	jiéguǒ	result; outcome	25
结业	結業	(VO)	jiéyè	to complete a course	26
借	借	(V)	jiè	to borrow; to lend	16

借书证	借書證	(N)	jièshūzhèng	library card	16
进步	進步	(N/V)	jìnbù	progress; advancement/to make progress	26
经过	經過	(V)	jīngguò	to pass; to go through; to go by	18
京剧	京劇	(N)	jīngjù	Beijing opera	19
景色	景色	(N)	jǐngsè	scene; scenery; landscape	23
旧	舊	(A)	jiù	old; past; used	18
就	就	(Adv)	jiù	exactly; precisely	15
舅舅	舅舅	(N)	jiùjiu	uncle (mother's brother)	24
舅妈	舅媽	(N)	jiùmā	aunt (wife of mother's brother)	24
举办	舉辦	(V)	jǔbàn	to conduct; to hold	26
剧团	劇團	(N)	jùtuán	opera troupe; theatrical group	22
觉得	覺得	(V)	juéde	to feel; to think	17
角色	角色	(N)	juésè	character; role	22

K

开车	開車	(VO)	kāichē	to drive a car	20
开门	開門	(VO)	kāimén	to open the door; to begin a day's business	19
开始	開始	(V)	kāishǐ	to start; to begin	17
开玩笑	開玩笑	(VO)	kāi wánxiào	to crack a joke; to make fun of	19
考	考	(V)	kǎo	to give or take an examination; to test	16
考试	考試	(V/N)	kǎoshì	to give or take an examination/examination; test	16
可不	可不	(IE)	kěbù	exactly; right; that's just the way it is	24
课本	課本	(N)	kèběn	textbook	16
客气	客氣	(A)	kèqi	polite; courteous	18
客厅	客廳	(N)	kètīng	living room	21
孔子	孔子	(PN)	Kǒngzǐ	Confucius	23
空白	空白	(N)	kòngbái	blank space	19
快	快	(A)	kuài	fast; quick; rapid	15

L

老	老	(A)	lǎo	old; experienced	19
老外	老外	(N)	lǎowài	foreigner	26
累	累	(A)	lèi	tired	23
离	離	(Prep)	lí	away; off; from	21
里(边)	里(邊)	(N)	lǐ(bian)	in; inside; within	18
历史	歷史	(N)	lìshǐ	history	26
辆	輛	(M)	liàng	(a measure word for vehicles)	24
聊	聊	(V)	liáo	to chat	26
零(下)	零(下)	(N)	líng(xià)	zero (below zero)	23
流利	流利	(A)	liúlì	fluent	15
龙	龍	(N)	lóng	dragon	23
路	路	(N)	lù	route	18
路上	路上	(N)	lùshang	on the road; on the way	20
绿	綠	(A)	lǜ	green	17

M

麻烦	麻煩	(V)	máfan	to bother sb.; to trouble sb.	17
马马虎虎	馬馬虎虎	(A)	mǎmǎhūhū	so-so; careless	19
马上	馬上	(Adv)	mǎshàng	right away; immediately	25
卖	賣	(V)	mài	to sell	17
慢	慢	(A)	màn	slow; slowly	16

没关系	没關系	（IE）	méi guānxi	never mind; it doesn't matter	17
美	美	（A）	měi	beautiful	19
美术馆	美術館	（N）	měishùguǎn	art gallery	19
门	門	（N）	mén	door; gate; entrance	18
米	米	（M）	mǐ	meter	21
民乐	民樂	（N）	mínyuè	folk music played with traditional instruments	20
民族	民族	（N）	mínzú	nation; nationality	20
明年	明年	（N）	míngnián	next year	26
明信片	明信片	（N）	míngxìnpiàn	postcard	15
墨	墨	（N）	mò	Chinese ink	19

N

拿	拿	（V）	ná	to take; to hold; to get	16
那样	那樣	（Pr）	nàyàng	such; so; like that	26
南	南	（N）	nán	south	26
难	難	（A）	nán	difficult; hard	22
年级	年級	（N）	niánjí	grade	24
年轻	年輕	（A）	niánqīng	young	15
农民	農民	（N）	nóngmín	farmer; peasant	24
努力	努力	（A）	nǔlì	to make great efforts; to endeavor; to exert oneself	26

P

爬	爬	（V）	pá	to climb	23
拍	拍	（V）	pāi	to pat; to beat; to take (a picture)	23
排	排	（N）	pái	line; row	22
排队	排隊	（VO）	páiduì	to form a line; to queue up	15
派出所	派出所	（N）	pàichūsuǒ	police substation	25
旁边	旁邊	（N）	pángbiān	side	20
跑	跑	（V）	pǎo	to run	19
陪	陪	（V）	péi	to accompany	26
匹	匹	（M）	pǐ	(measure word for horses)	19
篇	篇	（M）	piān	(a measure word for essays and articles)	20
便宜	便宜	（A）	piányi	cheap	17
票	票	（N）	piào	ticket	18
平方米	平方米	（M）	píngfāngmǐ	square meter	21
普通话	普通話	（N）	pǔtōnghuà	the common speech(mandarin)	15

Q

妻子	妻子	（N）	qīzi	wife	26
骑	騎	（V）	qí	to ride	25
齐白石	齊白石	（PN）	Qí Báishí	(name of a well-known Chinese painter)	19
旗袍	旗袍	（N）	qípáo	cheongsam; a long, formal dress with a slit skirt	17
起	起	（V）	qǐ	to rise; to get up	23
汽车	汽車	（N）	qìchē	automobile; motor vehicle; car	18
气温	氣溫	（N）	qìwēn	air temperature	23
千	千	（Nu）	qiān	thousand	15
前边	前邊	（N）	qiánbian	front; ahead	21
前门	前門	（PN）	Qiánmén	Qianmen (a place in Beijing)	18
前年	前年	（N）	qiánnián	the year before last year	24
情况	情況	（N）	qíngkuàng	situation	26

秋天	秋天	（N）	qiūtiān	autumn	23
球	球	（N）	qiú	ball	21
取	取	（V）	qǔ	to take; to get; to fetch	18
去年	去年	（N）	qùnián	last year	21

R

热	热	（A）	rè	hot	20
热情	热情	（A）	rèqíng	warm; warmhearted; enthusiastic	26
人民币	人民幣	（N）	rénmínbì	Renminbi（RMB）	15
认真	認真	（A）	rènzhēn	earnest; serious	26
如果	如果	（Conj）	rúguǒ	if	25

S

山	山	（N）	shān	hill; mountain	23
伤	傷	（V）	shāng	to hurt; to wound	25
商店	商店	（N）	shāngdiàn	shop; store	17
上	上	（V/N）	shàng	to go up; to get on / last; previous	16
上	上	（V）	shàng	to be engaged in（work，study，etc.）at a fixed time	24
上边	上邊	（N）	shàngbian	above; over; upward	21
上演	上演	（V）	shàngyǎn	to stage a show; to perform	22
少	少	（A）	shǎo	few; little	15
声调	聲調	（N）	shēngdiào	tone	26
生活	生活	（V/N）	shēnghuó	to live/life	16
实在	實在	（A/Adv）	shízài	honest/truly; really	26
试	試	（V）	shì	to try on; to have a try	17
收入	收入	（N）	shōurù	income; earnings	24
售货员	售貨員	（N）	shòuhuòyuán	shop assistant; salesclerk	17
售票员	售票員	（N）	shòupiàoyuán	ticket seller; conductor	18
蔬菜	蔬菜	（N）	shūcài	vegetable	24
书店	書店	（N）	shūdiàn	bookstore	21
数	數	（V）	shǔ	to count	15
束	束	（M）	shù	bunch（of flowers）	25
帅	帥	（A）	shuài	handsome; smart	17
涮羊肉	涮羊肉	（N）	shuànyángròu	thin slices of mutton boiled in water	20
水平	水平	（N）	shuǐpíng	level	21
丝绸	絲綢	（N）	sīchóu	silk	17
死	死	（V）	sǐ	to die	26
送	送	（V）	sòng	to take someone somewhere; to see someone off	25
虽然	雖然	（Conj）	suīrán	although; though	22
所以	所以	（Conj）	suǒyǐ	so	20

T

它	它	（Pr）	tā	it	19
它们	它們	（Pr）	tāmen	they（refering to things，animals）	19
太极拳	太極拳	（N）	tàijíquán	Taiji Boxing	17
泰山	泰山	（PN）	Tàishān	Taishan Mountain	23
躺	躺	（V）	tǎng	to lie（on，down）	25
套	套	（M）	tào	set; suit; suite	17
特别	特別	（Adv）	tèbié	extraordinary; especially; particularly	22
特点	特點	（N）	tèdiǎn	characteristic; feature	26
踢	踢	（V）	tī	to kick	21
提	提	（V）	tí	to put forward; to raise	23

提高	提高	（V）	tígāo	to improve; to increase	21
填	填	（V）	tián	to fill in; to write	16
条	條	（M）	tiáo	strip; long narrow piece; (a measure word for objects like rivers, dragons, trousers)	23
停	停	（V）	tíng	to stop; to park	25
通知单	通知單	（N）	tōngzhīdān	advice note; letter of notice	18
同学	同學	（N）	tóngxué	classmate; schoolmate	21
偷	偷	（V）	tōu	to steal	25
图片	圖片	（N）	túpiàn	photograph; picture	26
图书馆	圖書館	（N）	túshūguǎn	library	16
腿	腿	（N）	tuǐ	leg	25

W

外边	外邊	（N）	wàibian	outside	21
弯	彎	（V）	wān	to bend	25
完	完	（V）	wán	to finish; to run out of	25
王府井	王府井	（PN）	Wángfǔjǐng	(name of a famous commercial district in Beijing)	15
往	往	（Prep）	wǎng	to; toward	18
忘	忘	（V）	wàng	to forget	16
卫生间	衛生間	（N）	wèishēngjiān	washroom; bathroom	21
温室	溫室	（N）	wēnshì	greenhouse	24
文化	文化	（N）	wénhuà	culture; education; literacy	24
文章	文章	（N）	wénzhāng	essay; article	20
问路	問路	（V O）	wèn lù	to ask directions (a route)	24
卧室	臥室	（N）	wòshì	bedroom	21

X

西安	西安	（PN）	Xī'ān	(name of the capital of Shaanxi Province)	15
西边	西邊	（N）	xībian	west side	22
西方	西方	（N）	xīfāng	western; the West	20
西服	西服	（N）	xīfú	Western-style clothes; suit	17
习惯	習慣	（V/N）	xíguàn	to be accustomed to/habit	20
戏院	戲院	（N）	xìyuàn	theatre	22
虾	蝦	（N）	xiā	shrimp	19
下	下	（V/N）	xià	to go down; to get off/next	16
下边	下邊	（N）	xiàbian	below; underneath	21
夏天	夏天	（N）	xiàtiān	summer	23
下雪	下雪	（V O）	xià xuě	to snow	23
下雨	下雨	（V O）	xià yǔ	to rain	24
先	先	（Adv）	xiān	first; before	16
想像	想像	（V）	xiǎngxiàng	to imagine	19
向	向	（Prep）	xiàng	towards; to	24
像	像	（V）	xiàng	to be alike; to take after	24
消息	消息	（N）	xiāoxi	news	25
小孩	小孩	（N）	xiǎoháir	kid; child	24
小伙子	小夥子	（N）	xiǎohuǒzi	young man	26
小时	小時	（N）	xiǎoshí	hour	17
小说	小說	（N）	xiǎoshuō	novel; fiction	22
小偷	小偷	（N）	xiǎotōu	thief	25
小燕子	小燕子	（PN）	Xiǎo Yànzi	(name of a Chinese tour guide)	23
笑	笑	（V）	xiào	to laugh; to smile	25

些	些	（M ）	xiē	some	18
新	新	（A ）	xīn	new	16
辛苦	辛苦	（A ）	xīnkǔ	hard; toilsome	24
新年	新年	（N ）	xīnnián	new year	20
《新实用汉语课本》	《新實用漢語課本》	（PN ）	Xīn Shíyòng Hànyǔ Kèběn	*New Practical Chinese Reader*	16
信	信	（N ）	xìn	letter	15
行	行	（V ）	xíng	to be O.K.	23
性别	性別	（N ）	xìngbié	sex; gender	16
姓名	姓名	（N ）	xìngmíng	name	16
徐悲鸿	徐悲鸿	（PN ）	Xú Bēihóng	(name of a well-known Chinese painter)	19
学校	學校	（N ）	xuéxiào	school	21
雪	雪	（N ）	xuě	snow	23

Y

颜色	顏色	（N ）	yánsè	colour	17
演	演	（V ）	yǎn	to act; to perform; to play	22
演员	演員	（N ）	yǎnyuán	actor or actress; performer	22
演奏	演奏	（V ）	yǎnzòu	to give an instrumental performance	20
阳台	陽臺	（N ）	yángtái	balcony	21
样子	樣子	（N ）	yàngzi	shape; sample; model; pattern	17
医药费	醫藥費	（N ）	yīyàofèi	medical expenses	25
一定	一定	（Adv ）	yídìng	must; surely	17
一会儿	一會兒	（IE ）	yíhuìr	a little while	16
一样	一樣	（A ）	yíyàng	the same; alike	19
以后	以後	（N ）	yǐhòu	after; afterwards	21
已经	已經	（Adv ）	yǐjing	already	17
以前	以前	（N ）	yǐqián	before; ago; previously; formerly	22
以为	以爲	（V ）	yǐwéi	to think (with more subjectivity)	25
阴天	陰天	（N ）	yīntiān	cloudy sky; overcast sky	23
因为	因爲	（Conj）	yīnwèi	because	20
音乐会	音樂會	（N ）	yīnyuèhuì	concert	20
银行	銀行	（N ）	yínháng	bank	15
英镑	英鎊	（N ）	yīngbàng	pound sterling	15
英文	英文	（N ）	Yīngwén	English	18
赢	赢	（V ）	yíng	to win	21
用	用	（V ）	yòng	to use	15
优美	優美	（A ）	yōuměi	graceful; fine; exquisite; elegant	22
游	游	（V ）	yóu	to swim	19
油彩	油彩	（N ）	yóucǎi	greasepaint	19
邮费	郵費	（N ）	yóufèi	postage	18
油画	油畫	（N ）	yóuhuà	oil painting	19
游泳	游泳	（V ）	yóuyǒng	to swim	23
有的	有的	（Pr ）	yǒude	some	22
又	又	（Adv ）	yòu	again	20
右	右	（N ）	yòu	right	21
右边	右邊	（N ）	yòubian	the right side	21
雨	雨	（N ）	yǔ	rain	24
远	遠	（A ）	yuǎn	far	21
越剧	越劇	（N ）	yuèjù	the Shaoxing opera	22
越来越	越来越	（IE ）	yuè lái yuè	more and more	26
乐器	樂器	（N ）	yuèqì	musical instrument	20

| 乐曲 | 樂曲 | (N) | yuèqǔ | musical composition | 20 |

Z

在	在	(Adv)	zài	(used to indicate an action in progress)	24
咱们	咱們	(Pr)	zánmen	we, us	18
糟糕	糟糕	(A)	zāogāo	in a wretched state; in a mess; too bad	18
早	早	(A)	zǎo	early	15
展览	展覽	(N)	zhǎnlǎn	exhibition; show	26
站	站	(N)	zhàn	station; stop	18
站	站	(V)	zhàn	to stand	23
丈夫	丈夫	(N)	zhàngfu	husband	26
着急	著急	(VO/A)	zháojí	to feel anxious/anxious	20
照相机	照相機	(N)	zhàoxiàngjī	camera	20
着	著	(Pt)	zhe	(indicating the continuous aspect)	25
这么	這麼	(Pr)	zhème	so; such; like this	22
正式	正式	(A)	zhèngshì	formal	20
正在	正在	(Adv)	zhèngzài	in the process of; in the middle of; (key word of a progressive construction)	24
职业	職業	(N)	zhíyè	occupation; profession	16
只	只	(Adv)	zhǐ	only	19
纸	紙	(N)	zhǐ	paper	19
中餐	中餐	(N)	zhōngcān	Chinese food (meal)	26
中国化	中國化	(V)	zhōngguóhuà	to make Chinese in quality or characteristics; Sinicize	26
中国画	中國畫	(N)	zhōngguóhuà	traditional Chinese painting	19
中国通	中國通	(N)	zhōngguótōng	an expert of China	26
中式	中式	(A)	zhōngshì	Chinese style	17
种	種	(M)	zhǒng	kind; sort; type	22
种类	種類	(N)	zhǒnglèi	kind; sort; type; variety	22
种	種	(V)	zhòng	to grow; to plant	24
重	重	(A)	zhòng	serious; heavy	25
主角	主角	(N)	zhǔjué	leading actor or actress	22
主要	主要	(A)	zhǔyào	main	19
注意	注意	(V)	zhùyì	to pay attention to	25
抓	抓	(V)	zhuā	to clutch; to catch; to arrest	25
撞	撞	(V)	zhuàng	to knock; to collide	25
桌子	桌子	(N)	zhuōzi	table; desk	25
自己	自己	(Pr)	zìjǐ	oneself	16
自行车	自行車	(N)	zìxíngchē	bicycle	25
走	走	(V)	zǒu	to walk; to go	17
足球	足球	(N)	zúqiú	soccer	21
左边	左邊	(N)	zuǒbian	the left side	21
座	座	(M)	zuò	(a measure word for mountains, buildings and other similar immovable objects)	24
座位	座位	(N)	zuòwèi	seat	22

补充词汇
Supplementary Words

词条	繁体	词性	拼音	英译	课号
				A	
爱人	爱人	（N）	àiren	husband or wife；spouse	24
				B	
薄	薄	（A）	báo	thin	17
悲伤	悲傷	（A）	bēishāng	sad；sorrow	22
毕业	畢業	（VO）	bìyè	to graduate；to finish school	26
便饭	便飯	（N）	biànfàn	a simple meal	22
表	表	（N）	biǎo	watch	17
补	補	（V）	bǔ	to mend；to patch；remediation	25
布	布	（N）	bù	cloth；fabric	17
不怎么样	不怎麽樣	（IE）	bù zěnmeyàng	not so good	22
				C	
菜	菜	（N）	cài	food；a dish	15
菜单	菜單	（N）	càidān	menu	23
茶楼	茶樓	（N）	chálóu	tearooms；tea house	16
城市	城市	（N）	chéngshì	city	15，21
出差	出差	（V）	chūchāi	to go on a business trip	21
聪明	聰明	（A）	cōngming	clever；bright	18，22
				D	
打折	打折	（VO）	dǎzhé	to sell at a discount；to give a discount	17
刀	刀	（N）	dāo	knife	25
地方	地方	（N）	dìfang	place	15
地上	地上	（N）	dìshang	ground；floor	25
电影院	電影院	（N）	diànyǐngyuàn	cinema	21
掉	掉	（V）	diào	to drop；to fall	25
动	動	（V）	dòng	to move	23
冻	凍	（V）	dòng	to freeze	24
顿	頓	（M）	dùn	（a measure word for meals）	22
多余	多余	（A）	duōyú	superfluous；uncalled for；surplus	20
				E	
儿子	兒子	（N）	érzi	son	15，18
				F	
发抖	發抖	（V）	fādǒu	to shake；to tremble；to shiver	24
方法	方法	（N）	fāngfǎ	method	26
房间	房間	（N）	fángjiān	room	16
封	封	（M）	fēng	（measure word for letter）	18

G

钢琴	鋼琴	(N)	gāngqín	piano	19
公斤	公斤	(M)	gōngjīn	kilogram (kg.)	18
挂失	掛失	(VO)	guàshī	to report the loss of something	25
观点	觀點	(N)	guāndiǎn	opinion	19
管	管	(V)	guǎn	to discipline	19
广东	廣東	(PN)	Guǎngdōng	Guangdong Province	16
国籍	國籍	(N)	guójí	nationality	16

H

孩子	孩子	(N)	háizi	child	16,19
害怕	害怕	(V)	hàipà	to be afraid	23
杭州	杭州	(PN)	Hángzhōu	Hangzhou	21
后边	後邊	(N)	hòubian	back; behind	21
回忆	回憶	(V)	huíyì	to reminisce; to recollect; to recall	22
汇率	匯率	(N)	huìlǜ	exchange rate	15

J

机场	機場	(N)	jīchǎng	airport	24
纪念	紀念	(N)	jìniàn	commemorate	18
加元	加元	(N)	jiāyuán	Canadian dollar	15
贾宝玉	賈寶玉	(PN)	Jiǎ Bǎoyù	(name of the leading male character in *Dream of the Red Chamber*)	22
减肥	減肥	(VO)	jiǎnféi	to reduce; to be on diet	19
见面	見面	(VO)	jiànmiàn	to meet; to see	26
建筑师	建築師	(N)	jiànzhùshī	architect	21
将军	將軍	(N)	jiāngjūn	general	24
脚	腳	(N)	jiǎo	foot	20
教育	教育	(V)	jiàoyù	to teach; to educate	19
接(人)	接(人)	(V)	jiē(rén)	to pick up (someone)	24
结婚	結婚	(VO)	jiéhūn	to get married	22
节目	節目	(N)	jiémù	program	19
经验	經驗	(N)	jīngyàn	experience	26
警察	警察	(N)	jǐngchá	policeman	25
警车	警車	(N)	jǐngchē	police car; police van	25
句	句	(M)	jù	sentence	26

K

咖啡馆	咖啡館	(N)	kāfēiguǎn	coffee bar	21
开始	開始	(V)	kāishǐ	to start; to begin	16
棵	棵	(M)	kē	(a measure word for trees, plants)	23
渴	渴	(A)	kě	thirsty	23
客人	客人	(N)	kèrén	guest	26
哭	哭	(V)	kū	to cry; to weep	22
裤子	褲子	(N)	kùzi	trousers; pants	17

L

老人	老人	(N)	lǎorén	the elderly; the aged; old man or woman	16
离开	離開	(V)	líkāi	to leave; to depart from	22,26
凉快	涼快	(A)	liángkuai	cool	24
辆	輛	(M)	liàng	(a measure word for vehicle)	20
了不起	了不起	(IE)	liǎobuqǐ	amazing; terrific; extraordinary	17

了解	了解	(V)	liǎojiě	to understand; to realize	26
料子	料子	(N)	liàozi	material for making clothes	17
林黛玉	林黛玉	(PN)	Lín Dàiyù	(name of the leading female character in *Dream of the Red Chamber*)	22

M

美元	美元	(N)	měiyuán	U. S. dollar	15
目录	目錄	(N)	mùlù	catalogue; list	16

N

南边	南邊	(N)	nánbian	south side	21
年龄	年齡	(N)	niánlíng	age	16
暖和	暖和	(A)	nuǎnhuo	warm	24

O

欧元	歐元	(N)	ōuyuán	Euro	15

P

跑步	跑步	(VO)	pǎobù	to run, jog	19
骗	騙	(V)	piàn	to cheat; to trick	22

Q

骑	騎	(V)	qí	to ride; to sit on the back of	19
起飞	起飛	(V)	qǐfēi	to take off	23
晴天	晴天	(N)	qíngtiān	sunny sky	23
请客	請客	(VO)	qǐngkè	to feast; to treat sb. to sth. (a meal)	26

R

然后	然後	(Adv)	ránhòu	then	18
热闹	熱鬧	(A)	rènao	lively; bustling with noise and excitement	16

S

山	山	(N)	shān	hill; mountain	21
山水	山水	(N)	shānshuǐ	landscape	21
烧	燒	(V)	shāo	to burn	22
蛇	蛇	(N)	shé	snake	20
设计	設計	(V)	shèjì	to design	21
声	聲	(N)	shēng	sound; voice	24
生火	生火	(VO)	shēnghuǒ	to make a fire	24
生气	生氣	(VO)	shēngqì	to get angry; to take offense	19
诗	詩	(N)	shī	poem; poetry	22
诗人	詩人	(N)	shīrén	poet	21
士兵	士兵	(N)	shìbīng	soldier	24
手	手	(N)	shǒu	hand	25
手机	手機	(N)	shǒujī	cell phone	25
瘦	瘦	(A)	shòu	thin	19
输	輸	(V)	shū	to lose	21
书店	書店	(N)	shūdiàn	bookstore; bookshop	19
书法	書法	(N)	shūfǎ	handwriting; calligraphy	19
熟悉	熟悉	(V)	shúxī	to be familiar with	26
树	樹	(N)	shù	tree	23
双	雙	(M)	shuāng	pair	17
死	死	(V)	sǐ	to die	22,23

苏杭	蘇杭	(PN)	Sū Háng	Suzhou and Hangzhou	21
苏州	蘇州	(PN)	Sūzhōu	Suzhou	21
孙子	孫子	(N)	sūnzi	grandson	18

T

太太	太太	(N)	tàitai	wife; Mrs.	22
添	添	(V)	tiān	to add	20
天气预报	天氣預報	(N)	tiānqì yùbào	weather forecast	23
天堂	天堂	(N)	tiāntáng	heaven; paradise	21
条	條	(M)	tiáo	(a measure word for long, narrow objects, such as trousers, skirt, snake, etc.)	17,20
贴	貼	(V)	tiē	to stick; to paste	18
停	停	(V)	tíng	to stop; to cease	24
停车场	停車場	(N)	tíngchēchǎng	parking lot	23
头发	頭發	(N)	tóufa	hair	17
突然	突然	(A)	tūrán	sudden/suddenly	25

W

完	完	(V)	wán	to finish	20
万事如意	萬事如意	(IE)	wàn shì rú yì	May all your wishes come true.	20
危险	危險	(A)	wēixiǎn	dangrous	23
问答	問答	(N)	wèndá	questions and answers	16

X

吓	嚇	(V)	xià	to scare; to frighten	25
现金	現金	(N)	xiànjīn	cash	15
相爱	相愛	(V)	xiāng'ài	to fall in love	22
相声	相聲	(N)	xiàngsheng	comic dialogue; repartee	17
箱子	箱子	(N)	xiāngzi	box; case; trunk	24
项链	項鏈	(N)	xiàngliàn	necklace	25
小学	小學	(N)	xiǎoxué	primary school	20
鞋子	鞋子	(N)	xiézi	shoes	17
信封	信封	(N)	xìnfēng	envelope	18
信用卡	信用卡	(N)	xìnyòngkǎ	credit card	15,25
型号	型號	(PN)	xínghào	model; type	25
行李	行李	(N)	xíngli	baggage; luggage	24
幸福	幸福	(A)	xìngfú	happy	20
熊	熊	(N)	xióng	bear	23
修建	修建	(V)	xiūjiàn	to build; to construct	21
续借	續借	(V)	xùjiè	to renew	16

Y

亚洲学系	亞洲學系	(N)	yàzhōuxué xì	Department of Asian studies	15
研究	研究	(V)	yánjiū	to study; to discuss; to consider	22
钥匙	鑰匙	(N)	yàoshi	key	16
页	頁	(M)	yè	page	17
业余	業余	(A)	yèyú	amateur; spare time	19
一路平安	一路平安	(IE)	yílù píng'ān	to have a pleasant journey; *bon voyage*	24
以前	以前	(N)	yǐqián	before; formerly; previously	19
艺术	藝術	(N)	yìshù	art	26
意思	意思	(N)	yìsi	meaning	26
音乐厅	音樂廳	(N)	yīnyuètīng	concert hall	20
邮票	郵票	(N)	yóupiào	stamp	18

预订	预訂	（V）	yùdìng	to reserve; to book	16
元	元	（M）	yuán	(measure word for Chinese currency; *kuai*)	15
园林	園林	（N）	yuánlín	garden; park	21
远	遠	（A）	yuǎn	far	19
阅览室	閱覽室	（N）	yuèlǎnshì	reading room	16

Z

杂志	雜志	（N）	zázhì	magazine	16
站岗	站崗	（VO）	zhàngǎng	to stand guard	24
正常	正常	（A）	zhèngcháng	normal; regular	24
中国民航	中國民航	（PN）	Zhōngguó Mínháng	Civil Aviation Administration of China (CAAC)	23
装	裝	（V）	zhuāng	to pretend to be sth./sb.	23
准备	準備	（N/V）	zhǔnbèi	preparation/to prepare; to get ready	18,26
自行车	自行車	（N）	zìxíngchē	bike; bicycle	19
总是	總是	（Adv）	zǒngshì	always	17
足	足	（N）	zú	foot	20
足球场	足球場	（N）	zúqiúchǎng	soccer field	21
最	最	（Adv）	zuì	the most	20

汉字索引

Character Index